# A GRAMMAR OF BIBLICAL HEBREW

---

*Part One*

## An Introduction to Biblical Hebrew

---

*Part Two*

## Continuing Biblical Hebrew

---



Robert Bornemann

University Press of America,® Inc.
Lanham • New York • Oxford

**University Press of America,® Inc.**
4720 Boston Way
Lanham, Maryland 20706

12 Hid's Copse Rd.
Cummor Hill, Oxford OX2 9JJ


Printed in the United States of America
British Library Cataloging in Publication Information Available

**Library of Congress Cataloging-in-Publication Data**

Bornemann, Robert.
A grammar of biblical Hebrew / Robert Bornemann.
p. cm.
Includes index.
Contents: pt. l. An introduction to biblical Hebrew—pt. 2.
Continuing biblical Hebrew.
l. Hebrew language—Grammar. I. Title.
PJ4567.3.B67 1998 492.4'82421—dc21 98-20786 CIP

ISBN 0-7618-1185-0 (pbk: alk. ppr.)

™ The paper used in this publication meets the minimum requirements of American National Standard for Information Sciences—Permanence of Paper for Printed Library Materials, ANSI Z39.48—1984

# A GRAMMAR OF BIBLICAL HEBREW

## A PREFATORY NOTE

The present volume is in two parts, representing two different but related courses. *Part One* is an introduction to biblical Hebrew which can stand independently. *Part Two*, building on *Part One*, is a full course in grammar and reading.

*Part One: An Introduction to Biblical Hebrew* is specifically designed as a four-week intensive course of study. It is not, however, a traditional, full course in Hebrew grammar compressed into a single month, although students will have received the basic materials by which they can actually begin to read in the Hebrew Bible. *Part One* is an introduction to the language, expression and text of the Hebrew Bible to give some basic insights and tools for its study to those who may never do anything more with Hebrew

More specifically, *Part One* is designed to provide students with some of the basic linguistic tools for the study of the Hebrew Bible by enabling them (1) to have a basic grasp of the nature and structure of the language; (2) to use the Hebrew lexicon and concordance, and so be able to exercise some control over translations; (3) to develop a basic vocabulary of words significant for biblical thought and theology; (4) to understand the peculiar problems of the Hebrew text and its transmission; and (5) to use scholarly commentaries with understanding.

*Part One*, then, is not intended to turn out full-fledged Hebraists, but intelligent users of the Hebrew Bible. At the same time, however, it provides a firm basis on which interested and able students may continue their study of Hebrew by reading in the Hebrew Bible and inductively expanding their knowledge of the Hebrew language.

*Part Two: Continuing Biblical Hebrew* is designed for such students. It presents a full summary of Hebrew grammar and extensive notes on Hebrew syntax. The Elijah narratives in 1

Kings 17-19 are suggested as a text for beginning this inductive study. They are excellent Hebrew prose, and are not only a self-contained literary unit of reasonable length with easily divided sections, but also grammatically contain examples of nearly all the elements needed for a sound knowledge of biblical Hebrew. As in the case of any inductive study, how the materials will actually be used in the course of study depends upon the instructor and students.

A Hebrew-English glossary, designed to be used for both parts is included. It contains all the words used in *Part One* (except for the fully translated examples of Chapter XV) and all the words of 1Kings 17-19. An index for easy reference to all the materials completes the volume.

The *Grammar* has been many years in the making. *Part One: An Introduction to Biblical Hebrew* grew out of the Hebrew requirement for all M. Div. students at the Lutheran Theological Seminary at Philadelphia, where it has been in use with many revisions since 1973. *Part Two: Continuing Biblical Hebrew* has taken many forms before the present one. In all I would be remiss if I did not express my thanks to the excellent students with whom I have discussed this project many times; to my colleague, Foster McCurley, who freely shared the results of his teaching in this area; to Moshe Held, my teacher and friend, who went over the entire manuscript of the *Introduction*, making many valuable suggestions and improvements; and to my colleagues, Christopher Seitz and Robert Robinson, who have taught these materials with me and from whom I have learned much.

Robert Bornemann

Philadelphia, Pennsylvania
12 June 1993

# A GRAMMAR OF BIBLICAL HEBREW

## TABLE OF CONTENTS



## PART ONE: AN INTRODUCTION TO BIBLICAL HEBREW

## PART TWO: CONTINUING BIBLICAL HEBREW

Wilderness
[11] 1 Kings 19:9-18 The Theophany at Horeb
[12] 1 Kings 19:19-21 The Call of Elisha

## A SUMMARY OF HEBREW GRAMMAR

## NOTES ON HEBREW SYNTAX

# GLOSSARY
(233-260)

# INDEX OF SUBJECTS
(261-273)

# APPENDIX
(275-285)

Paradigm of the Strong Verb
Verbs with Weak Letters and Gutturals In Outline

-----------------------------

# A GRAMMAR OF BIBLICAL HEBREW

## PART ONE: AN INTRODUCTION TO BIBLICAL HEBREW

### AN INTRODUCTORY NOTE

Just as people in the ancient Near East lived in a thought-world very different from ours, so their languages are also very different from our modern, western languages. To understand the Hebrew Bible one must have some understanding of the language in which it is written, as well as the patterns of thought that go hand in hand with linguistic expression. The purpose of this introduction is to help students gain such an understanding by becoming acquainted with the basic characteristics of biblical Hebrew, and having at least an elementary grasp of the nature and structure of the language.

The study of Hebrew also becomes a help in gaining an insight into Semitic mentality. To be sure, one cannot re-create the thought-world of ancient Israel simply on the basis of language. At the same time, however, language does express one's understanding of the world, reflecting the way one thinks and approaches reality.

Because of the structure and orthography of Hebrew, an introduction to biblical Hebrew becomes also an introduction to textual criticism. The problems of text in the Hebrew Bible can only be understood and dealt with in terms of the language itself.

An essential aspect of biblical exegesis is the study of words and expressions--word study in the broad sense--in order to understand them not on the basis of etymology but of usage. To do this, one must not only know what the actual words and phrases are in Hebrew and where to find them, but also to see how they are used in context, what other words and notions are associated with them. Here a knowledge of Hebrew is necessary, and even a minimal knowledge will serve. Only in this way can a study of words and expressions in the Hebrew Bible be controlled, so that students can be sure they are dealing with the actual biblical terms and not a translator's interpretations.

*An Introduction to Biblical Hebrew* is designed to help students deal with these concerns: the language and thought-world of the Hebrew Bible, its text and diction; but it is not expected that it will make anyone *The Compleat Hebraist*! It is simply, as its name says, an introduction to the language, expression and text of the Hebrew Bible to give some basic insights and tools to those who may never do anything more with the study of Hebrew. Interested students may continue the study of biblical Hebrew in Part Two, building on the content of *An Introduction*; but the *Introduction* itself is a self-contained and independent course with its own purpose and goals.

In format *An Introduction* is divided into fifteen chapters. Of these, Chapter XV, which deals with the Hebrew text and its transmission, may well be postponed, incorporated into a basic course in Hebrew Bible, especially if it immediately follows the four-week period. The first week of study, Chapters I-IV, is devoted to the alphabet, vowels and reading; the second week deals with nouns and adjectives, Chapters V-VIII; the third week treats verbs, Chapters IX-XI; and the fourth week is concerned with participles, syntax and text, and finding roots, Chapters XII-XV.

In the course of *An Introduction to Biblical Hebrew* all the major elements essential to Hebrew grammar are presented. It cannot be expected, of course, that all of these can be fully mastered within four weeks.

There are, however, nine items that must be known *absolutely.* In order to read and pronounce Hebrew words, the students must know (1) the 22 letters of the alphabet, (2) the three letters used as vowels (the *matres lectionis*), and (3) the Masoretic vowel points. In order to have a basic grasp of nouns and adjectives, students must know (4) the pattern of the three declensions, (5) the nominal endings (the same for all declensions and there are no case endings), and (6) the elements attached to roots to make them nominal forms (basically only four). To have control of verbal forms, students must know (7) the names and definitions of the seven stems of the verb, (8) the conjugation of the simple (Qal) perfect (nine forms), and (9) the conjugation of the simple (Qal) imperfect (ten forms). It will be noted that these nine items are covered in the first three weeks of the month's study.

There are nine vocabularies, found in Chapters V through XIII. They have been developed around a basic vocabulary of about fifty words significant for biblical thought and theology. To this basic list have been added prepositions, adverbs and other words needed in the course of reading and translation. All told there are about 160 words, many of which are only different forms of the same roots. To be sure, many important and frequently used words in the Hebrew Bible are omitted; but this is unavoidable, given the aims and limits of an introduction such as this. The glossary includes all the words used in *An Introduction* except for the fully translated examples of textual criticism in Chapter XV. The glossary, purposely only Hebrew to English, follows the lexical arrangement of Brown-Driver-Briggs, *Lexicon.*

The reading and translation exercises, as much as possible within the limits of a greatly restricted vocabulary, reflect the literary structures and patterns of expression and word associations to be found in the Hebrew Bible. It goes without saying, of course, that in any given reading assignment students should be able to translate without recourse to crib notes or written-out translations! Throughout, the importance of reading aloud cannot be stressed too much. There is real truth in the dictum of my Israeli teacher, "If you can't say it, you don't know it!"

In this connection it should be noted that modern Israeli pronunciation is followed throughout. It is not only simpler, but it is the one most used in scholarly circles. The most obvious differences from the traditional academic pronunciation are in the treatment of the spirants (b, g, d, k, p, t) and the letter ו which is pronounced as a "v" instead of "w."

As early and as often as possible students should actually use an edition of the Hebrew Bible. Done best in small groups or tutorials, this can be especially helpful, not only in learning the alphabet and vowels and developing facility in reading Hebrew words, but also in becoming familiar with the Hebrew text itself. In addition it gives the instructor opportunity to point out things of interest along the way. Passages for these practice sessions are suggested in the assignments for the early chapters of the *Introduction.*

A word, finally, to those who use this volume. No claim is made that what is set forth here is תּוֹרָה מִסִּנַי, but hopefully it will help in understanding it.

--------------------

# AN INTRODUCTION TO BIBLICAL HEBREW

## I

### 1 HEBREW AND THE SEMITIC LANGUAGES

The Semitic languages are divided into three major families: (1) North-East Semitic [Akkadian, Babylonian and Assyrian]; (2) North-West Semitic [Canaanite and Aramaic]; and South-West Semitic [Arabic and Ethiopic].

Hebrew belongs to the North-West family of languages, and is specifically a Canaanite dialect. To this same Canaanite group belong (1) Ugaritic [witnessed mainly by the extensive literary remains discovered at Ras Shamra in Syria and which date from the 14th to the 13th centuries B.C.E.]; (2) the Amarna glosses [Canaanite explanations in cuneiform letters written to Egyptian pharaohs during the 14th century by petty kings and rulers in Palestine]; Phoenician and Punic [attested by many inscriptions found from Syria-Palestine to North Africa and dating from the 10th century B.C.E. to the 2nd century C.E.]; and (4) Moabite [known only from the Meša Inscription, the famous Moabite Stone, which dates from the 9th century B.C.E., and which also casts some interesting light on the biblical account of a battle between Moab and the Israelite kingdom in 2 Kings 3:4-27].

Of these languages Ugaritic is the most important for Hebrew. Indeed, today no sound study of Hebrew language and letters can be carried on apart from it. Among other Semitic languages significant for the study of Hebrew, Akkadian stands next to Ugaritic in importance to be followed by Aramaic; Arabic is least significant.

## THE HEBREW ALPHABET

| PRINTED | WRITTEN | NAME | SOUND | VALUE |
|---|---|---|---|---|
| א | א | ’alep̱ | ’ | 1 |
| ב | ב | bēṯ | b [ḇ=v] | 2 |
| ג | ג | gîmel | g [g] | 3 |
| ד | ד | dāleṯ | d [ḏ] | 4 |
| ה | ה | hê | h | 5 |
| ו | ו | vāv | v | 6 |
| ז | ז | zayin | z | 7 |
| ח | ח | ḥêṯ | ḥ | 8 |
| ט | ט | ṭêṯ | ṭ | 9 |
| י | י | yôḏ | y | 10 |
| כ ך | כ ך | kāp | k [ḵ=ḥ] | 20 |
| ל | ל | lāmeḏ | l | 30 |
| מ ם | מ ם | mêm | m | 40 |
| נ ן | נ ן | nûn | n | 50 |
| ס | ס | sāmeḵ | s | 60 |
| ע | ע | ‘ayin | ‘ | 70 |
| פ ף | פ ף | pê | p [p̱=f] | 80 |
| צ ץ | צ ץ | ṣāḏê | ṣ | 90 |
| ק | ק | qôp̱ | q [=ḳ] | 100 |
| ר | ר | rêš | r | 200 |
| שׂ | שׂ | śîn | ś | --- |
| שׁ | שׁ | šîn | š [=sh] | 300 |
| ת | ת | tāv | t [ṯ] | 400 |

א ב ג ד ה ו ז ח ט י כ ך ל מ ם נ ן ס ע פ ף צ ץ ק ר שׂ שׁ ת

## 2. THE HEBREW ALPHABET

Hebrew is written from right to left and employs an alphabet of twenty-two characters, all of which are consonants. They have been developed from pictographic writing on an acrophonic principle; that is, the form of the letters are adaptations of original pictographs and the phonetic values of the letters are the initial sounds of the words which are depicted.

| | | | | |
|---|---|---|---|---|
| ʾālep | ox |  | ʾ | [א] |
| bêṯ [bayiṯ] | house |  | b | [ב] |
| gîmel [gāmāl] | camel |  | g | [ג] |
| vāv | hook | 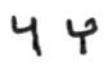 | v | [ו] |
| ḥêṯ | fence |  | ḥ | [ח] |
| mêm [mayim] | water | 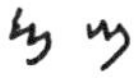 | m | [מ] |
| ʿayin | eye |  | ʿ | [ע] |
| rêš [rôʾš] | head |  | r | [ר] |
| šîn [šên] | tooth |  | š | [שׁ] |
| tāv | mark, sign | 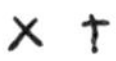 | t | [ת] |

The present "square" alphabet was borrowed from Aramaic, and has been in common use since the 6th century B.C.E. The accompanying chart gives the printed and written forms of the letters, their names and transliterations, the early form of the alphabet, and the numerical values of the letters. Note that five letters have a special form when written at the end of a word: כ (final form ך), מ (final form ם), נ (final form ן), פ (final form ף), and צ (final form ץ).

Care should be taken to distinguish among the following letters in their printed form:

| | |
|---|---|
| ז ו | ב כ |
| י ו ן | ג נ |
| ט מ | ד ר |
| ס ם | ד ך |
| ע צ ץ | ה ח ת |

In writing the letters think of putting them in squares; thus: כ = k, but נ = n; ר = r, but ו = v. Make full use of the *tittles* [note the upper right of ד and the lower right of ב ], and observe the squared and curved corners [note the lower left of final ם and ס ], so as to avoid confusion, for example, between:

| | | |
|---|---|---|
| ד and ר | ד = d | ר = r |
| ב and כ | ב = b | כ = k |
| ס and ם | ס = s | ם = final m |

## 3 THE SPIRANTS

Six letters are spirants and have both a hard and soft (aspirated) sound. They are ב ג ד כ פ ת . These letters have their normal *hard* sound whenever there is no vowel sound of any kind before them, but they have a *soft* (*aspirated*) sound when there is. These six letters have the mnemonic name, b$^{e}$gāḏk$^{e}$pāṯ. In pointed Hebrew a dot (called *dāgēš lēnē*) is placed in the bosom of these letters to show that the sound is to be hard: בּ גּ דּ כּ פּ תּ . In English transliteration the hard sound is indicated by the simple letters: b, g, d, k, p, t. To indicate the soft sound several ways are employed. Some add an h to the letters: bh, gh, dh, kh, ph, th. Others, to avoid introducing an extra letter, use Greek letters: β, γ, δ, χ, φ, θ. In this grammar the soft sound is indicated by a line under the letter: ḇ, g̱, ḏ, ḵ, p̱, ṯ.

Traditionally the aspirated sounds have been carefully distinguished from the hard: ḇ is pronounced as *v*, g like the *g* in German *Tage*, ḏ like the *th* in *thee*, ḵ like the *ch* in the German *doch*, p̱ as an *f*, and ṯ like the *th* in *thing*. This grammar, however, follows modern Israeli pronunciation, and so no distinction is made between the hard and soft forms of *d* or *t*, and very little in the case of *g*. For all practical purposes, only the soft forms of *b*, *k*, and *p* are observed: ḇ = v; ḵ = ḥ (no distinction between a soft *k* and a ח); and p̱ = f.

## 4 THE GUTTURALS

Hebrew has four gutturals: ח ה א ע [ר sometimes shares the characteristics of the gutturals.] Note of them is made because sometimes they affect the vowels of words; e.g. gutturals have a tendency to prefer *a* vowels.

## 5 WEAK CONSONANTS

Several of the consonants show weaknesses of various kinds. א ה ו י have full consonantal value at the beginniong of a syllable, but frequently lose their consonantal value at the end of a syllable, and on rare occasion they may not even be written. א and ה are of such weak character at the end of a syllable that one is sometimes used for the other. נ, when it has no vowel of its own, is usually assimilated into the consonant following it; and ו, ה and י may disappear by assimilation after prefixes.

## ASSIGNMENT

PRACTICE READING the letters of the alphabet in Genesis t1:1-5. See also the alphabetic acrostic in Psalm 111. Be sure to read from right to left.

TRANSLITERATE the following into Hebrew letters. Remember that English goes from left to right, but Hebrew from right to left.

| | | |
|---|---|---|
| ‘ṣ | mvt | npš |
| gdl | ’l | yš‘ |
| ’mn | ’p | ’mt |
| mzbḥ | ḥṭ’ | ’dny |
| bḥr | ’hb | śdh |
| r’h | brk | qsm |
| šmym | mṣvh | |

TRANSLITERATE the following into English letters. Remember that Hebrew goes from right to left, but English from left to right.

| | | |
|---|---|---|
| קדשׁ | כהן | אב |
| צוה | מלך | אדם |
| ארץ | עם | בן |
| משׁפט | פשׁע | רגל |
| סתר | צדק | זבח |
| שׂרף | שׁם | חסד |
| | שׁמע | ים |

---------------------------

# II

## 6 THE HEBREW VOWELS

The Semitic languages have three primary vowel sounds. These are: A I U. In Hebrew these form three classes of vowels:

| | |
|---|---|
| Class 1 | A |
| Class 2 | I and E |
| Class 3 | U and O |

Within these three classes there are four kinds of vowels. These vowels with their transliterations are as follows:

(a) *Pure short*: a i e u o

These vowels are short by nature and cannot be modified.

(b) *Pure long*: â î ê û ô

These vowels are long by nature and cannot be modified.

(c) *Tone long*: ā ē ō

These vowels are long by relation to the tone (= accent); there is only one tone long vowel for each class. They are used in a closed syllable under tone (= accented) or in an open syllable near the tone (= accent).

(d) *Indistinct*, or *šᵉvâ*: (1) ᵉ or ᵃ (2) ᵉ or ᵉ (3) ᵉ or ᵒ

These represent the reduction of tone long vowels to an indistinct sound, not counted as a full vowel. There are two forms having the same function: simple and composite, the latter used with gutturals.

## 7 THE HEBREW VOWEL LETTERS

Although spoken Hebrew made use of all these vowels and their gradations in sound, the writing of Hebrew was originally entirely consonantal; not even final vowels were written. While one could usually tell the form of the word from the context, many uncertainties still remained. The written consonants, *mlk*, for example, could be read in any one of the following ways:

| | |
|---|---|
| *melek̲* | king |
| *malkô* | his king |
| *malkî* | my king |
| *malkâ* | queen |
| *malkāh* | her king |
| *mālak̲* | he is king/ruler, he reigns |
| *mālek̲â* | she is queen/ruler, she reigns |
| *malek̲û* | they are rulers, they reign |

So it was that to alleviate this situation certain consonants were used to represent long, usually *pure long* and *final* vowels.

This practice developed on the principle of "historical writing," by which the consonant of a diphthong continues to be written even after the diphthong is resolved. For example, the word in Hebrew for *day* was originally *yawm(u)*, and so written יום; but when the diphthong was resolved from *-aw-* to *ô*, the ו was still written, although now it represented the vowel *ô*. The use of consonants as vowels in written Hebrew was introduced about the 9th century B.C.E. The weak letters of the alphabet were chosen to serve this purpose, one for each of the three classes of vowels.

(1) ה (and later א ) = final *â*
(2) י = *î* or *ê*
(3) ו = *û* or *ô*

The grammarians called these letters *matres* (singular, *mater*) *lectionis*, "mother(s) of reading," because they provided the source for correct interpretation.

## ASSIGNMENT

PRACTICE reading the letters of the alphabet in Isaiah 40:1-2, noting possible *matres lectionis.*

TRANSLITERATE INTO HEBREW, indicating only the circumflexed vowels by *matres lectionis.*

| | |
|---|---|
| ʼādôn | māšîaḥ |
| berāḵâ | miṣvâ |
| berîṯ | qādôš |
| yešûʻâ | šālôm |
| kāḇôḏ | tôrâ |

TRANSLITERATE INTO ENGLISH, indicating alternative readings where necessary

| | |
|---|---|
| טובה | אישׁ |
| יום | גוי |
| מה | דוד |
| קום | דומה |
| שׁיר | טוב |

---

# III

## 8 THE MASORETIC VOWEL POINTS

The use of vocalic consonants for major vowels, while helpful, was still not enough to safeguard the correct reading of the text. Many words, for instance, do not have pure long vowels, and so where the context is not clear the way they are to be read is ambiguous. Is one, for example, to read **מטה** as *maṭṭeh* (staff, rod), or as *miṭṭâ* (bed)? Just this question appears in Genesis 47:31, where the Hebrew tradition rightly reads *bed* ("Then Israel bowed himself upon the head of his bed"), but the Septuagint reads *staff*, which mistranslation is quoted in Hebrews 11:21: "By faith Jacob, when dying, blessed each of the sons of Joseph, bowing in worship over the head of his staff."

A similar misunderstanding may lie behind Amos 9:12, where the Hebrew text now reads *Edom* (**אדום**), while the Greek must have read *men* (**אדם**). See Acts 15:17, where once again the New Testament text follows the Septuagint.

Or again, in 1 Chronicles 17:19 the phrase **וכלבך** is interpreted in the present Hebrew text as "and according to your heart" (*ûḵelibbeḵā*), but it should almost certainly be read, "and your dog" (*veḵalbeḵā*). It is an interesting problem, because its solution involves not only the Hebrew text, but also life in the ancient world. As the Hebrew text now stands, the verse reads: "Yahveh, on behalf of your servant and according to your heart you have done all this greatness....." The early Hebrew interpreters had taken the consonants, **וכלבך**, as ו + כ + לב + ך (lit.: "and + according to + heart + your"). The same consonants, however, can also be read ו + כלב + ך (lit.: "and + dog + your"). This is probably the correct reading.

In the ancient Near East it was quite common for one even of high estate to refer to himself as servant or dog as a sign of humility. This way of speaking is known not only from

Babylonian materials, but also from the Hebrew Bible itself. In 2 Kings 8:13, for example, Hazael, who was to become king of Aram, says to Elisha, "What is your servant, the dog, that he [Yahveh] should do this great thing?" Again, in 2 Samuel 9:8 Mephibosheth, son of Jonathan and grandson of Saul, responds to David's showing mercy to him after Saul's death, "What is your servant that you should turn to the dead dog such as I [am]?" There is little doubt that 1 Chronicles 17:19 should be read in this fashion: "Yahveh, on behalf of your servant and your dog you have done this greatness....."

Even with words that employed one or more of the *matres lectionis* there could be problems in reading correctly. This is apparent from the exercise in the previous chapter, where without knowing the language one could not know whether a י stood for *ê* or *î*, or whether the ו of דוד is a mater lectionis to be read *dôḏ* (uncle), or a consonant to be read *Dāvîḏ*.

Even early Jewish interpreters had problems with the correct reading of the *matres*. A famous case in point is the word צלמות which was taken as a compound word: *ṣal-māveṯ*, made up of צל *shadow* and מות *death*, and translated as *shadow of death.* Actually, however, there is no such word, for Hebrew has no compounds. It is now known that the root of the word is צלם *to be dark*, and that the form is a noun with the common ending *-ûṯ*, and is to be read *ṣalmûṯ* with the meaning *darkness.* The word occurs eighteen times in the Hebrew Bible including the well-known passage in Psalm 23:4. It is interesting for the history of Bible translation to note that *RSV* knew the meaning of צלמות and translated it (rightly or wrongly) as *deep darkness* in every place except Psalm 23, where the traditional rendering, "the valley of the shadow of death," was retained. *NRSV* translates it as *the darkest valley.*

The problems surrounding a basically consonantal text together with the high place accorded the Scriptures in Jewish life made it necessary to find some way of establishing and preserving a correct and standard reading of the text. To achieve this end the Masoretes, Jewish scholars devoted to the study and interpretation of the tradition (*masôrâ*), began in the 6th century C.E. to employ a system of signs which would indicate the precise vowel sounds [*vocalization*] of the words. The signs were principally dots and short lines, and came to be called *points*. Thus to indicate the vowels of a word is known as *pointing*, or sometimes as *punctuation* (from *punctus*, point).

This system of Masoretic points was complete in itself, but it did not replace the system of *matres lectionis*, for these *vocalic consonants* were by now part of the official consonantal text. The two systems were simply combined. So it is that a pure long *o* may be indicated by ˙ over the consonant, or by וֹ after the consonant (the combination of the *mater* ו and the Masoretic point ˙ ). When both the Masoretic point and the *mater lectionis* are used, the word is said to be written fully (*plēnē*); when the *mater* is not used for a pure long vowel, but only the point, the word is said to be written defectively (*dēfectivē*).

The following charts give the Masoretic points and their combination with the *matres* for each of the three classes of vowels. They follow the outline of the Hebrew vowels given above in § 6.

## FIRST CLASS VOWELS

| | | |
|---|---|---|
| pure short | a ַ | pataḥ |
| pure long | â ָה (final) ָ | qāmeṣ |
| tone long | ā ָ | qāmeṣ |
| indistinct ($š^e$vâ) | e/a ְ / ֲ | $š^e$vâ / ḥaṭep pataḥ |

## SECOND CLASS VOWELS

| | | | | | |
|---|---|---|---|---|---|
| pure short | i | ִ | e | ֶ | ḥîreq & segôl |
| pure long | î | ִי / ִ | ê | ֵי / ֵ | ḥîreq & ṣērê |
| tone long | ē | ֵ | | | ṣērê |
| indistinct (š$^{e}$vâ) | e/e | ְ / ֱ | | | š$^{e}$vâ / ḥaṭep̱ segôl |

## THIRD CLASS VOWELS

| | | | | | |
|---|---|---|---|---|---|
| pure short | u | ֻ | o | ָ | qibbûṣ & qāmeṣ ḥāṭûp̱ |
| pure long | û | וּ / ֻ | ô | וֹ / ֹ | šûreq / qibbûṣ & ḥōlem |
| tone long | ō | ֹ | | | ḥōlem |
| indistinct (š$^{e}$vâ) | e/o | ְ / ֳ | | | š$^{e}$vâ/ḥaṭep̱ qāmeṣ |

Note in the above charts how the Masoretic points are combined with the *matres lectionis.* Note also that ָ can represent either a long *ā* (qāmeṣ) or a short *o* (qāmeṣ ḥāṭûp̱). The ָ is a *qāmeṣ* in an open syllable or in a closed syllable that is accented; it is a *qāmeṣ ḥāṭûp̱* in a closed unaccented syllable.

## 9 THE WRITING OF HEBREW

Hebrew is written from right to left. Note, however, that when transliterating into English, the English order from left to right is to be followed, for example: אָדָם = 'āḏām.

The vowel points are written under or above the consonants with which they go; for example, lā = לָ ; lî = לִ, lô = לֹ, lû = לֻ
Note how the matres lectionis and Masoretic points are combined: lâ = לָה ; lî = לִי ; lô = לוֹ ; lû = לוּ .

In transliteration the ševâ is written above the line to distinguish it from the short vowel, for example, בָּחִיר = bāḥîr, but בְּרִית = b$^{e}$rîṯ.

Every syllable in Hebrew must begin with a consonant, but never with more than two. Every syllable must have a full vowel; note that in this regard vocal ševâ is not counted as a full vowel. Thus:

(a) דָּבָר (dāḇār) is divided: dā-ḇār
(b) בָּחִיר (bāḥîr) is divided: bā-ḥîr
(c) אֶרֶץ ('ereṣ) is divided: 'e-reṣ
(d) תּוֹרָה (tôrâ) is divided: tô-râ
(e) דְּבָרִים (d$^{e}$ḇārîm) is divided: d$^{e}$ḇā-rîm

## ASSIGNMENT

MEMORIZE the Masoretic points thoroughly

| | | |
|---|---|---|
| קֹדֶשׁ | טוֹב | אָב |
| רָשָׁע | יָם | אֲדֹנָי |

| | | |
|---|---|---|
| אֱמֶת | יְשׁוּעָה | שׁוּב |
| בָּחַר | מָוֶת | שֵׁם |
| בָּרָא | סֵפֶר | שָׁמַיִם |
| בְּרָכָה | עֶבֶד | תּוֹרָה |
| גּוֹי | צְדָקָה | |

TRANSLITERATE the following into Hebrew letters. Remember that the letters, בגדכפת , when hard have a dot in their bosom, and when soft (aspirated) no dot.

| | |
|---|---|
| ’ēl | meleḵ |
| ’$^{e}$mûnâ | nāḇî’ |
| b$^{e}$rîṯ | pešaʿ |
| ḥeseḏ | qāḏôš |
| kāḇôḏ | šālôm |

PRACTICE READING the Hebrew words, putting together consonants and vowels in the words above and in Genesis 1:1-5. Be sure to read aloud.

-------------------

## IV

### 10 THE SYLLABLE IN HEBREW

The *šᵉvâ* and the *dāḡēš* are two signs peculiar to Hebrew, but essential for reading and writing the language. Because they are related to syllabification the following summary of the nature of the syllable in Hebrew will help in understanding their uses.

Hebrew has two kinds of syllables: an *open* syllable, which ends with a vowel, and a *closed* syllable, which ends with a consonant. Every syllable must have a full vowel (thus excluding *šᵉvâ*). The vowel of an open syllable is long, although it may be short if accented. The vowel of a closed syllable is short, although it may be long if accented.

Every syllable must begin with a consonant, but never with more than two. [The conjunction, ו, is the only exception to this rule: usually pointed with *vocal šᵉvâ* (וְ), it becomes וּ before labials or another *vocal šᵉvâ*, thus forming a purely vocalic syllable.] Only one consonant may stand at the end of a closed syllable within a word; no more than two consonants may stand at the end of a closed syllable which is the final syllable of the word.

### 11 THE ŠᵉVÂ

The *šᵉvâ* is used to mark the beginning and the end of a syllable. There are two kinds of *šᵉvâ*: *vocal* ševâ and *silent* ševâ. Except with gutturals (see the chart of Masoretic vowel points in § 8) the signs for vocal and silent ševâ are the same, namely ְ. There is little difficulty in distinguishing them, however, because *vocal* š$^e$vâ can stand only at the beginning of a syllable, and *silent* š$^e$vâ can stand only at the end of a syllable.

The rules for the use of *š$^e$vâ* are as follows:

(a) *Vocal š$^e$vâ* is placed under the first of two consonants beginning a syllable.

Examples: בְּרִית and יְשׁוּעָה
With gutturals a *composite* š$^e$vâ is used, as in אֱמֶת and חֲסָדִים

Note: As it will be seen later, vocal š$^e$vâ is often the result of inflection, for example, when tone long vowels are reduced.

(b) *Silent š$^e$vâ* is placed (i) under the single sounded consonant ending a syllable if it is not the final consonant of the word, or (ii) under the two consonants ending a word if both consonants are sounded.

Examples: מִשְׁפָּט (mišpāṭ) and שָׁם (šām)
קֹשְׁטְ (qōšṭ) and מָלַכְתְּ (mālaḵt), but
חֵטְא (ḥēṭ') and לִקְרָאת (liqrā'ṯ) because the 'ālep is quiescent

Remember: vocal š$^e$vâ can stand only at the beginning of a syllable, while silent š$^e$vâ can stand only at the end of a syllable. When two š$^e$vâs appear together, the first must be silent and the second vocal, as in יִמְלְכוּ (yiml$^e$ḵû).

(c) Frequently in composition and inflection two vocal š$^e$vâs come together, setting up an unpronounceable succession of sounds. When this happens, the following adjustments in vocalization are made.

(i) If both š$^{e}$vâs are simple š$^{e}$vâs, the first becomes a short vowel, usually a ḥîreq: ִ ְ < ְ ְ; as, for example, in the following:

לִמְלָכִים < לְמְלָכִים < לְ + מְלָכִים
דִּבְרֵי < דְּבְרֵי < דְּבָרִים

(ii) If one of the š$^{e}$vâs is a composite š$^{e}$vâ, the first becomes the short vowel of the composite: ֶ ֱ < ְ ֱ or ַ ֲ < ְ ֲ; as, for example, in the following:

בֶּאֱמוּנָה < בְּאֱמוּנָה < בְּ + אֱמוּנָה
חַכְמֵי < חֲכְמֵי < חֲכָמִים
וַעֲמוֹד < וְעֲמוֹד < וְ + עֲמוֹד

## 12 THE DĀG̱ĒŠ

The *dāgēš* is a dot placed in the middle of a consonant. There are two kinds: *dāgēš lēnē* (which hardens the spirants) and *dāgēš fortē* (which doubles the consonant). Although they are identical in form, they are mutually exclusive in function, and so there is little difficulty in distinguishing the one from the other. The following summary makes clear their uses.

(a) *Dāgēš lēnē* is used only with the spirants, בגדכפת, and indicates their hard sound. It is placed in the spirants only when there is no vowel sound whatsoever (including vocal š$^{e}$vâ) immediately before them.

Examples: דָּבָר and דְּבָרִים
עֶבֶד and עֲבָדִים, but עַבְדֵי

(b) *Dāgēš fortē* is used in all letters except the gutturals, אהחע, and ר. It cannot be used in the first or last consonants of a word, but only within the word, where its function is to double the consonant. The doubled consonant ends one syllable and begins the next, and so the *dāgēš fortē* can only follow a full vowel (thus excluding vocal šᵉvâ), because every syllable must have a full vowel. Since the syllable ended by the doubled consonant is now closed, its vowel is short if it is unaccented, but may be long if accented.

Examples: צַדִּיק (ṣad-dîq)
יָם in the plural is יַמִּים (yam-mîm)
עַתָּה (ʻat-tâ), but also עָתָּה (ʻāt-tâ)

Remember: Dāgēš lēnē *cannot* follow a vowel, but dāgeš fortē *must*!

## ASSIGNMENT

LEARN the rules for the syllable, šᵉvâ, and dāgēš.

PRACTICE READING aloud Amos 5:18-20 and Psalm 23.

TRANSLITERATE the following into English letters. Practice pronouncing the Hebrew words, being sure to say them aloud.

| | | |
|---|---|---|
| מִשְׁתֶּה | אֲדֹנַי | אָב |
| עִמָּנוּ-אֵל | מִדְבָּר | קִדֵּשׁ |
| יִשְׂרָאֵל | אַפַּיִם | בְּרָכָה |
| אַהֲבָה | דָּבָר | חַסְדּוֹ |
| מַלְכֵי | אֱלֹהִים | יְקַדְּשׁוּ |

יָדַעְתִּי    זֶבַח    יִרְמְיָהוּ

הַבְּרָכוֹת    הַלְלוּ-יָהּ    נֶפֶשׁ

יִלָּחֵם    אָרְכּוֹ    הִשְׁתַּחֲווּ

מַלְכְּךָ

TRANSLITERATE the following into Hebrew letters.

| | |
|---|---|
| ’āḏôn | ‘aḇāḏîm |
| miṣvâ | šāṯâ |
| yiḵtōḇ | ḥasāḏîm |
| dibbēr | yiššāḇe‘û |
| yiṣḥāq | kōhanîm |
| ’emeṯ | hannāḇî’ |
| mišpāṭ | ḥaḇaqqûq |
| ’ap̄ | |

--------------------

# V

## 13 THE NOUN: GENERAL REMARKS

The characteristics of the noun in Hebrew may be summarized as follows.

There are *two genders* in Hebrew: masculine and feminine. Hebrew has no neuter gender.

Nouns have *three numbers*: singular, plural, and dual. In biblical Hebrew the dual is restricted primarily to the numeral two and to natural body pairs, such as eyes, ears, and feet. Verbs and adjectives have no dual number, and so use the plural with nouns in the dual.

Nouns have *two states*: (1) the absolute state, used for the subject, direct and indirect objects, and the last member of a genitival relationship; and (2) the construct state, used for the first member of a genitival relationship.

There are *no case endings* in biblical Hebrew. This was not always so. At one time Hebrew employed case endings in common with other ancient Semitic languages: *u* for the nominative, *i* for the genitive, and *a* for the accusative. Only a trace of this early usage remains in biblical Hebrew.

There are *three declensions* [or, *patterns of declension*] of nouns. (1) The *first declension* is characterized by *a* vowels and the reduction of tone long vowels in open syllables distant from the tone (accent). Examples of noun patterns in this declension are דָּבָר, נָבִיא, כָּבֵד, קָטוֹן, and כּוֹכָב. Nominal forms with unchangeable vowels, such as סוּס, שִׁיר, צַדִּיק, are also included within this first declension pattern. (2) The *second declension* is based on original monosyllables, and is characterized by nouns having the accent on the penult, a s$^{e}$gôl in the last syllable and the return of the original mononsyllabic vowel in inflection, for example מֶלֶךְ, סֵפֶר, and בֹּקֶר (3) The *third declension* is characterized by an unchangeable vowel in the first syllable and a ṣērê in the second syllable, which is reduced to š$^{e}$vâ when in the course of inflection it falls in an open syllable near the tone (accent). Examples of this declension are אוֹכֵל and מִסְפֵּד.

The singular, plural and dual endings are *the same* for all three declensions.

## 14 THE ENDINGS FOR THE ABSOLUTE STATE

Masculine nouns have no special ending for the singular. Plural and dual endings are placed directly on the simple masculine singular form.

| | | | |
|---|---|---|---|
| *Masculine:* | *sing.* | --- | סוּס |
| | *plur.* | ִים | סוּסִים |
| | *dual* | ַיִם | סוּסַיִם |

Feminine nouns have two forms: one, like the masculine nouns, with no special ending for the singular, and one with the ending ה (sometimes ת, which was the original feminine stem). Note that this original ת reappears as part of the dual stem in nouns that end in ה.

| | | | |
|---|---|---|---|
| *Feminine:* | *sing.* | --- | יָד |
| | *plur.* | וֹת | יָדוֹת |
| | *dual* | ַיִם | יָדַיִם |
| | | OR | |
| | *sing.* | ָה | סוּסָה |
| | *plur.* | וֹת | סוּסוֹת |
| | *dual* | ָת + ַיִם | סוּסָתַיִם |

When endings are placed on the words, modifications in the pointing take place, because the accent shifts when endings are added. These are explained in §§ 15-17, where each of the three declensions is described in detail. The *construct state*, used in genitival relationships, is simply a modification of the *absolute* forms, and is discussed below in VII, §§ 23-25.

## 15 THE FIRST DECLENSION

The first declension is characterized by nouns with a tone long ָ in the tone (accented) syllable, or in the pretone, or in both. Adjectives and nouns with unchangeable vowels are also included in this declension. Typical patterns are כּוֹכָב, קָדוֹשׁ, זָקֵן, בָּחִיר, דָּבָר ; cf. also צַדִּיק, שִׁיר, סוּס .

Except for the vowels written with *matres*, the vowels of first declension nouns are tone long, that is, long because of their nearness to the tone (accent); for example, in דָּבָר the ָ of -בָר is tone long because it is in a closed syllable under tone (with the accent); the ָ of -דָּ is also tone long because it is in an open syllable near (just before) the tone.

When an ending is placed on a noun or adjective, another syllable is added to the word; and because the endings take the accent the syllabification of the word is also changed; for example: דָּבָר has two syllables, the tone syllable -בָר and the near open (pretone) -דָּ ; with the addition of the plural ending ִים there are now three syllables: דָּבָרִים , the tone syllable -רִים , the pretone, or near open syllable -בָ- , and the distant (more than one syllable before the tone) open syllable -דָּ .

The rule for inflection of first declension nominal forms is that tone long vowels in distant open syllables are reduced to vocal šᵉvâ. Note the following examples.

דָּבָר + ִים > דָּבָרִים > דְּבָרִים

זָקֵן + ִים > זָקֵנִים > זְקֵנִים

בָּחִיר + ִים > בָּחִירִים > בְּחִירִים

*but* כּוֹכָב + ִים > כּוֹכָבִים > כּוֹכָבִים

(Note that while the syllable -כּוֹ is distant open, the vowel is pure long.)

## 16 THE SECOND DECLENSION

Second declension nouns were originally monosyllabic, as for example, *malk(u)* (king), *sipr(u)* (book), *buqr(u)* (morning). With the dropping of case endings a helping vowel came to be placed between the second and third consonants (or, radicals) to aid pronunciation: *malku* > *malk* > *malek̲* > *melek̲*; or, *sipru* > *sipr* > *sip̲er* > *sep̲er*; or again *buqru* > *buqr* > *buqer* > *boqer*.

The accent of these nouns was on the original thematic vowel, and in the simple singular form remained there even with the added helping vowel. In inflection, however, the helping vowel disappears, and the accent shifts to the ending; for example מֶ֫לֶךְ *king*, but מַלְכִּ֫י *my king*. Exactly the same thing happens in English with the word *prism*, which has a helping vowel (unwritten) between the last two consonants, but in other forms of the word, such as *prismatic*, the helping vowel disappears and the accent changes. Because of the wide use of s^e^gôl as the helping vowel, the nouns of the second declension are often called *segolates*.

There are three classes of segolate nouns, corresponding to the three classes of vowels: *a*, *i/e*, and *o/u*. Using the paradigm קטל , they are called *qaṭl*, *qiṭl*, and *quṭl*.

(1) qaṭl (original ַ )  מֶ֫לֶךְ < מַלְךְ

(2) qiṭl (original ִ )  סֵ֫פֶר < סִפְר
צֶ֫דֶק < צִדְק

(3) quṭl (original ֻ or ָ / ֹ)  בֹּ֫קֶר < בָּקְר

Note that gutturals prefer *a* vowels, especially before them, so that a second declension noun with a guttural for its third radical has ַ instead of ֶ before it, as for example זֶ֫רַע *seed* and מֶ֫לַח *salt.* If the second radical is a guttural the s$^{e}$gôls before and after the guttural become pataḥ, as in בַּ֫עַל *Ba'al* and שַׁ֫חַר *dawn.*

In the singular the inflection of masculine and feminine nouns is the same; so masculine nouns like מֶ֫לֶךְ *king*, סֵ֫פֶר *book* and בֹּ֫קֶר *morning* appear similar to feminine nouns like אֶ֫רֶץ *earth*, צֶ֫דֶק *righteousness* and אֹ֫זֶן *ear*. With suffixes the original monosyllabic forms with their original thematic vowels reappear, but again masculine and feminine nouns are treated in the same way: מַלְכִּי *my king*, סִפְרוֹ *his book*, בָּקְרָהּ *her morning*, אַרְצִי *my earth*, צִדְקוֹ *his righteousness*, and אָזְנָהּ *her ear*.

In the dual the regular dual ending is placed directly on the original monosyllabic form; for example:

| | | | |
|---|---|---|---|
| רֶ֫גֶל | *foot* | רַגְלַ֫יִם < ־ַיִם + רַגְל | *feet* |
| אֹ֫זֶן | *ear* | אָזְנַ֫יִם < ־ַיִם + אָזְן | *ears* |

In the plural second declension nouns appear to follow a first declension analogy (tone long *a* vowels with reduction of distant open syllables). This may be due to an original internal plural stem (compare English *man* and its plural form *men*) to which has been added the usual plural endings. In any case, the plural of all second declension nouns may be formed by assuming an internal plural stem, namely ָ ָ , for all three classes (qaṭl, qiṭl, quṭl) of nouns; so the masculine nouns -מָלָךְ , -סָפָר , and -בָּקָר , and the feminine nouns -אָרָץ , -צָדָק , and -אָזָן . To these one adds the appropriate plural ending, reducing the resulting distant open ָ to vocal š$^{e}$vâ (using the composite š$^{e}$vâ with gutturals), as in the following.

| | |
|---|---|
| מְלָכִים < מָלָכִים < ִים + -מָלָךְ | *kings* |
| סְפָרִים < סָפָרִים < ִים + -סָפָר | *books* |
| בְּקָרִים < בָּקָרִים < ִים + -בָּקָר | *mornings* |
| אֲרָצוֹת < אָרָצוֹת < וֹת + -אָרָץ | *lands* |
| צְדָקוֹת < צָדָקוֹת < וֹת + -צָדָק | *saving acts* |
| אֲזָנוֹת < אָזָנוֹת < וֹת + -אָזָן | *ears* |

## 17 THE THIRD DECLENSION

Third declension nouns are characterized by an unchangeable vowel in the pretone (the next to the last syllable ) and a ֵ in the tone (accented) syllable. An unchangeable vowel is either a short vowel in an unaccented closed syllable, as in מַמְלָכָה , or a pure long vowel such as ִי , ֵי , וּ , and וֹ (often written *defectivé* as a simple ֹ ). Note the following examples of third declension nouns: מִסְפֵּד *mourning*, מַקֵּל *staff*, מְחַדֵּשׁ *one who renews*, [שֹׁפֵט] שׁוֹפֵט *ruler*; cf. also שֵׁם *name.*

With vocalic endings (endings that begin with a vowel) third declension nouns reduce the near open ṣērê to vocal š$^{e}$vâ. Note that this is just the opposite of first declension nouns, which reduce when possible the distant open. Note the following examples.

| | |
|---|---|
| מִסְפְּדִים < מִסְפֵּדִים < ִים + מִסְפֵּד | mournings |
| מַקְלוֹת < מַקֵּלוֹת < וֹת + מַקֵּל | staves |
| מְקַדְּשִׁים < מְקַדֵּשִׁים < ִים + מְקַדֵּשׁ | renewers |
| שׁוֹפְטִים < שׁוֹפֵטִים < ִים + שׁוֹפֵט | rulers |

With consonantal endings (endings that begin with a consonant) third declension nouns modify the near open ṣērê to s[e]gôl, as in the following.

| | | |
|---|---|---|
| מִסְפֶּדְךָ < ךָ + מִסְפֵּד | | your mourning |
| מַקֶּלְךָ < ךָ + מַקֵּל | | your staff |
| מְחַדֶּשְׁךָ < ךָ + מְחַדֵּשׁ | | your renewer |
| שׁוֹפֶטְךָ < ךָ + שׁוֹפֵט | | your ruler |

## VOCABULARY

אֶרֶץ *n.f.* earth, country

שָׁמַיִם *n.m., only dual* heaven(s)

דָּבָר *n.m.* word, thing, event

טוֹב *adj.* good, pleasing, pleasant

רַע *adj.* evil, harmful, unpleasant

כָּבוֹד *n.m.* glory

מֶלֶךְ *n.m.* king

נָבִיא *n.m.* prophet

קֹדֶשׁ *n.m.* holiness

קָדוֹשׁ *adj.* holy

צֶדֶק *n.m.* righteousness, saving activity

צְדָקָה *n.f.* righteousness, righteous or saving act

צַדִּיק *adj.* righteous

רוּחַ *n.f.* wind, spirit*

תּוֹרָה *n.f.* instruction, revelation, law

* Pronounced *rû-aḥ*. The paṯaḥ is a *furtive paṯaḥ*, inserted before a final guttural without an *a* vowel to help keep the guttural sound. In inflection when the guttural is no longer final, the paṯaḥ disappears, e.g. רוּחִי *my spirit.*

## ASSIGNMENT

This chapter presents the noun as a whole, all three declensions in the absolute state. It may be desirable to divide the materials into two parts, the first dealing only with the first declension, and the second with all the materials together. The assignment is divided accordingly: Assignment A deals only with the first declension, while Assignment B deals with all three.

### ASSIGNMENT A

(a) Write the plural of the following nouns.

אָדוֹן   דּוֹד   זָהָב   חָכְמָה   שִׁירָה

(b) Write the dual and plural of the following nouns.

יָד   שָׂפָה

(c) Write the masculine plural and the feminine singular and plural of the following adjectives and participles.

גָּדוֹל   מַזְכִּיר   נִכְבָּד   צַדִּיק   רָשָׁע

### ASSIGNMENT B

(a) Write the plural of the following nouns.

מִסְפֵּד   מֶלֶךְ   כָּבוֹד   דָּבָר   אֶרֶץ

תּוֹרָה   רוּחַ   צְדָקָה   נָבִיא   מִצְוָה

(b) Write the dual of the following nouns.

יָד רֶ֫גֶל שָׂפָה אֹ֫זֶן בֶּ֫רֶךְ

(c) Write the masculine plural and the feminine singular and plural of the following adjectives and participles.

טוֹב שָׁמֵן אוֹכֵל קָדוֹשׁ חוֹטֵא

PRACTICE READING AND RECOGNIZING NOUNS in Isaiah 6:1-3 and Psalm 23.

--------------------

# VI

## 18 THE DEFINITE ARTICLE

English has both definite and indefinite articles. Hebrew has only a definite article: . הַ (הַ followed by dāgēš fortē). It is attached directly to the noun or adjective. See the following examples.

(a) word דָּבָר
the word הַדָּבָר < דָּבָר + . הַ

(a) saving act צְדָקָה
the saving act הַצְּדָקָה < צְדָקָה + . הַ

A problem arises, however with the gutturals (אהחע) and ר, which cannot take a dāgēš fortē. Because of this the pointing of the article before these consonants is modified in a variety of ways. It is not necessary here to learn all these variations by memory, but one should be aware of the possibilities in pointing the article, for this is important for getting to the root of a word. The following chart outlines these possibilities.

. הַ Before all consonants except gutturals and ר
הַ Before ה and ח (except with ָ )*
הָ Before א, ר, ע (except unaccented עָ ) and accented הָ **
הֶ Before חָ, חֳ and unaccented הָ and עָ ***

*Examples: הַחֵטְא *the sin*; הַֽהֵיכָל הַהוּא *that palace.* Note the small mark under the first ה ; this is called a *meṯeg* (bridle), and is placed on the second (counting vocal š$^{e}$vâ) full syllable before the tone if that syllable is open. It serves to protect a full vowel in an open syllable distant from the tone. It also serves to indicate a secondary accent within a word.

**Examples: הָאָב *the father*; הָאִישׁ *the man*; הָֽרָשָׁע *the wicked (one)*; הָעִיר *the city*; הָהָר *the mountain.*

***Examples: הֶחָג *the festival*; הֶֽחָבֵר *the friend, companion*; הָֽחֳלִי *the sickness*; הֶֽעָפָר *the ground, dust.*

## 19 THE INSEPARABLE PREPOSITIONS

Like the article, certain very common prepositions are attached directly to the nominal form. Because they cannot stand alone, they are called inseparable prepositions. These are:

בְּ *in, by, with, at, from*
כְּ *like, according to, as*
לְ *to, for*

The usual pointing of these prepositions is with vocal šᵉvâ; for example, בְּשָׁלוֹם *in peace,* כְּאֵל *like a god,* לְגוֹי *for a people.* Before another vocal šᵉvâ, however, the pointing is modified as follows.

Before a simple vocal šᵉvâ the inseparable preposition is pointed with ḥîreq:

לִמְלָכִימ < לְמְלָכִים < מְלָכִים + לְ *for kings*

Before a composite ševâ the inseparable preposition is pointed with the short vowel of the composite:

לַאֲדֹנִי < לְאֲדֹנִי < אֲדֹנִי + לְ *to my lord*
בֶּאֱמוּנָה < בְּאֱמוּנָה < אֱמוּנָה + בְּ *by faithfulness*

When an inseparable preposition is placed on a word which has the definite article, the preposition replaces the ה of the article, but retains the pointing of the article.

בַּדָּבָר < בְּהַדָּבָר < הַדָּבָר + בְּ *by the word*
כֶּעָפָר < כְּהֶעָפָר < הֶעָפָר + כְּ *as the dust*
לַהֵיכָל < לְהַהֵיכָל < הַהֵיכָל + לְ *to the palace*

The preposition מִן *from, out of*, sai may stand by itself; as for example in מִן סֵפֶר *from a book*, or מִן הַהֵיכָל *from the palace.* It may also be joined to its object by a *maqqēp̱* (hyphen), for example מִן-סֵפֶר and מִן-הַהֵיכָל.

> Note that all words before the maqqēp lose their accent, and so tone long vowels in closed syllables become short, for example, אֵת כֹּל הַדָּבָר *all the word*, but with maqqēp, אֶת-כָּל-הַדָּבָר.

The preposition מִן may also be attached directly to the noun, as are the inseparable prepositions. This is because of the weakness of נ, which when it has no vowel of its own tends to be assimilated into the next consonant. The same phenomenon is known in English, where the *n* of the negative particle *in-* when used with a word like *mobile* becomes *m*: so *in* + *mobile* > *inmobile* > *immobile.* The same thing happens in Hebrew when מִן is attached directly to a nominal form.

When מִן is attached directly to a noun, the נ of מִן is assimilated into the first consonant of the noun by dāgēš fortē:

מִסֵּפֶר < מִנְסֵפֶר < סֵפֶר + מִן *from a book*

Before gutturals, however, the נ cannot be assimilated since gutturals cannot take dāgēš fortē. In this case the נ is dropped, and compensation for the loss of the נ is made by raising the ḥîreq of מִן to its tone long, ṣērê.

מֵעִיר < מִעִיר < מִנְעִיר < עִיר + מִן *from a city*

Note that with words that have the article, מִן with maqqēp is most often used: מִן-הָאָרֶץ instead of מֵהָאָרֶץ.

## 20 THE CONJUNCTION VAV [וּ]

The conjunction וְ *and* is similar to the inseparable prepositions in that is placed directly on the word which it introduces. Like the inseparable prepositions it too is pointed with vocal š$^{e}$vâ, as in וְדָבָר *and a word.* There are differences, however, when וְ comes before a simple vocal š$^{e}$vâ or one of the labials [ב ו מ פ].

Before simple vocal š$^{e}$vâ and the labials [ב ו מ פ] וְ becomes וּ, and is the only exception to the rule that every syllable must begin with a consonant.

וּצְדָקָה < וְצְדָקָה < צְדָקָה + וְ *and righteousness*

וּמִצְוָה < וְמִצְוָה < מִצְוָה + וְ *and a commandment*

Before a composite ševâ the וְ takes the short vowel of the composite; cf. the inseparable prepositions.

וֶאֱמוּנָה < וְאֱמוּנָה < אֱמוּנָה + וְ *and faithfulness*

Note that the conjunction וְ does not replace the ה of the article.

## 21 THE USE OF THE ADJECTIVE

In Hebrew, as in other languages, the adjective must agree in gender and number with the noun it modifies, remembering, of course, that the adjective has no dual form, and so uses the plural form with nouns in the dual. The adjective may be used in two ways: as a qualifying adjective and as a predicate adjective.

The qualifying adjective stands after the noun it modifies. If the noun is definite, having the article, so must also the adjective be definite, having the article. If more than one adjective is used with a definite noun, each is definite and so each must have the definite article. Note the following examples of the qualifying adjective.

| | |
|---|---|
| מֶלֶךְ חָכָם | *a wise king* |
| הַמֶּלֶךְ הֶחָכָם | *the wise king* |
| הַמֶּלֶךְ הֶחָכָם וְהַטּוֹב | *the wise and good king* |

The predicate adjective does not take the article, and usually stands before the subject.

| | |
|---|---|
| חָכָם הַמֶּלֶךְ | *The king is wise.* |
| חָכָם וְטוֹב הַמֶּלֶךְ | *The king is wise and good.* |

Note: מֶלֶךְ חָכָם *a wise king,*
but חָכָם מֶלֶךְ *A king is wise.*

Hebrew has no special forms for comparison of adjectives, such as *good, better, best.* To express the *comparative* degree, Hebrew uses the adjective followed by מִן, for example: טוֹב מִן־הַמֶּלֶךְ הוּא, which means literally, *He is good from the king*; that is, *He is better than the king.* The *superlative* degree may be expressed by using the definite article with the adjective, for example: הַקָּדוֹשׁ הוּא, literally, *He is the Holy (One),* where the context may make it clear that what is meant is, *He is the Holiest.* The superlative may also be expressed in such phrases as *the holy of holies*, that is, *the most holy*; or by simple repetition, as in *Holy, holy, holy is Yahveh of hosts.*

## 22 THE COPULATIVE AND HEBREW

While the notion of existence, *there is* and *there is not*, is expressed in Hebrew by יֵשׁ and אֵין, and the active notions of *to become* and *to happen* are expressed by הָיָה , the simple verb *to be* in such a sentence as *The king is wise*, does not exist. There is no copula in Hebrew, and so it has to be supplied when translating into English. This means that the choice of form and tense, even position within the sentence, is a matter of interpretation, and needless to say is often the occasion for sharp differences of opinion.

The Ten Commandments, for example, begin with the words, אָנֹכִי יהוה אֱלֹהֶיךָ , literally: *I Yahveh your-God.* Should this be translated, *I [am] Yahveh, your God*, as it is traditionally, or should it be translated in the style of ancient royal decrees, *I, Yahveh, [am] your God*?

Or again, in Amos 7:14 the prophet is speaking about the validity of his ministry at Bethel, and in answer to his being told to go back to Judah and earn his living there, he says (according to the traditional rendering which is continued in the main text of the *NRSV*:

> *I am no prophet, nor a prophet's son [or: one of the sons of the prophets]; but I am a herdsman, and a dresser of sycamore trees, and the LORD took me from following the flock, and the LORD said to me, Go, prophesy to my people Israel. Now therefore, hear the word of the LORD.*

This has generally been taken as drawing a sharp distinction between Amos and the prophets, suggesting that while he may have fulfilled a prophetic function, he is not to be regarded as an official prophet or part of the prophetic movement. This has significant implications for the interpreter of the Hebrew Bible (and also for Christians who look for biblical patterns for understanding the nature of ministry). The passage, however, can, and probably should be read differently. At the beginning of verse 14 the Hebrew reads quite simply:

לֹא-נָבִיא אָנֹכִי וְלֹא בֶן-נָבִיא אָנֹכִי כִּי-בוֹקֵר אָנֹכִי
וּבוֹלֵס שִׁקְמִים . . .

[Literally: *not prophet I and-not son-of a-prophet*
*I but herdsman I and-tender-of sycamores* . . .]

This passage can be read: *I (was) not a prophet, nor (was) I* a son of a prophet [that is, a member of a prophetic guild], *but I (was) a herdsman and a tender of sycamores, and Yahveh took me from the flock and said to me, Go, be a prophet* [the verb is derived from the noun] *to my people Israel. Now hear the word of Yahveh!* Such a translation represents quite a different understanding of Amos' relation to the prophets and ultimately of the nature of Israelite prophecy itself.

Another example of the problems raised because Hebrew has no copula is seen in the *Šᵉma' Yiśrā'ēl* in Deuteronomy 6:4: שְׁמַע יִשְׂרָאֵל יהוה אֱלֹהֵינוּ יהוה אֶחָד. Literally translated the passage reads: *Hear Israel Yahveh our-God Yahveh one/only/alone.* Depending upon where one places the copula, the verse may be translated in any one of four ways:

> *Hear, O Israel, Yahveh our God is one Yahveh.*
> [This is the traditional rendering, which, of course, substitutes LORD for the name Yahveh.]
> *Hear, O Israel, Yahveh our God, Yahveh is one.*
> *Hear, O Israel, Yahveh is our God, Yahveh is one.*
> *Hear, O Israel, Yahveh is our God, Yahveh alone.*

## VOCABULARY

אָב *n.m.* father; pl. אָבוֹת

בֵּן *n.m.* son, offspring, child; pl. בָּנִים

אָדוֹן *n.m.* lord

אֲדֹנָי *n.m. pl. (of majesty)* (lit. my lords) the Lord, i.e. Yahveh

אַיִן *subst. (particle of negation)* there is not

יֵשׁ *subst. (particle of existence)* there is
אִישׁ *n.m.* man; *pl.* אֲנָשִׁים
אִשָּׁה *n.f.* woman; *pl.* נָשִׁים
אֵל *n.m.* god
אֱלֹהִים *n.m. pl. (of majesty)* god(s), God
אָמֵן *vb.* to be firm, stable
אֱמֶת *n.f.* truth, faithfulness
אֱמוּנָה *n.f.* faithfulness
הַר *n.m.* mountain
חֵטְא *n.m.* sin
כּוֹל / כֹּל *n.m.* all, whole
עִיר *n.f.* city; *pl.* עָרִים
בְּ *prep.* in, by, with, at, against, from
כְּ *prep.* like, according to, as
לְ *prep.* to, for
מִן *prep.* from, out of, at
רָשָׁע *adj.* wicked

## ASSIGNMENT

PRACTICE READING AND RECOGNIZING NOUNS, noting their prefixed elements in Exodus 20:1-6.

READ ALOUD AND TRANSLATE into English.

1. יהוה הָאֱלֹהִים :

2. הַתּוֹרָה מֵאֱלֹהִים :

3. טוֹב הָאָב לַבֵּן :

4. רָשָׁע הָאִישׁ בֶּאֱמֶת ׃

5. יֵשׁ לַמֶּלֶךְ אֶרֶץ רָעָה ׃

6. הַמְּלָכִים הַטּוֹבִים כִּנְבִיאִים מִן-הַשָּׁמַיִם ׃

7. אֵין צֶדֶק בַּשָּׁמַיִם וּבָאָרֶץ ׃

8. כָּאָב כַּבֵּן ׃

9. אֵין נָבִיא בְּכָל-הָאָרֶץ ׃

TRANSLATE into Hebrew.

1. The man and woman are righteous.

2. Faithfulness is in the city.

3. The evil word is from the Holy One.

--------------------

# VII

## 23 THE CONSTRUCT STATE OF THE NOUN

The noun in Hebrew, as noted above in § 13, has two states: (1) *the absolute state*, which is the basic form used for subjects and objects and the last member of a genitival relation; and (2) *the construct state*, used only as the first member of a genitival relation. In the phrase, *great of heart*, *great of* is in the construct state and *heart* is in the absolute. Again, in the phrase, *word of the king*, the first element, *word of*, is in the construct, and the second, *the king*, is in the absolute. In Hebrew the genitival relationship can only be expressed in this full form. There is nothing in Hebrew to correspond to the English use of *'s* to express possession, as in *the king's word*; in Hebrew one must always say *the word of the king*.

The first word of a genitival relationship is put in the construct state. Since it is dependent for its completion on the last word of the phrase (the word in the absolute state) it is reduced to its shortest form. Beginning with the absolute form, this is done in two ways: (1) by the reduction of tone long vowels, and (2) by the contraction of endings.

(1) *The reduction of tone long vowels* affects the pointing in two ways:

(i) tone long vowels in near open syllables are reduced to vocal ševâ, for example:

גְדוֹל < גָדוֹל　　　　קְדוֹשׁ < קָדוֹשׁ

(ii) tone long vowels in closed accented syllables are reduced to short vowels, for example:

כּוֹכָב > כּוֹכַב      דָּבָר > דְּבַר

It is as if the word in construct had no accent at all; indeed, the word in construct is frequently joined to the word in absolute by a maqqēp, as in דְּבַר-הַמֶּלֶךְ *the word of the king.*

(2) *The contraction of endings* for words in construct is as follows:

(i) the masculine plural ִים and the masculine and feminine dual ַיִם are contracted to ֵי , for example:

סוּסִים > סוּסֵי      דְּבָרִים > דִּבְרֵי      שְׂפָתַיִם > שִׂפְתֵי

Note in the last two examples that the reduction of tone long vowels to vocal š$^{e}$vâ results in two vocal š$^{e}$vâs together. This happens frequently in forming the construct, and the regular rules as outlined in § 11 are followed. Note also that whenever the ending ֵי occurs, it can only be a plural or dual construct form.

(ii) the feminine singular ending ָה is contracted to ַת (the primitive feminine stem), for example:

סוּסָה > סוּסַת      צְדָקָה > צִדְקַת

Note that the feminine plural ending וֹת remains unchanged.

## 24 THE INFLECTION OF NOUNS IN THE CONSTRUCT STATE

The inflection of *first declension* nouns in the construct state may be summarized by the following examples.

| | | | | |
|---|---|---|---|---|
| Masculine: | sg. | ------ | סוּס | דָּבָר |
| | pl. | ֵי < ִים | סוּסֵי | דִּבְרֵי |
| | du. | ֵי < ַיִם | סוּסֵי | דִּבְרֵי |

| | | | |
|---|---|---|---|
| Feminine | sg. | ------ | יָד |
| | pl. | וֹת < וֹת | יְדוֹת |
| | du. | ֵי < ַיִם | יְדֵי |

OR

| | | | | |
|---|---|---|---|---|
| Feminine | sg. | ַת < ָה | סוּסַת | שְׂפַת |
| | pl. | וֹת < וֹת | סוּסוֹת | שִׂפוֹת |
| | du. | ְתֵי < ָתַיִם | סוּסְתֵי | שִׂפְתֵי |

In the *second declension* nouns in the singular have the same form for both the absolute and construct states; only the context can determine which. In the construct dual and plural second declension nouns are similar to the first declension, contracting endings and reducing tone long vowels. One difference from the first declension, however, is that in second declension nouns when two vocal šᵉvâs come together, the first does not become a ḥîreq, but the original thematic vowel of the noun. This happens only in the plural. Note the following examples.

| | |
|---|---|
| מַלְכֵי < מְלְכֵי < מְלָכִים | מֶלֶךְ |
| סִפְרֵי < סְפְרֵי < סְפָרִים | סֵפֶר |
| בָּקְרֵי < בְּקְרֵי < בְּקָרִים | בֹּקֶר |
| נַפְשׁוֹת < נְפְשׁוֹת < נְפָשׁוֹת | נֶפֶשׁ |

Note that the šᵉvâ of the construct plural is a vocal šᵉvâ (despite the short vowel of the first syllable), because it is the reduction of a tone long ָ . Since the dual of second declension nouns is built on the original monosyllabic form, there is no reduction of tone long vowels in forming the construct, only the contraction of the ending ַיִם, for example רַגְלֵי < רַגְלַיִם and אָזְנֵי < אָזְנַיִם.

In the *third declension* the singular construct is usually the same as the absolute, except with nouns like מִזְבֵּחַ which because of the gutteral form their construct with pataḥ: מִזְבַּח. In the plural, because tone long vowels are already reduced, only the dual and masculine plural endings need to be contracted.

## 25 THE USE OF THE CONSTRUCT

A word in construct cannot take the definite article. If the word in the absolute is definite, the *whole expression* is definite.

| | |
|---|---|
| דְּבַר-הַמֶּלֶךְ | *the word of the king* |
| דְּבַר-דָּוִד | *the word of David* |

If one wishes to say a word of the king, one must use a construction such as דָּבָר לַמֶּלֶךְ, literally *a word belonging to the king*, that is, *a word of the king.*

A word in construct immediately precedes the word in the absolute with which it goes. There can be no intervening words. Note, however, that there can be a chain of constructs, as in דְּבַר אֱלֹהֵי הַשָּׁמַיִם *the word of the God of the heavens.*

An adjective modifying a word in construct follows the whole expression, and while agreeing in gender and number with the word in construct is in the absolute state.

| | |
|---|---|
| דִּבְרֵי הַמֶּלֶךְ הַטּוֹבִים | *the good words of the king* |
| תּוֹרַת הָאֱלֹהִים הַקְּדוֹשָׁה | *the holy law of God* |
| דִּבְרֵי מֶלֶךְ אֲרָם גְּדוֹלִים | *the great words of the king of Aram* |
| דִּבְרֵי מֶלֶךְ אֲרָם הַגָּדוֹל | *the words of the great king of Aram* |

Ambiguities can of course arise; for example, דְּבַר הַמֶּלֶךְ הַטּוֹב can be translated either as *the good word of the king*, or as *the word of the good king.* Only the context can make the choice clear.

## 26 PERSONAL AND DEMONSTRATIVE PRONOUNS

(a) The *personal pronouns* in Hebrew are used only in the nominative case. For direct objects, for objects of prepositions, or for showing possession pronominal suffixes are used; see § 28.

| | | |
|---|---|---|
| 1c sg | אָנֹכִי, אֲנִי | I |
| 2m sg | אַתָּה | you (masc.) |
| 2f sg | אַתְּ | you (fem.) |
| 3m sg | הוּא | he |
| 3f sg | הִיא | she |
| 1c pl | אֲנַחְנוּ | we |
| 2m pl | אַתֶּם | you (masc.) |
| 2f pl | אַתֵּן, אַתֵּנָה | you (fem.) |
| 3m pl | הֵם, הֵמָּה | they (masc.) |
| 3f pl | הֵנָּה | they (fem.) |

(b) The demonstrative pronouns are closely related to the third person forms of the personal pronouns.

| | | | |
|---|---|---|---|
| זֶה | this (masc.) | הוּא | that (masc.) |
| זֹאת | this (fem.) | הִיא | that (fem.) |
| אֵלֶּה | these (com.) | הֵם (הֵמָּה) | those (masc.) |
| | | הֵנָּה | those (fem.) |

When used as the subject, the demonstrative stands first in the sentence and agrees in gender and number with the predicate.

| | |
|---|---|
| זֶה הָאִישׁ : | *This [is] the man.* |
| זֹאת הָאָרֶץ : | *This [is] the land.* |
| אֵלֶּה הַדְּבָרִים : | *These [are] the words.* |

When used as a qualifying adjective, the demonstrative can only modify a definite noun, because as a demonstrative it points to what is definite. Like the adjective it follows the noun, agrees in number and gender, and takes the definite article.

| | | | |
|---|---|---|---|
| הָאִישׁ הַזֶּה | this man | הָאָרֶץ הַהִוא | that land |
| הָאִישׁ הַהוּא | that man | הַדְּבָרִים הָאֵלֶּה | these words |
| הָאָרֶץ הַזֹּאת | this land | הַדְּבָרִים הַהֵם | those words |

## 27 THE THIRD MASCULINE SINGULAR PERFECT OF THE VERB

Although formal treatment of the verb in Hebrew is not taken up until Chapter IX, some verbs in their simple form are included from now on in the working vocabularies for the sake of variety and interest in the reading exercises. Most verbs in Hebrew have three consonants (called *radicals*, or root letters), and in their simplest and most basic form appear in *the third masculine singular perfect*. The usual pointing for the verb is ָ ַ as in בָּחַר *he chose*, or שָׁפַט *he ruled*. Note that the subject, *he*, is part of the verb form itself, so that it is not necessary to use a personal pronoun. Some verbs have the pointing pattern of ָ ֵ as in אָהֵב *he loved*. Often verbs with this pattern are intransitive and express a state as in זָקֵן *he is/was old*, or כָּבֵד *he is/was heavy*. When the last letter of a verb is weak, א or ה, the pataḥ is lengthened to qāmeṣ, as in בָּרָא *he created*, or רָאָה *he saw*. With such forms only the context can distinguish between a verb and a first declension noun.

When referring to the roots of Hebrew words, which are mostly triliteral, this simple third masculine singular form of the verb is usually used. So, for example, the root of מִשְׁפָּט *justice, judgment* is שׁפט; to pronounce it one says שָׁפַט. Note that it is this form that is listed in the vocabularies, and while it is third masculine singular in form, the definition is given as an infinitive, for example: בָּחַר *vb.* to choose, elect.

## VOCABULARY

אֶת / אֵת *part.* (*nota accusativa*) a particle placed before a definite direct object, but is not translated

בָּחַר *vb.* to choose, to elect (the object is often introduced by ב )

בָּחִיר *n.m.* elect, chosen one

גָּדוֹל *adj.* great

זָבַח *vb.* to sacrifice

זֶבַח *n.m.* sacrifice

מִזְבֵּחַ *n.m.* altar; *pl.* מִזְבְּחוֹת

חָטָא *vb.* to sin [cf. חֵטְא ]

פָּשַׁע *vb.* to sin, to rebel

פֶּשַׁע *n.m.* sin, transgression

כֹּהֵן *n.m.* priest

כֶּסֶף *n.m.* silver, money

זָהָב *n.m.* gold

מָלַךְ *vb.* to be king, to reign [cf. מֶלֶךְ ]

מָשִׁיחַ *n.m.* anointed one, messiah

שָׁפַט *vb.* to rule, to judge

מִשְׁפָּט *n.m.* justice, judgment

## ASSIGNMENT

PRACTICE READING Psalm 1, generally reviewing the noun.

TRANSLATE into English.

1. גָּדוֹל כְּבוֹד הַמֶּלֶךְ
מְשִׁיחַ יהוה הוּא
וּבְחִיר אֱלֹהֵי יִשְׂרָאֵל׃

2. יהוה מָלַךְ
זִבְחֵי צֶדֶק לְכֹהֲנֵי הָאָרֶץ
וּדְבַר יהוה לִנְבִיאֵי הָאֱלֹהִים :

3. הַמֶּלֶךְ שָׁפַט אֶת-הָאָרֶץ בְּצֶדֶק וּבְמִשְׁפָּט :

4. דִּבְרֵי הַנְּבִיאִים כְּדִבְרֵי הָאֱלֹהִים וּכְתוֹרָה מִסִּינָי :

5. הָאִישׁ פָּשַׁע בָּאֱלֹהִים וּבַמֶּלֶךְ :

6. יהוה בָּחַר בְּהַר צִיּוֹן לְמִזְבַּח-כָּל-יִשְׂרָאֵל :

7. הַכֹּהֵן הַגָּדוֹל זָבַח לֵאלֹהֵי-הַשָּׁמַיִם בְּהַר-הַקֹּדֶשׁ

TRANSLATE into Hebrew.

1. Justice and truth are in the land of God,
   righteousness and faithfulness in the holy
   mountain.

2. The spirit of righteousness be for the king,
   and justice for the anointed of Yahveh.

--------------------

# VIII

## 28 THE PRONOMINAL SUFFIXES

The pronoun in Hebrew is employed only in the nominative case. For all other cases *pronominal suffixes* are used, attached directly to nouns, prepositions, verbs, and the special sign of the definite direct object. It is not expected in an introduction to Hebrew such as this that all the suffixes and their workings be fully mastered. At the same time it is necessary to be sufficiently familiar with them to recognize the possibility of their use as one analyzes a word to find its root. Note that a noun with a pronominal suffix is definite, and so does not take a definite article.

### (a) SUFFIXES WITH NOUNS

#### (i) Suffixes on Singular Nouns

| | | | | | |
|---|---|---|---|---|---|
| 1c sg | ִי | *my* | דְּבָרִי | בִּרְכָתִי | חַסְדִּי |
| 2m sg | ְךָ | *your* | דְּבָרְךָ | בִּרְכָתְךָ | חַסְדְּךָ |
| 2f sg | ֵךְ | *your* | דְּבָרֵךְ | בִּרְכָתֵךְ | חַסְדֵּךְ |
| 3m sg | וֹ | *his* | דְּבָרוֹ | בִּרְכָתוֹ | חַסְדּוֹ |
| 3f sg | ָהּ | *her* | דְּבָרָהּ | בִּרְכָתָהּ | חַסְדָּהּ |

| | | | | | |
|---|---|---|---|---|---|
| 1c pl | ֵנוּ | *our* | דְּבָרֵנוּ | בִּרְכָתֵנוּ | חַסְדֵּנוּ |
| 2m pl | ְכֶם | *your* | דְּבַרְכֶם | בִּרְכַתְכֶם | חַסְדְּכֶם |
| 2f pl | ְכֶן | *your* | דְּבַרְכֶן | בִּרְכַתְכֶן | חַסְדְּכֶן |
| 3m pl | ָם | *their* | דְּבָרָם | בִּרְכָתָם | חַסְדָּם |
| 3f pl | ָן | *their* | דְּבָרָן | בִּרְכָתָן | חַסְדָּן |

### (ii) Suffixes on Plural Nouns

Note that the following suffixes include the contraction of the noun's plural and/or dual endings as in the following example: דִּבְרֵיכֶם < כֶם + דְּבָרִים.

| | | | | | |
|---|---|---|---|---|---|
| 1c sg | ַי | *my* | דְּבָרַי | בִּרְכוֹתַי | חֲסָדַי |
| 2m sg | ֶיךָ | *your* | דְּבָרֶיךָ | בִּרְכוֹתֶךָ | חֲסָדֶיךָ |
| 2f sg | ַיִךְ | *your* | דְּבָרַיִךְ | בִּרְכוֹתַיִךְ: | חֲסָדַיִךְ |
| 3m sg | ָיו | *his* | דְּבָרָיו | בִּרְכוֹתָיו | חֲסָדָיו |
| 3f sg | ֶיהָ | *her* | דְּבָרֶיהָ | בִּרְכוֹתֶיהָ | חֲסָדֶיהָ |
| 1c pl | ֵינוּ | *our* | דְּבָרֵינוּ | בִּרְכוֹתֵינוּ | חֲסָדֵינוּ |
| 2m pl | ֵיכֶם | *your* | דִּבְרֵיכֶם | בִּרְכוֹתֵיכֶם | חַסְדֵיכֶם |
| 2f pl | ֵיכֶן | *your* | דִּבְרֵיכֶן | בִּרְכוֹתֵיכֶם | חַסְדֵיכֶן |
| 3m pl | ֵיהֶם | *their* | דִּבְרֵיהֶם | בִּרְכוֹתֵיכֶן | חַסְדֵיהֶם |
| 3f pl | ֵיהֶן | *their* | דִּבְרֵיהֶן | בִּרְכוֹתֵיכֶן | חַסְדֵיהֶן |

## (b) SUFFIXES WITH VERBS

The pronominal suffixes for verbs are the same as those for nouns and prepositions with the following exceptions:

(i) The suffix for the first person singular is נִי ; e.g. קְטָלַנִי *he killed me*; יִקְטְלֵנִי *he kills me.*

(ii) With verbs in the imperfect the third masculine singular suffix is ֵהוּ , and the third feminine singular is ֶהָ ; e.g. יִקְטְלֵהוּ *he kills him*; יִקְטְלֶהָ *he kills her.*

## (c) SUFFIXES WITH PREPOSITIONS AND THE SIGN OF THE ACCUSATIVE

### (i) The Inseparable Prepositions

| | | | | |
|---|---|---|---|---|
| 1c sg | בִּי | כָּמוֹנִי | לִי | מִמֶּנִּי |
| 2m sg | בְּךָ | כָּמוֹךָ | לְךָ | מִמְּךָ |
| 2f sg | בָּךְ | ----- | לָךְ | מִמֵּךְ |
| 3m sg | בּוֹ | כָּמוֹהוּ | לוֹ | מִמֶּנּוּ |
| 3f sg | בָּהּ | כָּמוֹהָ | לָהּ | מִמֶּנָּה |
| 1c pl | בָּנוּ | כָּמוֹנוּ | לָנוּ | מִמֶּנּוּ |
| 2m pl | בָּכֶם | כָּכֶם | לָכֶם | מִכֶּם |
| 2f pl | בָּכֶן | ----- | לָכֶן | מִכֶּן |
| 3m pl | בָּהֶם / בָּם | כָּהֶם | לָהֶם | מֵהֶם |
| 3f pl | בָּהֶן | כָּהֵנָּה | לָהֶן | מֵהֶן |

### (ii) The Prepositions אֶל to, עַל for, אֵת with, and the Accusative Particle אֵת / אֶת־

| | [אֶל] | [עַל] | [אֵת] | [אֵת / אֶת־] |
|---|---|---|---|---|
| 1c sg | אֵלַי | עָלַי | אִתִּי | אֹתִי |
| 2m sg | אֵלֶיךָ | עָלֶיךָ | אִתְּךָ | אֹתְךָ |
| 2f sg | אֵלַיִךְ | עָלַיִךְ | אִתָּךְ | אֹתָךְ |
| 3m sg | אֵלָיו | עָלָיו | אִתּוֹ | אֹתוֹ |
| 3f sg | אֵלֶיהָ | עָלֶיהָ | אִתָּהּ | אֹתָהּ |
| 1c pl | אֵלֵינוּ | עָלֵינוּ | אִתָּנוּ | אֹתָנוּ |
| 2m pl | אֲלֵיכֶם | עֲלֵיכֶם | אִתְּכֶם | אֹתְכֶם |
| 2f pl | אֲלֵיכֶן | עֲלֵיכֶן | אִתְּכֶן | אֹתְכֶן |
| 3m pl | אֲלֵיהֶם | עֲלֵיהֶם | אִתָּם | אֹתָם |
| 3f pl | אֲלֵיהֶן | עֲלֵיהֶן | אִתָּן | אֶתְהֶן |

## VOCABULARY

אֶל *prep.* to

עַל *prep.* upon, over, concerning, against, on behalf of, to

אֵת *prep.* with

בֹּקֶר *n.m.* morning

עֶרֶב *n.m.* evening

יוֹם *n.m.* day; *pl.* יָמִים

לַיְלָה *n.m.* night; *pl.* לֵילוֹת

בָּרָא *vb.* to create, to make

גּוֹי *n.m.* nation

עַם *n.m.* people; *pl.* עַמִּים

חֶסֶד *n.m.* steadfast love, covenant loyalty, mercy

עָשָׂה *vb.* to do, to make, to work

יָשַׁע *vb.* to be wide, spacious

הוֹשִׁיעַ *vb., causative stem of* ישע to save, to deliver

יְשׁוּעָה *n.f.* salvation

שָׁלוֹם *n.m.* wholeness, well-being, prosperity, peace

מִלְחָמָה *n.f.* battle, war

צָבָא *n.m.* host, army, time of service; *pl.* צְבָאוֹת

צִוָּה *vb., intensive stem of* צוה to command

מִצְוָה *n.f.* commandment

## ASSIGNMENT

PRACTICE READING Deuteronomy 6:4-9.

READ ALOUD AND TRANSLATE into English.

1. הָאֱלֹהִים בָּרָא אֶת-הַשָּׁמַיִם וְאֵת-הָאָרֶץ
וְעָשָׂה אֶת-הַיּוֹם וְאֶת-הַלָּיְלָה ׃

2. יהוה אִישׁ מִלְחָמָה
קְדוֹשׁ יִשְׂרָאֵל אֵל יְשׁוּעָתֵנוּ :

3. בְּצִדְקָתוֹ אֱלֹהִים הוֹשִׁיעַנִי
שְׁפָטַנִי בְּמִשְׁפָּט :

4. אֱלֹהִים תּוֹרָתְךָ הַמֶּלֶךְ צִוָּה :

5. יהוה צְבָאוֹת עָשָׂה חֶסֶד וֶאֱמֶת
וְהוֹשִׁיעַ דָּוִד מְשִׁיחוֹ :

6. יהוה בָּחַר בָּנוּ
עַמּוֹ אֲנַחְנוּ

שָׁלוֹם לָנוּ כָּל-הַיּוֹם
צֶדֶק וּמִשְׁפָּט כָּל-הַלַּיְלָה :

7. עַמְּךָ אֲנַחְנוּ גּוֹי כְּבוֹדֶךָ :

TRANSLATE into Hebrew,

1. God created peace upon his land.

2. The commandments of God are righteous,
his judgments are the revelation of truth.

3. The king judged the nations in truth; to his
people he showed mercy and righteousness.

--------------------

# IX

## 29 THE VERB: GENERAL REMARKS

(a) *The Root of the Verb.* The simplest form of the verb is the third person masculine singular qal (simple stem) perfect. It is this form, rather than the infinitive, that is usually cited as the verb root. As indicated in § 27, the most common pointing pattern is ◌ַ ◌ָ , as in שָׁמַע or בָּחַר . Variations in this pattern occur, for example, in verbs expressing a state (the statives), where a frequent pattern is ◌ֵ ◌ָ , as in כָּבֵד or זָקֵן ; or in those verbs having a final quiescent consonant, where the pointing is ◌ָ ◌ָ , as in בָּרָא or עָשָׂה .

The major exception to listing the root of the verb by the third person masculine singular qal perfect is in the case of verbs whose second radical (letter) is ו or י , such as בּוֹא *to enter*, שׁוּב *to return*, or שִׁיר *to sing*. This class of verbs is called *middle hollow*, because they in effect have only two consonants, the first and the third, with the second or middle one missing. For these verbs the *actual infinitive* is cited as the root, as above: בּוֹא, שׁוּב, שִׁיר. The simple third masculine singular perfect of these verbs is בָּא *he entered*, שָׁב *he returned*, or שָׁר *he sang*. Note that while these verbs have only two consonants, they reflect the usual pointing of the perfect with ◌ָ , as in בָּחַר *he chose*, כָּבֵד *he was/is heavy*, or רָאָה *he saw*.

The three root letters (or, *radicals*) are given names in Hebrew grammar. These are derived from the verb פעל *to work*, which was the paradigm word in the medieval grammars. The first letter of a verb root is called *Pē* (פ ), the second letter is called *'Ayin* (ע ), and the third letter is called *Lāmeḏ* (ל ). They form a kind of grammatical shorthand. For example, one can refer to the *middle hollow* verbs as ע״ו ('ayin vāv) or ע״י ('ayin yôḏ) verbs: this means the ע , or second letter, is ו

or י. Or, another example, בָּרָא, which ends in a quiescent letter and so the usual verbal pointing pattern is modified, may be referred to as a ל״א verb, that is, one whose third consonant is an א. So it is that נָתַן *to give* is called a פ״ן verb, שָׁמַע *to hear* is called a ל *gutteral*, and so on.

(b) *The Forms (or, Aspects) of the Verb.* Hebrew verbs have only two *forms*, or *aspects*: the *perfect* and the *imperfect*. These are often called tenses, but this terminology is very misleading. The terms, *perfect* and *imperfect*, in biblical Hebrew do not express the time of an action, but the quality of an action. The *perfect form* designates an action as *complete*, finished (and so, perfect); and this action may be thought of as taking place in the past, present or future. The *imperfect form* describes an action as incomplete, still going on (and so, imperfect); and this also may be thought of as happeneing in the past, present or future. An awareness of this *time-lessness* in Hebrew verbal forms is of great importance for the interpretation of the Hebrew Bible. This is what is involved, for example, in the so-called *prophetic perfect* by which the future is described as a *fait accompli*; or, again, in the alternation of perfect and imperfect in Hebrew poetry, where the change is not a reference to time, but only a literary device, as in Psalm 93:3 or Psalm 38:12.

In actual practice, of course, a completed action (*perfect*) is usually associated with what has happened, the past, while an incomplete action (*imperfect*) is usually associated with what is happening now or will be happening, the present or future. Only the context, however, can make the precise meaning clear. A good rule of thumb is to begin by translating an *imperfect* in the present tense and a *perfect* in the past tense until the context makes the thought clear.

It may be noted in passing that with regard to verbal forms and tenses modern Hebrew is very different from biblical Hebrew. Modern Hebrew has been adapted to the requirements of modern languages and thought patterns, and so verb forms indicate actual tenses: the participle is used for the present tense, the perfect for the past, and the imperfect the future.

(c) *The Voices of the Verb.* As in Greek, the Hebrew verb has not only an *active* and *passive* voice, but also a *reflexive.*

(d) *The Stems of the Verb.* By modifying the basic three consonants of the verbal root a variety of meanings, all related to the basic meaning of the root, may be achieved. This is done by adding prefixes or by doubling consonants. These modified forms are called *stems.* There were originally at least nine of these stems, arranged in three groups, but the process of simplification in the language has reduced the number to seven, and all verbs do not have all stems.

Of the three groups of stems there are first of all the *simple stems*, which express the basic idea of the root. These occur now in biblical Hebrew only in the active and reflexive voices. That there was originally a simple passive stem is certain, but (except for the simple passive participle) it has for the most part disappeared. The simple reflexive stem serves for the passive as well.

The second group, the *intensive-repetitive stems*, appear in all three voices: active, passive and reflexive. These stems are characterized by a doubling of the middle radical of the root. In meaning these stems intensify the simple meaning of the verb root either by the degree of intensity, or by the notion of habit and repetition. So, for example, סָפַר means *to count*, but סִפֵּר, the *intensive-repetitive stem* (note the doubled פּ ) means *to recount, to tell, to narrate.* Again, the basic meaning of the root גנב is *to steal*, but the intensive-repetitive form גַּנָּב means a *thief*, that is, one who repeatedly steals.

Finally, there are the *causative stems*, which are formed primarily by prefixing a ה (rarely a שׁ ) to the root. If סָפַר means *to count*, and סִפֵּר means *to recount*, then הִסְפִּיר, the causative stem, means *to cause to count.* The causative stems originally had all three voices, but by the time of biblical Hebrew they were for all practical purposes restricted to the active and passive

It should be noted that not all verbs have all three stems, and that often there is little distinction in meaning between stems.

The following chart indicates the scheme of the verb stems, using the most basic form of the verb, the third masculine singular simple (or qal) perfect. The names of the stems come from the old paradigm word פעל, and are still used although the paradigm word now employed is קטל. Both should be learned. Note that while their roots are different, both the old names and the corresponding paradigm examples have the same basic pattern.

| | Active | Passive | Reflexive |
|---|---|---|---|
| Simple | qal קָטַל | ---------- | nip'al נִקְטַל |
| Intensive | pi'ēl קִטֵּל | pu'al קֻטַּל | hitpa'ēl הִתְקַטֵּל |
| Causative | hip'îl הִקְטִיל | hop'al הָקְטַל | ---------- |

To master the Hebrew verb it is *absolutely essential to know* these stems. Indeed, if one knows the basic third person masculine singular perfect and imperfect of all the stems--only fourteen forms in all, six of which are the names of the stems--half the battle in learning the verbs is already won!

The following chart lists the paradigm forms for the *perfect* (the same as in the chart above) and also the corresponding *imperfect* forms. Note that the initial י on the imperfect forms is the pronominal prefix for the third person masculine singular of the imperfect, and it will change with the change of persons. These forms are basic for the conjugation of the verb, and *must be learned thoroughly.*

| | | | Perfect | Imperfect |
|---|---|---|---|---|
| Simple | Active | qal | קָטַל | יִקְטֹל |
| | Reflexive | nip‘al | נִקְטַל | יִקָּטֵל* |
| Intensive | Active | pi‘ēl | קִטֵּל | יְקַטֵּל |
| | Passive | pu‘al | קֻטַּל | יְקֻטַּל |
| | Reflexive | hiṯpa‘ēl | הִתְקַטֵּל | יִתְקַטֵּל |
| Causative | Active | hip‘îl | הִקְטִיל | יַקְטִיל |
| | Passive | hop‘al | הָקְטַל | יָקְטַל |

* The נ of the nip‘al is assimilated into the first radical by dāḡēš fortē.

## VOCABULARY

אָהֵב *vb.* to love

אַהֲבָה *n.f.* love

אָמַר *vb.* to say

בָּרַךְ *vb.* to kneel, to bend the knee; *intensive* בֵּרֵךְ to bless

בְּרָכָה *n.f.* blessing

זָכַר *vb.* to remember

יָדַע *vb.* to know

כָּרַת *vb.* to cut; note the idiom כָּרַת בְּרִית to make a covenant

מוּת *vb.* to die; *qal perf.* מֵת ; *causative* הֵמִית to kill

מָוֶת *n.m.* death; *construct* מוֹת

סָפַר *vb.* to count; *intensive* סִפֵּר to recount, relate

שׁוּב *vb.* to turn, return, to repent; *qal perf.* שָׁב

**שָׁמַע** *vb.* to hear, to obey
**שָׁמַר** *vb.* to keep, to watch over, to guard

## ASSIGNMENT

IDENTIFY THE VERBAL STEMS of each of the following forms and translate them. Note that they are all third person masculine singular.

| | | | |
|---|---|---|---|
| דִּבֵּר | יַשְׁמִיעַ | נִכְרַת | הִתְקַדֵּשׁ |
| יִשְׁמֹר | סֻפַּר | יִתְאַמֵּ | יְקֻדַּשׁ |
| אָהֵב | יִתְקַדֵּשׁ | יִבָּרֵא | הִכְרִית |
| סִפֵּר | יְדַבֵּר | הָכְרַת | הִתְחַטֵּא |
| יְצַוֶּה | יָשׁוּב | הִקְדִּישׁ | יְסֻפַּר |
| נִשְׁמַע | יֵאָמֵר | יְדֻבַּר | יַזְכִּיר |
| שָׁב | קִדֵּשׁ | הִשְׁתַּמֵּר | נִשְׁפַּט |
| דֻּבַּר | יָכְרַת | עָשָׂה | יֶחֱטָא |
| נִדְבַּר | אָמַר | בֵּרֵךְ | הֵמִית |
| הוּמַת | זִבַּח | יִתְבָּרֵךְ | יִשְׁמַע |

--------------------

# X

## 30 THE CONJUGATION OF THE VERB

(a) In conjugating the verb in Hebrew the person of the subject is indicated by additions to the stem. For the *perfect* these additions are at the end (*afformatives*), and for the *imperfect* they are primarily at the beginning (*preformatives*). These afformatives and preformatives are as follows.

| | Perfect | Imperfect |
|---|---|---|
| 3m sg | ______ | ______ י |
| 3f sg | ָה ______ | ______ת |
| 2m sg | תָּ ______ | ______ת |
| 2f sg | תְּ ______ | ִי ____ת |
| 1c sg | תִּי ______ | ______א |
| 3m pl | וּ ______ | וּ _____ י |
| 3f pl | וּ ______ | נָה ____ת |
| 2m pl | תֶּם ______ | וּ _____ת |
| 2f pl | תֶּן ______ | נָה ____ת |
| 1c pl | נוּ ______ | ______ נ |

These indications of the person are the same for all stems. This means that if one knows the *stem pattern* (the third masculine singular form), the above *afformatives and preformatives*, and *two simple statements* about accent and consonantal endings given below, one can conjugate the verb in all its stems.

In conjugating the verb one always begins with the *simple basic form of the verb stem*, the third masculine singular form. In qal, for example, this would be קָטַל for the perfect and יִקְטֹל for the imperfect. To these basic perfect and imperfect forms *the afformatives* are added in accordance with *the two statements* given below. Note that with imperfect stems the preformatives change according to the person; see the chart above and the paradigm in § 32.

(b) *The Two Statements.* The accent in the Hebrew verbs is affected by the kind of afformative used, whether it is *vocalic* (an ending beginning with a vowel, e.g. וּ or ִי ), or *consonantal* (an ending beginning with a consonant, e.g. תָּ or נוּ ), or *heavy* (an ending beginning and ending with a consonant, e.g. תֶּם or תֶּן.

*Statement One: Concerning the Accent*

The accent remains where it is on the ultima of the basic form (קָטַל or יִקְטֹל) except:

(a) with vocalic endings (except in hip'îl), in which case the accent shifts to the ultima and the penult becomes vocal š$^{e}$vâ.

קָטְלָה < קָטַלָה < ָה + קָטַל
יִקְטְלוּ < יִקְטֹלוּ < וּ + יִקְטֹל

(b) with heavy endings, in which case the accent shifts to the ultima and the pointing follows a first declension analogy (the distant open syllable is reduced to š$^{e}$vâ if possible).

קְטַלְתֶּם < קָטַלְתֶּם < תֶּם + קָטַל

*Statement Two: Concerning Consonantal Afformatives*

Before consonantal afformatives the vowels ◌ִי and ◌ֵ become ◌ַ, except:

(a) with pi'ēl imperfect, where the ◌ֵ remains unchanged; and
(b) with hip'îl imperfect, where ◌ִי becomes ◌ֵ.

קִטֵּל + תָּ > קִטֵּלְתָּ > קִטַּלְתָּ
הִקְטִיל + תָּ > הִקְטִילְתָּ > הִקְטַלְתָּ
Cf. also אָהֵב + תָּ , אָהֵבְתָּ , אָהַבְתָּ

[Note that this second statement concerning vowel changes with consonantal afformatives applies primarily to the pi'ēl, hiṯpa'ēl and hip'îl stems; in qal it only affects verbs having the pattern ◌ָ◌ֵ.]

## 31 THE QAL PERFECT

| | Singular | Plural |
|---|---|---|
| 3m | קָטַל | קָטְלוּ |
| 3f | קָטְלָה | |
| 2m | קָטַלְתָּ | קְטַלְתֶּם |
| 2f | קָטַלְתְּ | קְטַלְתֶּן |
| 1c | קָטַלְתִּי | קָטַלְנוּ |

### VOCABULARY

אָדָם *n.m.* man, humankind
אֲדָמָה *n.f.* land, ground, earth
בְּרִית *n.f.* covenant
חַיִּים *n.m., pl.* life

חָכְמָה *n.f.* wisdom
יָם *n.m.* sea, ocean; *pl.* יַמִּים
לֹא / לוֹא *adv.* not, no
נָהָר *n.m.* stream, flood, river; *pl.* נְהָרִים and נְהָרוֹת
נֶפֶשׁ *n.f.* self, (living) being, life
עֶבֶד *n.m.* slave, servant, devotee
רָאָה *vb.* to see
שְׁאֵרִית *n.f.* remnant, rest, that left over
שֵׁם *n.m.* name, reputation, fame; *pl.* שְׁמוֹת

## ASSIGNMENT

LEARN THE QAL PERFECT PARADIGM

For practice say and write the qal perfect of the following verbs: אָהֵב, זכר, שׁפט, משׁל

READ ALOUD AND TRANSLATE into English.

1. אָהַבְתִּי אֶת-יִשְׂרָאֵל בְּאַהֲבַת אָב לִבְנוֹ
וְעַמִּי לֹא זָכַר אֶת-בְּרִיתִי
וְלֹא שָׁמַר אֶת-מִצְוֹתָי ׃

2. יהוה אָמַר לַאֲדֹנִי
בְּנִי אַתָּה
אֲנִי הַיּוֹם בְּחַרְתִּ֫יךָ ׃

3. נַפְשִׁי יָדְעָה חַסְדֵי יהוה
וְהוּא הוֹשִׁיעַ אֶת-חַיַּי מִמָּוֶת ׃

4. גְּדוֹלָה חָכְמַת אֲדֹנַי
טוֹבִים כָּל־דְּבָרָיו ׃

5. אֲנִי אֵל וְלֹא אָדָם
לֹא כָרַתִּי אֶת־עַמִּי מֵאֶרֶץ הַחַיִּים ׃

6. שְׁאֵרִית הַגּוֹי שָׁבָה אֶל־יְרוּשָׁלַםִ ׃

7. אָנֹכִי לֹא זָכַרְתִּי פִּשְׁעֵיכֶם וְאַתֶּם לֹא זְכַרְתֶּם חֲסָדָי ׃

8. הַנְּבִיאִים יָדְעוּ חֵטְא־יִשְׂרָאֵל
וּבְנֵי הַנְּבִיאִים פֶּשַׁע יַעֲקֹב ׃

9. גָּדוֹל יהוה אֱלֹהֵינוּ
עַל־כָּל־הָאָרֶץ כְּבוֹדוֹ

כָּל־הַגּוֹיִם רָאוּ צִדְקָתוֹ
וְעַמֵּי הָאָרֶץ יְשׁוּעָתוֹ ׃

10. אֵין הָעֶבֶד גָּדוֹל מֵאֲדֹנוֹ ׃

TRANSLATE into Hebrew.

1. We kept the commands of God,
   the words of truth we remembered.

2. I said, O king, you judged your people in
   righteousnmess,
   and, priests, you watched over their children.

3. Sea and flood recounted the glory of our God,
   and earth knew the salvation of the Lord.

# XI

## 32 THE QAL IMPERFECT

| | Singular | Plural |
|---|---|---|
| 3m | יִקְטֹל | יִקְטְלוּ |
| 3f | תִּקְטֹל | תִּקְטֹלְנָה |
| 2m | תִּקְטֹל | תִּקְטְלוּ |
| 2f | תִּקְטְלִי | תִּקְטֹלְנָה |
| 1c | אֶקְטֹל | נִקְטֹל |

Note that the usual pointing for the personal prefix is ◌ִ , but because of the guttural א of the 1c singular it is pointed with ◌ֶ .

The usual pointing of the qal imperfect is with ◌ֹ . Some verbs, however, especially intransitives and verbs with ע or ח as their third radical, form their imperfects with ◌ַ ; e.g. יִכְבַּד *he is heavy*, יִשְׁמַע *he hears*, and יִבְטַח *he trusts*. ל״א verbs keep the ◌ָ in the imperfect, e.g. יִבְרָא *he creates*; and ל״ה verbs form their imperfects with ◌ֶ , e.g. יִהְיֶה *he becomes*. Despite such variations because of weak letters and gutturals, the basic structure of the qal imperfect is easily recognized.

## 33 THE IMPERATIVE

The imperative is based on the second person imperfect forms. Consistent with the peremptory character of a command, the imperative is simply a shortened form of the imperfect. It is formed by dropping the personal prefix of the second person imperfect form, making any necessary modifications in pointing or stem protection occasioned by dropping the prefix. The imperative for the qal is as follows.

| | |
|---|---|
| קְטֹל < תִּקְטֹל | masculine singular |
| קִטְלִי < קְטְלִי < תִּקְטְלִי | feminine singular |
| קִטְלוּ < קְטְלוּ < תִּקְטְלוּ | masculine plural |
| קְטֹלְנָה < תִּקְטֹלְנָה | feminine plural |

## 34 THE NEGATIVE COMMAND

In Hebrew the imperative form cannot be used with the negative. To express a negative command one of the following alternatives must be used:

(i) the imperfect with לֹא , as in לֹא תִּגְנֹב *You shall not steal*; or

(ii) the jussive (a form often identical with the imperfect, see below at § 35) with אַל , as in אַל תִּגְנֹב *Let you not steal = Do not steal.*

## 35 THE JUSSIVE AND COHORTATIVE

The *jussive* is a form of the imperfect which is used only with the second and third persons of the verb. It is characterized by a tendency to pull back the accent where possible, which sometimes results in modifying the pointing. For the most part, however, the jussive is identical in form with the imperfect. This can lead to questions in translating. Psalm 29:11, for example, reads יהוה עֹז לְעַמּוֹ יִתֵּן יהוה יְבָרֵךְ אֶת-עַמּוֹ בַשָּׁלוֹם . Should the verbs be read as imperfects and the verse translated as *Yahveh gives strength to his people, Yahveh blesses his people with peace*; or should one take the verbs as jussives and so translate, *May Yahveh give strength to his people, may*

*Yahveh bless his people with peace*? Whichever, the translation is dependent upon the context and one's understanding of it.

Note the following examples of the jussive and its translation. The example in the hip'îl shows how a jussive form may modify the usual imperfect form.

[אַל] תִּקְטֹל *Let you [not] kill. / May you [not] kill. / Do [not] kill!*

[אַל] יִקְטֹל *Let him [not] kill. / May he [not] kill.*

יַקְטֵל < יַקְטִיל *Let him cause to kill / May he cause to kill*

The *cohortative* is used only for the first person. It is formed by adding ה ָ to the first person imperfect form of the verb, making the necessary changes in pointing in accordance with the rule about vocalic afformatives; see Statement One in § 30. Note the following examples.

אֶקְטְלָה < אֶקְטֹלָה < ה ָ + אֶקְטֹל *Let me kill / May I kill*

נִקְטְלָה < נ1קְטֹלָה < ה ָ + נִקְטֹל *Let us kill / May we kill*

## VOCABULARY

אוֹר *n.m.* and f. light; *pl.* אוֹרִים

חֹשֶׁךְ *n.m.* darkness, obscurity

בָּטַח *vb.* to trust

הָיָה *vb.* to become, to happen *

חָיָה *vb.* to live, to be alive *

זָקֵן *adj.* old; *as a noun:* elder

כִּי *conj.* for, that, when, yea; כִּי אִם but rather
כָּבֵד *vb.* to be heavy; *intensive stem*: to honor
כָּבוֹד *n.m.* glory
כּוֹכָב *n.m.* star
כָּתַב *vb.* to write
לֵבָב *n.m.* heart, mind, will
לֵב *n.m.* heart, mind, will; *pl.* לִבּוֹת
מַעֲשֶׂה *n.m.* work, deed
סָלַח *vb.* to forgive (the object is introduced by ל )
עַד *n.m.* perpetuity, ever
עַד *prep.* to, unto, until
עוֹלָם *n.m.* long duration, perpetuity, age, eternity

*Note that ל״ה verbs not only form their qal imperfect with ֶ , as for example יִהְיֶה *it happens*, but with vocalic endings the ה is dropped, as for example, in the imperfect plural: יִהְיוּ < וּ + יִהְיֶה .

## ASSIGNMENT

LEARN THE QAL IMPERFECT PARADIGM

For practice say and write the qal imperfect of the following verbs:

מלך, בטח, שׁמר, משל

READ ALOUD AND TRANSLATE into English

1. צַדִּיק בֶּאֱמוּנָתוֹ יִחְיֶה :

2. אֶכְתֹּב אֶת-שִׁמְךָ בְּסֵפֶר הַחַיִּים
וּפִשְׁעֲךָ לֹא אֶזְכּוֹר :

3. אָמַרְתִּי לְנַפְשִׁי
בִּטְחִי בְּיהוה אֱלֹהַיִךְ
כִּי הוּא יִשְׁפֹּט עַמּוֹ בְּצֶדֶק
וּבְרִיתוֹ יִשְׁמֹר עַד-עוֹלָם :

4. שְׁמַע יִשְׂרָאֵל: יהוה אֱלֹהֵיכֶם

כִּי הוּא יִבְרָא עֲלֵיכֶם אוֹר גָּדוֹל
כְּכוֹכְבֵי הַשָּׁמַיִם יִהְיֶה חַסְדּוֹ

כֹּהֲנֵיכֶם יִזְבְּחוּ זִבְחֵי-צֶדֶק
נְבִיאֵיכֶם דְּבַר-יהוה יַשְׁמִיעוּ
וְחָכְמַת-אֱלֹהֵינוּ זְקֵנֵיכֶם יְדַבֵּרוּ

מַלְכֵי-הָאָרֶץ יִשְׁמְרוּ מִצְוֹתָיו
וְכָל-הָעַמִּים יְכַבְּדוּ שְׁמוֹ

הַשָּׁמַיִם יְסַפְּרוּ כְּבוֹד אֵל
וְכָל-הָאָרֶץ מַעֲשֵׂה יָדָיו :

5. אַזְכִּיר כָּל-אֲשֶׁר אָמַרְתִּי אֶל דָּוִד מְשִׁיחִי
בְּנִי אַתָּה וַאֲנִי אָבִיךָ

אַתָּה וּבָנֶיךָ תִּשְׁמְרוּ אֶת-מִצְוֹתַי
וְתִשְׁפְּטוּ אֶת-הָעָם בְּצֶדֶק וּבֶאֱמוּנָה :

6. שׁוּב אֶל-יהוה בְּכָל-לִבְּךָ
וַחֲטָאֶיךָ יִסָּלְחוּ לָֽךְ :

7. אֲסַפְּרָה אֶת-מַעֲשֵׂה יהוה
אַשְׁמִיעָה אֶת-יְשׁוּעַת אֱלֹהֵינוּ :

8. זְכוֹר צַדִּיק
בָּאָרֶץ חַיֵּהוּ
וְרָשָׁע מֵהָאָרֶץ יִכָּרֵת :

TRANSLATE into Hebrew.

1. The messiah, the king of peace, will cut off war from the land.

2. He will create light for the righteous (pl.), but on the wicked darkness.

3. Forgive, God of my salvation, for I trust in you.

--------------------

# XII

## 36 THE PARTICIPLES

Each stem of the Hebrew verb has its own participle, usually built on the basic perfect or imperfect form. Qal, however, has two participles, an active and also a passive, reflecting the lost simple passive stem. As nominal forms they follow the usual rules for the declension of nouns.

(a) *Participles of the Simple Stems.*

The *qal active* participle belongs to the third declension, and so reduces when possible the near open ◌ֵ to vocal š$^{e}$vâ.

| | |
|---|---|
| קֹטֵל [קוֹטֵל] | qal masculine singular |
| קֹטְלִים | qal masculine plural |
| קֹטְלָה or קֹטֶלֶת | qal feminine singular |
| קֹטְלוֹת | qal feminine plural |

The *qal passive* participle belongs to the first declension, and so reduces the distant open when possible.

| | |
|---|---|
| קָטוּל | qal masculine singular |
| קְטוּלִים | qal masculine plural |
| קְטוּלָה | qal feminine singular |
| קְטוּלוֹת | qal feminine plural |

The *nip'al* participle is a nominal version of the third masculine singular perfect. It follows a first declension pattern.

| | |
|---|---|
| נִקְטָל | nip'al masculine singular<br>[cf. perfect נִקְטַל] |
| נִקְטָלִים | nip'al masculine plural |
| נִקְטָלָה | nip'al feminine singular<br>[cf. perfect נִקְטְלָה] |
| נִקְטָלוֹת | nip'al feminine plural |

(b) *The Participles of the Intensive-Repetitive Stems.*

The *intensive-repetitive* participles are all closely related to the basic stem forms of the imperfect, and are formed by replacing the pronominal prefix with מ, a common nominal prefix. Note the characteristic doubled middle radical as well as the ְ under the introductory consonant. *Pi'ēl* and *hiṯpa'ēl* follow the third declension pattern, and *pu'al* the first.

| | |
|---|---|
| מְקַטֵּל | pi'ēl masculine<br>[cf. imperfect יְקַטֵּל] |
| מְקַטְּלָה | pi'ēl feminine |
| מְקֻטָּל | pu'al masculine<br>[cf. imperfect יְקֻטַּל] |
| מְקֻטָּלָה | pu'al feminine |
| מִתְקַטֵּל | hiṯpa'ēl masculine<br>[cf. imperfect יִתְקַטֵּל] |
| מִתְקַטְּלָה | hiṯpa'ēl feminine |

(c) *The Participles of the Causative Stems.*

The causative participles reflect the basic imperfect forms of the stems, and replace the nominal prefix with מ . They follow the first declension pattern.

| | |
|---|---|
| מַקְטִיל | hip'îl masculine<br>[ cf. imperfect יַקְטִיל] |
| מַקְטִילָה | hip'îl feminine |
| מָקְטָל | hop'al masculine<br>[ cf. imperfect יָקְטַל] |
| מָקְטָלָה | hop'al feminine |

## 37 THE PARTICIPLE IN HEBREW

In meaning and use the Hebrew participle shares the characteristics of both noun and verb. In form it is a noun, but in meaning it expresses a continuing action.

As a noun it may be translated as "one who does such and such;" for example, שׁוֹמֵר or הַשּׁוֹמֵר *one who keeps* or *the one who keeps*; אוֹהֵב *one who loves*, that is *a lover*. Note Psalm 146:6-9, where no fewer than nine participles are used in a series to describe how God acts.

As a verb, the participle may be compared to the English use of the auxiliary verb *to be*; הָאִישׁ יוֹצֵא מִן-הָעִיר *The man [is] going out of the city*, in effect, *The man goes out of the city*. Indeed, in modern Hebrew the participle is used for the present tense. As a verb the participle may also take an object, as in Genesis 9:6: שֹׁפֵךְ דַּם הָאָדָם בָּאָדָם דָּמוֹ יִשָּׁפֵךְ *He who sheds the blood of man, by man his blood shall be shed*. The participle often has a sense of the imminent, that which is about to happen. In the famous "virgin" passage of Isaiah 7:14, for example, the text reads . . . הִנֵּה הָעַלְמָה הָרָה וְיֹלֶדֶת בֵּן for which the translation is, *Behold, the young woman is pregnant and about to bear a child . . .*

## 38 THE INFINITIVES

The infinitive is a kind of *verbal noun.* It is like a word in English that ends in *-ing*; for example, *To dance is to live* can also be said, *Dancing is living.* There are two infinitives in Hebrew: the *infinitive construct* and the *infinitive absolute.*

The *infinitive construct*, which is frequently identical in form to the masculine singular imperative, is used much as the infinitive in English; and frequently has the preposition לְ *to* joined to it; as for example, בָּא לִשְׁפּוֹט אֶת-הָאָרֶץ *He came* (or, *comes*) *to judge the earth.* Often the infinitive construct is like a noun in *-ing*, and may take personal suffixes (either as subject or object of the infinitive) and prepositional prefixes. Note the following examples: בִּשְׁמוֹר *in keeping*; בְּשָׁמְרִי *in my keeping*, that is, *while I keep / kept*; בְּשָׁמְרֵנִי *in keeping me*, or temporally, *while keeping me.* Note that with suffixes the infinitive reflects a second declension pattern.

The *infinitive absolute*, like the infinitive construct has a nominal character: אָכוֹל *eating*; רָאֹה *seeing*; שָׁמוֹר *keeping.* It may also be used in the sense of a command: *Eat! See! Keep!* Unlike the infinitive construct, the infinitive absolute cannot take either prefixes or suffixes.

The most common use of the *infinitive absolute* in the Hebrew Bible is to give emphasis to the main verb of a clause. When it is used *before* the main verb, it strengthens the verbal idea itself, as for example in the frequent formula, מוֹת תָּמוּת , literally *dying you shall die*, that is, *you shall surely die.* When the infinitive absolute *follows* the verb, it expresses the notion of continuance, as in Isaiah 6:9, where it follows plural imperatives: שִׁמְעוּ שָׁמוֹעַ וְאַל-תָּבִינוּ וּרְאוּ רָאוֹ וְאַל-תֵּדָעוּ . Literally translated the text reads, *Hear, hearing and do not understand;*

*see, seeing and to not comprehend*; cf. *NRSV*, *Keep listening, but do not comprehend; keep looking, but do not understand.*

## VOCABULARY

אָכַל *vb.* to eat, to consume, to devour

אַשְׁרֵי pl. construct of אֶשֶׁר *happiness* happy, blest, blessed; cf. בָּרוּךְ

בּוֹא *vb.* to come, to enter; *qal perf.* בָּא

בָּשָׂר *n.m.* flesh

לֶחֶם *n.m.* food, bread

מַיִם *n.m. only in dual* water(s), drink, sea, deeps

הָלַךְ *vb.* to go, to walk

הִנֵּה *demonstrative particle* behold, lo

יָרֵא *vb.* to fear, to be in awe, to tremble

יָצָא *vb.* to go forth; *hip̄ʿîl* הוֹצִיא to bring out, to bring forth

יָשַׁב *vb.* to sit, to dwell, to inhabit, to be enthroned

כֹּה *demonstrative adv.* thus, so

עָוֹן *n.m.* guilt, iniquity, punishment

עָמַד *vb.* to stand

קוּם *vb.* to stand, to arise, to establish; *qal perf.* קָם

מָקוֹם *n.m.* place

רָעֵב *vb.* to be hungry

צָמֵא *vb.* to be thirsty

שָׂבַע *vb.* to be sated, to be satisfied

שָׁתָה *vb.* to drink

מָלֵא *vb.* to be full, to fill

תַּחַת *prep.* under, below, beneath

## ASSIGNMENT

READ ALOUD AND TRANSLATE into English.

1. אַשְׁרֵי-הָאִישׁ יָרֵא אֶת-יהוה
בּוֹטֵחַ בֵּאלֹהֵי יְשׁוּעָתֵנוּ

עֹשֶׂה שָׁמַיִם וָאָרֶץ
אֶת-הַיָּם וְכָל-אֲשֶׁר בָּם

הַשֹּׁמֵר אֱמֶת לְעוֹלָם
עֹשֶׂה חֶסֶד לָעַד

יהוה אוֹהֵב צַדִּיקִים
וְסֹלֵחַ לַעֲוֹנָם :

2. שִׁמְעוּ מַלְכֵי הָאָרֶץ
וּדְעוּ שֹׁפְטֵי הָעַמִּים

כִּי יהוה צְבָאוֹת בָּא
אִישׁ מִלְחָמָה הוּא

כִּי בָא לִשְׁפּוֹט הָאָרֶץ
יִשְׁפֹּט עַמִּים בְּצֶדֶק
גּוֹיִם בְּמִשְׁפָּט :

3. בָּרוּךְ אַתָּה אֲדֹנַי אֱלֹהֵינוּ מֶלֶךְ הָעוֹלָם הַמּוֹצִיא לֶחֶם מִן-הָאָרֶץ
בָּרוּךְ אַתָּה אֲדֹנַי אֱלֹהֵינוּ מֶלֶךְ הָעוֹלָם בּוֹרֵא פְּרִי * הַגָּפֶן ** :

* fruit   ** vine

4. הַמֶּלֶךְ בָּא אֶל-הַכֹּהֵן לִשְׁמוֹעַ אֶת-דְּבַר יהוה :

5. כֹּה אָמַר אֲדֹנָי
הִנֵּה יָמִים בָּאִים עֲלֵיכֶם
וְלֹא יִהְיֶה לֶחֶם לָרָעֵב לֶאֱכֹל
וּמַיִם לַצָּמֵא לִשְׁתּוֹת :

6. אַשְׁרֵי-צָמֵא לְצֶדֶק
רָעֵב לִדְבַר יהוה :

7. הָעָם הַהֹלְכִים בַּחֹשֶׁךְ
רָאוּ אוֹר גָּדוֹל
יֹשְׁבֵי בְּאֶרֶץ צַלְמָוֶת *
אוֹר נָגַהּ ** עֲלֵיהֶם :

* Repoint the MT to read צַלְמוּת *darkness*
** *shined*

8. הַשְּׁאֵרִית הַנֶּאֱמָנָה בּוֹטַחַת בְּאוֹהֲבָהּ :

TRANSLATE into Hebrew.

1. Yahveh keeps [participle] Israel day and night,
   seeing their good,
   knowing their evil.

2. The priest is standing in the holy mountain; he is hearing the word of God in the place of sacrifice.

3. Death is for the sinner, and life for the doer of the word of God.

--------------------

# XIII

## 39 THE COORDINATE NATURE OF HEBREW EXPRESSION

The structure of the Hebrew sentence is coordinate and not subordinate; that is, while in English a main clause is surrounded by clauses subordinate in form and expression to it, in Hebrew the structure is more like a series of main clauses, or short sentences, joined by *and* [וְ]. When Jacob blesses the sons of Joseph in Genesis 48:14, the *Revised English Bible* translates: *he stretched out his right hand and laid it on Ephraim's head, although he was the younger . . .* The Hebrew text, however, literally says here, *And Israel stretched out his right hand and he set upon the head of Ephraim and he [was] the young one.* In other words, for the sake of a smooth translation this last clause, introduced (as all of them are) by the simple conjunction וְ, has been made into a subordinate clause. Again, when in Judges 16:15, Delilah scolds Samson for tricking her, the Hebrew text reads, וַתֹּאמֶר אֵלָיו אֵיךְ תֹּאמַר אֲהַבְתִּיךְ וְלִבְּךָ אֵין אִתִּי. *NRSV* translates, *Then she said to him, "How can you say, 'I love you,' when your heart is not with me?"* Both *then* and *when* are translations of the simple connective. The passage literally reads, *And she said to him, "How do you say, 'I love you,' and your heart is not with me?"*

Even relative clauses in Hebrew are essentially two separate sentences joined by a *relative particle*, אֲשֶׁר, a word which does not really correspond to our relative pronouns, such as *who* or *which.* אֲשֶׁר is simply a word that indicates that what has gone before in the sentence is somehow related to what follows, the precise relationship to be determined by the context. In Numbers 10:29, for example, Moses says to his father-in-law, *We are journeying to the place of which Yahveh said, "I will give it to you."* The Hebrew text reads as follows:

נֹסְעִים אֲנַחְנוּ אֶל-הַמָּקוֹם אֲשֶׁר אָמַר יהוה אֹתוֹ אֶתֵּן לָכֶם

2 1

Clause 1: We are journeying to the place.
Clause 2: Yahveh said, "I will give it to you."
These two sentences are simply joined by אֲשֶׁר .

Again, in the Book of the Covenant there is a law dealing with a place of refuge for one who has committed involuntary manslaughter (Exodus 21:13). There it is said:

וְשַׂמְתִּי לְךָ מָקוֹם אֲשֶׁר יָנוּס שָׁמָּה

2 1

Clause 1: And I shall appoint for you a place.
Clause 2: He will flee thither.
The two sentences are joined by אֲשֶׁר , so that they read, *And I shall appoint for you a place to which he may flee.*

It is as if Hebrew presents us with a series of realities joined only by a neutral וְ or אֲשֶׁר , and in the midst of these juxtaposed realities we become active participants in determining how they are related to each other, and our decision is determined by the way we understand the situation and relationships. Behind the smooth and polished readings of our English translations there lies a whole history of interpretation, which often conceals the straight-forward, simple realism of Hebrew thought and expression.

## 40 THE VAV CONSECUTIVE

The coordinate character of Hebrew is clearly shown in the narrative device known as *vav consecutive.* It is peculiar to biblical Hebrew, and is employed to express a continuous series of actions within a narrative, as for example in the story of Sarah's conceiving a child (Genesis 21:1-3). Literally the Hebrew reads:

> *And Yahveh visited Sarah as he said, and Yahveh did to Sarah as he spoke, and Sarah became pregnant and she bore a son to Abraham in his old age. . . and Abraham called the name of his son . . . . . Isaac . . . [*and so on through the whole chapter] . . . . .

Each of these verbs begins a clause, and each is joined to what has gone before by the conjunction ו .

To express *consecutive narrative in the past* the first verb is in the perfect (completed action) or its equivalent, and all the following verbs are in the imperfect and prefixed with . וַ , or before א (which cannot be doubled) וָ . Note that the pointing of the ו in vav consecutive is exactly that of the definite article. This narrative device is called *vav consecutive imperfect.*

To illustrate how vav consecutive works for narrative in the past, see the following sentence and its translation into Hebrew.

> *Moses went to the mountain and God spoke with him there and he wrote the words in a book and he and the people made a covenant with God and they kept his commandments.*

מֹשֶׁה הָלַךְ אֶל-הָהָר וַיְדַבֵּר אֱלֹהִים אִתּוֹ שָׁם וַיִּכְתֹּב אֶת-הַדְּבָרִים
בְּסֵפֶר וַיִּכְרְתוּ הוּא וְהָעָם בְּרִית אֶת-אֱלֹהִים וַיִּשְׁמְרוּ מִצְוֹתָיו :

Note that each verb immediately begins the clause with no intervening words, and is connected with what has gone before by ו pointed as the article.

For *consecutive narrative in the present or future* the process is simply reversed. The first verb is in the imperfect (incomplete action) or its equivalent (including the imperative), and all the following verbs are in the perfect and prefixed with ו pointed exactly like the simple conjuction וְ . This narrative device is known as *vav consecutive perfect.*

To illustrate how vav consecutive perfect works for narrative in the present or future note the following version of the sentence used above.

*Moses will go to the mountain and God will speak with him there and he will write the words in a book and he and the people will make a covenant with God and they will keep his commandments.*

מֹשֶׁה יֵלֵךְ אֶל-הָהָר וְדִבֵּר אֱלֹהִים אִתּוֹ שָׁם וְכָתַב אֶת-הַדְּבָרִים
בְּסֵפֶר וְכָרְתוּ הוּא וְהָעָם בְּרִית אֶת-אֱלֹהִים וְשָׁמְרוּ מִצְוֹתָיו :

In using vav consecutive the following four notes should be carefully observed.

(a) With vav consecutive *the verb must stand first* in the clause with no intervening word however small, When such a word is necessary, as for example לֹא *not* or כִּי *for*, the continuity of verbs, that is, the consecutive narrative is broken, and one must start all over again. Note the following version of the illustrative sentence.

*Moses went to the mountain and God spoke with him there, and he did not write the words in a book and he and the people made a covenant with God and they kept his commandments.*

מֹשֶׁה הָלַךְ אֶל-הָהָר וַיְדַבֵּר אֱלֹהִים אִתּוֹ שָׁם וְלֹא כָתַב אֶת-דְּבָרִים
בְּסֵפֶר וַיִּכְרְתוּ הוּא וְהָעָם בְּרִית אֶת-אֱלֹהִים וַיִּשְׁמְרוּ מִצְוֹתָיו :

(b) In vav consecutive imperfect the *accent is usually drawn back to the penult* if open, and this sometimes results in a shortening of vowels; for example, וַיָּשָׁב < וַיָּשׁוּב < יָשׁוּב . As the example suggests, this happens most often with middle hollow verbs and with verbs having weak consonants. Note in this regard ל״ה verbs, which often lose the final ה in vav consecutive imperfect. The most common example is with the verb הָיָה : its qal imperfect is יִהְיֶה , but with vav consecutive imperfect it is apocopated to וַיְהִי . Despite the modified pointing, however, one always knows that the form is an imperfect because of the pointing of the ו.

With the accent in vav consecutive perfect just the opposite happens: *the accent is usually thrown forward to the ultima*, but with no change in the pointing. Note the following example: וְקָטַלְתִּי < וְקָטַלְתִּי < קָטַלְתִּי. This shift in the accent is often a clue as to whether the ו is a vav consecutive or simply a vav conjunctive.

(c) The vav consecutive imperfect may follow an implied (unexpressed) perfect or action in the past. So it is that the book of Ruth begins with a vav consecutive imperfect. The same principle applies to the vav consecutive perfect; it too may follow an implied (unexpressed) imperfect or imperative.

(d) In putting the vav consecutive into smooth English translators will often subordinate one clause to another, translating the ו with such words as *but*, *although*, and *therefore* or *then*, or they may ignore the ו altogether. For example, the illustrative sentence used above could be rendered:

> *Moses went to the mountain and when God spoke with him there he wrote the words in a book. Then he and the people made a covenant with God, keeping his commandments.*

One could also shift the emphasis somewhat and translate the same passage as follows:

> *Moses went to the mountain where God spoke with him. When he had written the words in a book, he and the people made a covenant with God, and they kept his commandments.*

Dealing only with English translations in cases such as this can be very misleading; but even the most superficial checking of the Hebrew text can indicate the vav consecutive structure of a passage, so that one can deal with the text itself and not simply with the niceties of a translator's diction.

## VOCABULARY

אוֹיֵב / אֹיֵב *participle m.* enemy

שָׂנֵא *vb.* to hate, to be an enemy

אָז *adv.* then, at that time

אֲשֶׁר *relative particle* that

אַחֵר *adj.* another, other

אַחֲרֵי *prep.* behind, after

בַּיִת *n.m.* house; *pl.* בָּתִּים

הֵיכָל *n.m.* palace, temple

לָחַם *vb. (in reflexive)* to fight, to do battle

נוּס *vb.* to flee, to escape; *qal perf.* נָס

פּוּץ *vb.* to be dispersed, to be scattered; *qal perf.* פָּץ

חָדָשׁ *adj.* new

פֹּה *adv.* here

שָׁם *adv.* there

נָתַן *vb.* to give, to set, to appoint

פָּנִים *n.m. only in pl.* face

לִפְנֵי *prep.* before, in front of

מָה *pron., interrogative and indefinite* what, how

לָמָּה *adv.* for what, why

עוֹד *adv.* still, yet, again

עָנָה *vb.* to speak, to answer, to respond

קוֹל *n.m.* thunder, noise, roar, voice; *pl.* קֹלוֹת

שִׁיר *vb.* to sing

שִׁירָה / שִׁיר *n.m. and f.* song

שֹׁרֶשׁ *n.m.* root, stump, stock

## ASSIGNMENT

READ ALOUD AND TRANSLATE into English.

1. וַיְהִי בִּימֵי יְשַׁעְיָה וַיָּקָם אֲרָם עַל-יְהוּדָה וַיָּבֹאוּ כָל-
מַלְכֵי-הָאָרֶץ לַמִּלְחָמָה וַיִּלָּחֵם יהוה צְבָאוֹת לְיִשְׂרָאֵל
עִמּוֹ וַיִּרְאוּ אוֹיְבֵי-יִשְׂרָאֵל כִּי יַד-הָאֱלֹהִים בָּם וַיָּנוּסוּ
אֶל-אַרְצוֹתֵיהֶם :

2. שְׁמֹר אֶת-מִצְוֹתַי וּשְׁמַע אֶת-דְּבָרַי וּכְתַבְתִּיךָ בְּסֵפֶר-
הַחַיִּים וְהָיִיתָ לִּי לָעָם :

3. הַכֹּהֵן הָלַךְ לִשְׁכֶם לִזְבּוֹחַ זֶבַח לְיהוה וַיְדַבֵּר דְּבָרָיו
לָעָם אֲשֶׁר בַּהֵיכָל וַיִּשְׁמְעוּ אֶת-דְּבַר-יהוה וַיֹּאמְרוּ:
בָּרוּךְ יהוה אֱלֹהֵי יִשְׂרָאֵל אֲשֶׁר דְּבָרוֹ אֱמֶת וָצֶדֶק :

4. יָקוּם אֱלֹהִים
יָפוּצוּ אוֹיְבָיו
וְיָנוּסוּ מְשַׂנְאָיו :

5. הַנָּבִיא וְהַכֹּהֵן הָלְכוּ אֶל-הַמֶּלֶךְ וַיְהִי בְּבוֹאָם לַהֵיכָל
וַיִּשְׁאַל עֶבֶד-הַמֶּלֶךְ לֵאמוֹר: מָה אַתֶּם עוֹשִׂים פֹּה
וַיַּעֲנוּ וַיֹּאמְרוּ: בָּאנוּ לְדַבֵּר אֶל-הַמֶּלֶךְ וַיְבִיאֵם
הָעֶבֶד אֶל-הַמֶּלֶךְ וַיְדַבְּרוּ אֶל-הַמֶּלֶךְ לֵאמוֹר: אַתָּה
שֹׁרֶשׁ יִשַׁי וּמָשִׁיחַ בֶּן-דָּוִד וַיֹּאמֶר הַמֶּלֶךְ: אֱמֶת
דִּבְרֵכֶם וַיִּשְׁאֲלוּ וַיֹּאמְרוּ: לָמָּה לֹא שָׁמַעְתָּ אֶת-קוֹל-
יהוה לִשְׁמוֹר מִצְוֹתָיו :

6. וַיְדַבֵּר אֱלֹהִים אֶת-כָּל-הַדְּבָרִים הָאֵלֶּה לֵאמֹר: אָנֹכִי
יהוה אֱלֹהֶיךָ אֲשֶׁר הוֹצֵאתִיךָ מֵאֶרֶץ מִצְרַיִם מִבֵּית
עֲבָדִים לֹא יִהְיֶה-לְךָ אֱלֹהִים אֲחֵרִים עַל-פָּנָי :

7. מֵעוֹלָם בְּחַרְתִּיךָ וּמֵאָז אֲהַבְתִּיךָ וְאַתָּה פָּשַׁעְתָּ בִּי
וַתֶּחֱטָא חֲטָאָה גְדוֹלָה כִּי לֹא שָׁמַרְתָּ תוֹרָתִי וַתְּהִי
לְאֹיֵב לִי וָאֶתֵּן אוֹתְךָ לְגוֹי אֲשֶׁר לֹא יָדַע אוֹתִי
וַיָּפֶץ בָּנֶיךָ עַל-פְּנֵי-כָל-הָאָרֶץ וְעוֹד הָלַכְתָּ אַחֲרֵי
אֱלֹהִים אֲחֵרִים וַתִּזְבַּח לָהֶם. שׁוּבָה אֵלַי עַמִּי וּבוֹא
לְבֵית קָדְשִׁי כִּי אֶסְלַח לְחַטָּאתְךָ וַעֲוֹנְךָ לֹא אֶזְכֹּר
עוֹד וּבַיּוֹם הַהוּא תָּשִׁיר שִׁירָה חֲדָשָׁה :

--------------------

# XIV

# FINDING THE ROOT

A major problem in Hebrew is finding the root of a word, important to know because most lexicons and concordances are arranged on the basis of roots. The problem is difficult because Hebrew is a language that makes full use of prefixes and afformatives of all kinds, and in addition has its share of weak letters that assimilate or otherwise disappear. The situation is not hopeless, however, and in these introductory materials the student has the basic elements to deal with it.

The process is primarily one of stripping away the additions and so to get to the root itself. To do this one has to know what the possibilities are: what it is that Hebrew adds to the beginnings and ends of words, what letters are weak, and which ones can be assimilated. These possibilites are spread throughout the preceding chapters. The following notes provide a summary of them.

## 41 FINDING THE ROOT OF NOUNS AND NOMINAL FORMS

The first question to ask in finding the root of nominal forms is what it is that can be added to the root. Note the following possibilties.

(1) *Feminine gender* may be indicated by the addition of ה or ת to the end of the root, e.g.:

| | |
|---|---|
| מַלְכָּה | f. sg. absolute from מלך |
| מַלְכַּת | f. sg. construct from מלך |
| אֹכֶלֶת | f. sg. qal participle from אכל |

(2) *Dual and plural endings* are added to both the absolute and construct forms of nouns.

| | | | |
|---|---|---|---|
| absolute | ִים | construct | ֵי |
| | ַיִם | | |
| | וֹת | | וֹת |

(3) The *conjunction* וְ and its variations, e.g. וּ.

(4) The *article* הַ. and its variations; see § 18.

(5) The *inseparable prepositions*: בְּ, כְּ, לְ, מִן [ . מִ / מֵ ]. Note that these prepositions may also be used with the infinitive construct, which is really a verbal noun.

(6) The *pronominal suffixes*; see § 28.

(7) Nouns may be formed by placing a *preformative* on the root letters. The most common nominal preformatives are מ and ת.

(a) Examples of nouns with preformative מ:

| | | | |
|---|---|---|---|
| קום | *to stand* | מָקוֹם | *a place* |
| זבח | *to sacrifice* | מִזְבֵּחַ | *an altar* |
| שׁתה | *to drink* | מִשְׁתֶּה | *a feast* |
| שׁפט | *to judge* | מִשְׁפָּט | *a judgment* |

There can be no confusion between this preformative מ and the preposition מִן when it is prefixed to a noun, for the מ of the preposition must have a dāgēš fortē following it (because of the assimilated ן ) or be pointed with tone long ֵ by compensation.

The *participles of the intensive-repetitive and causative stems* also belong to this class of nouns formed by preformative מ.

| | |
|---|---|
| מְקַטֵּל | intensive-repetitive |
| מְקֻטָּל | |
| מִתְקַטֵּל | |
| | |
| מַקְטִיל | causative |
| מָקְטָל | |

(b) Examples of nouns with preformative ת:

| | | | |
|---|---|---|---|
| קוה | *to hope* | תִּקְוָה | *hope* |
| ירה | *to instruct* | תּוֹרָה | *instruction* |

The only other place that ת is used as a prefix is with the imperfect of the verb. Since the nouns with preformative ת do not correspond to any verbal patterns, there can be no confusion.

## 42 FINDING THE ROOT OF VERBAL FORMS

As with nouns, the basic question is what can be added to the verb root. The following items are fundamental.

(1) The perfect and imperfect preformatives and afformatives; see §§ 30-32.

(2) The stem preformatives, such as the נ of the nip̄ʻal, the הִת of the hiṯpaʻēl, and the ה of the hip̄ʻîl and hop̄ʻal. It is essential to know the third masculine singular perfect and imperfect of all the stems; see § 29.

(3) The pronominal suffixes; see § 28 (b).

(4) The ו conjunctive and consecutive.

With verbs like שׁפט, עבד, and קטל there is no difficulty in getting to the root, for as one peels away preformatives and afformatives one can go no farther than their three root letters, for their consonants are such that they cannot be dropped or assimilated. Not all verb roots are so strong. Sometimes when the peeling-away process is completed, one is left with only two consonants (upon occasion only one!) instead of the usual three. This may be due to two reasons:

(i) The root may be a middle hollow verb, such as שׁוּב or שִׁיר , or it may be an ע״ע verb such as לבב , a verb whose middle radical is repeated as the third.

(ii) There may be a weak consonant in the verb root, a letter which may assimilate or simply disappear altogether in inflection. These letters are: נ and י when they are the first consonant of the root, and ה when it is the third.

In a brief introduction such as this only the major possibilities of what happens with these weak letters can be pointed out.

(1) *Verbs whose first radical is* נ [ פ״ן verbs]. Whenever the נ has no vowel of its own, it is assimilated into the following consonant by dāgēš fortē.

| | |
|---|---|
| נָפַל | *he fell* |
| יִפֹּל < יִנְפֹּל | *he falls* |
| נָגַשְׁתָּ | *you drew near* |
| תִּגַּשׁ < תִּנְגַּשׁ | *you draw near* |

Where this assimilation takes place the imperative often drops the נ , as in גַּשׁ *draw near!*

(2) *Verbs whose first radical is* י [ פ״י and פ״ו verbs]. In the qal imperfect the י is usually assimilated into the personal prefix, which is then pointed not with ◌ִ but with ◌ֵ . Note that these verbs form their imperfects with ◌ֵ rather than with ◌ֹ or ◌ַ or ◌ֶ .

| | |
|---|---|
| יָשַׁב | *he sat, dwelled* |
| יֵשֵׁב < יִיְשֵׁב | *he sits, dwells* |

Note that the assimilation goes in the opposite direction from that of the פ״ן verbs. Note also that the imperative of these verbs drops the personal preformative, so that the command to sit would be שֵׁב sit!

Most of these verbs originally had ו as their first radical, and this ו reappears in the prefixing stems: nip'al, hip'îl and hop'al. See the following examples with ישׁע *to save* and ידע *to know.*

| | |
|---|---|
| nip'al | נוֹשַׁע < נִיְשַׁע |
| hip'îl | הוֹשִׁיעַ < הִיְשִׁיעַ |
| hop'al | הוּשַׁע < הֻיְשַׁע |
| hiṯpa'ēl | הִתְוַדַּע < הִתְיַדַּע |

The change from י to ו should cause no difficulty, for in peeling away endings one is still left with the three consonants, ושׁע = ישׁע .

Note that the very common verb הָלַךְ *to go* belongs to this class of verbs.

(3) *Verbs whose third radical is* ה [ ל״ה , originally ל״י verbs]. Note the following characteristics.

With *vocalic endings*:

(a) ה before וּ and ִי is dropped.

עָשׂוּ < עָשְׂהוּ < וּ + עָשָׂה *they did*

(b) ה before ָה becomes ת.

הָרְתָה < הָרְהָה < ָה + הָרָה *she was pregnant*

With *consonantal endings*: ה becomes its original י

עָשִׂיתִי < עָשָׂהְתִּי < תִּי + עָשָׂה *I did*

With the *infinitive construct*: ה becomes וֹת .

שְׁתוֹת / לִשְׁתּוֹת *to drink*

Not all the problems can be solved by what has been presented in this introduction, but it should be possible to find the roots of most of the words in a text. It may not be possible to translate the text, but one can discover the Hebrew terms behind the words of an English translation, a necessary prerequisite for word study and sound exegesis.

## ASSIGNMENT

PRACTICE READING the passages listed below, and FIND THE ROOTS OF THE WORDS. You are not asked to translate the passages, although all the words are in the glossary, and on the basis of what has been covered in the grammar, you could do so.

Psalm 19:2
Jeremiah 31:31-34
Amos 8:11-12
Psalm 24:1-4

--------------------

# XV

# THE HEBREW TEXT

## 43 THE PROBLEM OF A CONSONANTAL TEXT

In working with the Hebrew Bible it is important to remember that one is dealing primarily with a consonantal text. This fact, together with the basically triliteral character of the language (which seems to make everything look alike), means that one wrongly written consonant is far more serious textually than a similar typographical error in English, where the word structure and the manner of writing safeguard the meaning. In Hebrew, however, one changed consonant can create a totally different root, thereby radically altering the meaning of a whole text--a circumstance which can help explain difficult passages, but which also has given rise to untold (and sometimes unprincipled) numbers of emendations and conjectures! Scholarly excesses notwithstanding, it is true that the very nature of a consonantal text does carry with it many possibilities for textual corruption.

## 44 ERRORS IN THE CONSONANTAL TEXT

Students of the Hebrew Bible should be aware of at least the following major sources of error attendant on the transmission of the Hebrew consonantal text. For an exhaustive study in this area see Friedrich Delitzsch, *Die Lese- und Schreibfehler im Alten Testament* (Berlin, 1920).

### (1) Wrong division of the consonants.

Hosea 6:5 וּמִשְׁפָּטֶיךָ אוֹר יֵצֵא *and your judgments [are] light [that] goes forth.* The consonants should be redivided so as to read, וּמִשְׁפָּטִי כָאוֹר יֵצֵא *and my judgment like light goes forth*, a reading that exactly fits the context of the verse.

Isaiah 8:8 מְלֹא רֹחַב-אַרְצְךָ עִמָּנוּ אֵל *filling the breadth of your land, Immanuel.* It seems likely that the line should read מְלֹא רֹחַב-אֶרֶץ כִּ[י] עִמָּנוּ אֵל *filling the breadth of the land, for / but God is with us*; see the same expression in verse 10.

**(2) Dittography, the repetition of letters, even whole words.**

Numbers 19:12 הוּא יִתְחַטָּא-בוֹ בַּיּוֹם הַשְּׁלִישִׁי וּבַיּוֹם הַשְּׁבִיעִי יִטְהָר *he shall cleanse himself (lit. de-sin himself) by / with it on the third day, and on the seventh day he shall be clean.* The בּוֹ *by / with it*, which has no antecedent, is to be omitted as dittography. Note that *NRSV* supplies the word *water* to make sense of the בּוֹ.

Isaiah 38:11 אָמַרְתִּי לֹא-אֶרְאֶה יָהּ יָהּ בְּאֶרֶץ הַחַיִּים *I said, I do not see Yah Yah in the land of the living.* Omit the second יָהּ (with the Dead Sea Isaiah scroll), or perhaps combine the two to read יהוה.

**(3) Haplography, the omission of letters, even whole words.**

Genesis 1:26 וְיִרְדּוּ בִדְגַת הַיָּם וּבְעוֹף הַשָּׁמַיִם וּבַבְּהֵמָה וּבְכָל-הָאָרֶץ וּבְכָל-הָרֶמֶשׂ הָרֹמֵשׂ עַל-הָאָרֶץ *and they shall rule over the fish of the sea and over the fowl of the heavens and over the animals and over all the earth and over all the creeping things that creep on the earth.* It is clear from the context, verse 25, that a word has been omitted in the phrase *and over all the earth*; one must insert חַיַּת *beast[s] of* and read וּבְכָל-חַיַּת הָאָרֶץ *and over all the beasts of the earth.*

Psalm 88:2 יהוה אֱלֹהֵי יְשׁוּעָתִי ‖ יוֹם-צָעַקְתִּי בַלַּיְלָה נֶגְדֶּךָ *God of my salvation, ‖ day I cry out, at night before you.* Grammatically, instead of יוֹם *day*, one should expect the adverbial form יוֹמָם *at day*, the מ having dropped out by haplography. The emendation also improves the parallelism.

**(4) The influence of neighboring words.**

Many errors are caused by the influence of words close by, so that the consonant of one word is inadvertently repeated on another. When this happens at the beginning of a word it is called *homoiarkton.* See Ezekiel 45:16 where the grammatically impossible כֹּל הָעָם הָאָרֶץ should be read כֹּל עַם הָאָרֶץ *all the people of the land*; by homoiarkton ("like-beginnings") the ה was wrongly placed on the word in construct. If the error is at the end of a word, it is called *homoioteleuton* ("like-endings"). See Numbers 16:1, where וַיִּקַּח קֹרַח *and Qorah took* should be read וַיָּקָם קֹרַח *and Qorah rose up*; by the similarity to the end of the word קֹרַח a ח was written in the first word instead of a מ.

**(5) Confusion of letters.**

Similarities among the forms of the written letters has given rise to a large number of errors. Among the most commonly confused letters are the following.

**(a) ו and י**

In Isaiah 40:21 the phrase מוֹסְדוֹת הָאָרֶץ *the foundations of the earth* should be written מִיסֻדוֹת.

The well-known passage in Habakkuk 2:4 וְצַדִּיק בֶּאֱמוּנָתוֹ יִחְיֶה *and a righteous one shall live by his faithfulness* was read by the Greek translator of the Septuagint as וְצַדִּיק בֶּאֱמוּנָתִי יִחְיֶה *and a righteous one shall live by my faithfulness*, suggesting a quite different theological understanding. The New Testament quotations offer no help here; they do not use any possessive pronoun at all.

**(b) ד and ר**

Genesis 22:13 וְהִנֵּה-אַיִל אַחַר נֶאֱחָז בַּסְּבַךְ בְּקַרְנָיו *and behold a ram behind caught in the thicket by his horns.* Traditionally אַחַר has been translated *behind him*, although the text has no pronoun. Rather than supply a word, one should read אֶחָד *one/a certain*, as most translations now do (along with all the ancient versions and some forty Hebrew manuscripts).

In Isaiah 8:9 רֹעוּ *be broken / confounded* is not impossible, but in view of the context it is more likely that one should read with the Septuagint: דְּעוּ *know!* Cf. also קשר and קדש in Isaiah 8:12-13.

**(c) ה and ח**

Hosea 9:4 כְּלֶחֶם אוֹנִים לָהֶם כָּל-אֹכְלָיו יִטַּמָּאוּ *like food of mourners to them, all eating it are defiled.* For לָהֶם *to them* one must read לֶחֶם *food* and add the suffix ָם (lost by haplography) to make the word לַחְמָם, so that the verse reads *like food of mourners [is] their food, all eating it are defiled.*

Isaiah 11:1 וְיָצָא חֹטֶר מִגֵּזַע יִשָׁי וְנֵצֶר מִשָּׁרָשָׁיו יִפְרֶה *a shoot will go forth from the stump of Jesse, and a branch from his stock will bear fruit.* Better than יִפְרֶה would be יִפְרַח *will sprout.*

**(d) ה and ת**

In Isaiah 42:25 the difficult phrase חֵמָה אַפּוֹ *heat, his anger* should no doubt be read חֲמַת אַפּוֹ *the heat of his anger.*

Psalm 132:4 אִם-אֶתֵּן שְׁנַת לְעֵינָי לְעַפְעַפַּי תְּנוּמָה *I will not give the sleep of / to my eyes slumber.* The grammar and parallelism both suggest reading שֵׁנָה, the absolute rather than the construct of the noun *sleep.*

**(e) ב and כ**

1 Kings 22:20 וַיֹּאמֶר זֶה בְּכֹה וְזֶה אֹמֵר בְּכֹה. The meaning of the sentence is that *one said one thing and another said another thing.* The

idiom, however, is not בְּכֹה . . . בְּכֹה *by thus . . . by thus*, but rather כָּכָה . . . כָּכָה *like so . . .like so*, as it correctly appears in the parallel passage in 2 Chronicles 18:19.

Joel 2:23 מוֹרֶה וּמַלְקוֹשׁ בָּרִאשׁוֹן *the early rain and the latter rain in the beginning.* It is generally accepted that the Septuagint is correct in reading כָּרִאשׁוֹן *as in the beginning*, i.e. *as before* (instead of בָּרִאשׁוֹן) , a reading which fits the context of promise and vindication.

**(f) ע and צ**

1 Samuel 28:16 וַיהוה סָר מֵעָלֶיךָ וַיְהִי עָרֶךָ *and Yahveh has turned from you and become your . . ? . .* The word עָר is unknown. Most commentators emend to צָר , a very common word for *adversary.*

**(6) Metathesis, a change in the order of letters.**

Psalm 22:16 יָבֵשׁ כַּחֶרֶשׂ כֹּחִי ‖ וּלְשׁוֹנִי מֻדְבָּק מַלְקוֹחָי *my strength is dried up like a potsherd, ‖ and my tongue cleaves to my jaws.* It is likely that כֹּחִי should be read חִכִּי *my mouth, my palate*, especially in parallelism with *tongue.*

Isaiah 38:11 speaks about being with the יוֹשְׁבֵי חָדֶל *the inhabitants of cessation.* The word חָדֶל appears only here and makes no sense. חֶלֶד *world* is to be read instead.

**(7) Confusion of similar sounding consonants and words.**

1 Kings 1:18 וְעַתָּה הִנֵּה אֲדֹנִיָּה מָלָךְ וְעַתָּה אֲדֹנִי הַמֶּלֶךְ לֹא יָדָעְתָּ *and now behold Adonijah is king, and now, my lord the king, you did not know.* The second עַתָּה must be read as אַתָּה *you*; but עַתָּה was written because of similarity in sound. A similar

mistake was made in Psalm 49:8 between a כ and a ח, which sound the same after a vowel. Instead of אָח *brother* one must read אַךְ *yea, surely.*

## 45 ERRORS IN INTERPRETING THE CONSONANTS

(a) In the long history of transmission errors other than those affecting the consonants themselves came into the text. For example, some words were apparently misunderstood, or at least the *consonants incorrectly read.* We have already spoken of צלמות, which was incorrectly vocalized as צַלְמָוֶת *shadow of death*; the correct vocalization as we know now is צַלְמוּת *darkness.* Another example of misreading the consonants is כבד . It seems likely that sometimes כבד has been wrongly read as כָּבֹד *glory*, and should have been vocalized כָּבֵד *liver*, meaning the inner-self, the seat of the emotions; it is a Canaanite idiom. For examples of this see Genesis 49:6 where the parallel is נֶפֶשׁ ‖ כָּבֹד where the Greek reads *liver.* See also Psalm 7:6 נֶפֶשׁ ‖ חַיִּים ‖ כָּבוֹד ; Psalm 16:9 and Psalm 108:2 לֵב ‖ כָּבוֹד .

In Isaiah 1:19-20 it is said that if Israel is willing and obeys טוּב הָאָרֶץ תֹּאכֵלוּ *you will eat the good of the land*, but if he refuses and rebells חֶרֶב תְּאֻכְּלוּ *(by) a sword you will be eaten.* Instead of reading חֶרֶב *sword*, it has been suggested that one should read חָרוּב *ḥarob* (a very humble, low kind of food), and take the verb as active to get the following rendering: *you will eat ḥarobs.* By this reading syntactical difficulties are removed, and the parallelism is made sound.

(b) *Abbreviations* were used in writing and the failure to recognize them has led to misreadings of the consonantal text. This seems, for example, to be the case in the difficult text of Jeremiah 7:4, where Jeremiah takes the people to task for a blind trust in the temple and its cultus. He quotes the people as saying, הֵיכַל יהוה הֵיכַל יהוה הֵיכַל יהוה הֵמָּה *the temple of Yahveh, the temple of Yahveh, the temple of Yahveh they.* What are the

הֵמָּה *they*? The word is likely an abbreviation: ה״ הם״ which stands for הַמָּקוֹם הַזֶּה *this place*, so that the cry is, *The temple of Yahveh, the temple of Yahveh, the temple of Yahveh is this place.*

Wrong interpretations of abbreviations may also be found. One such case may be in Isaiah 7:10, where the text reads וַיּוֹסֶף יהוה דַּבֵּר אֶל-אָחָז *and Yahveh spoke again to Ahaz.* It is thought by many that instead of reading יהוה the name יְשַׁעְיָה *Isaiah* should logically be read. It is quite possible that the abbreviation י״ was simply wrongly rendered in the text.

(c) *Ancient linguistic devices* which left their traces in the consonantal text were not always known, and so were misunderstood. A very common example is that of the *enclitic* מ , well-known in Akkadian and Ugaritic. It is the particle *-ma*, or *-mi*, attached to the end of a word, apparently without any special meaning, its function being for rhythm and balance. A celebrated example of this *mem enclitic* is found in Psalm 29, a very ancient psalm, believed by many to have been originally a Canaanite hymn to Ba'al and later adapted to the Yahveh cult. The text of verse 6 reads: וַיַּרְקִידֵם כְּמוֹ-עֵגֶל ‖ לְבָנוֹן וְשִׂרְיֹן כְּמוֹ בֶן-רְאֵמִים *he makes them to dance like a calf* ‖ *Lebanon and Sirion like offspring of buffalo.* As it stands the poetic structure is clearly off; it is unbalanced in meter and the parallelism is defective. The problem is with the third person plural suffix on the verb. Most commentators have emended by removing the suffix מ from the verb. This, however, is unnecessary, for the מ is not the personal suffix, but an enclitic used here in good Canaanite fashion. The text therefore reads: וַיַּרְקֶד-םָ כְמוֹ-עֵגֶל לְבָנוֹן ‖ וְשִׂרְיֹן כְּמוֹ בֶן-רְאֵמִים *he makes Lebanon dance like a calf* ‖ *and Sirion like the offspring of buffalo.*

## 46 SCRIBAL EMENDATIONS AND ADDITIONS

In addition to the unintentional and inadvertent errors which arose during the long years of its transmission, the text was also affected by deliberate changes. These were made by the scribes, the סוֹפְרִים, whose duty it was to protect the text and its interpretation. The changes and additions were made in the interest of doctrine and piety as well as clarity.

Scribal tradition says that there were eighteen emendations made by the scribes, the תִּקּוּנֵי סוֹפְרִים. An examination of the rabbinical listings, however, shows more than eighteen, and there are probably others that have not been remembered. Genesis 18:22 is a well-known example of these תִּקּוּנֵי סוֹפְרִים. The passage comes in the story of Sodom, how Yahveh and the two angels come to Abraham in the form of three men. When the two companions go on to Sodom the text says: וַיִּפְנוּ מִשָּׁם הָאֲנָשִׁים וַיֵּלְכוּ סְדֹמָה וְאַבְרָהָם עוֹדֶנּוּ עֹמֵד לִפְנֵי יהוה *and the men turned from there and went to Sodom, and Abraham was still standing before Yahveh.* According to the scribal tradition the last part of the sentence has been emended. Originally the names of Abraham and Yahveh were reversed, so that the original text read, *and Yahveh was still standing before Abraham. To stand before someone*, however, is a phrase sometimes used with the meaning *to wait upon, to be subservient to.* It was not fitting that such a suggestion be used of God, so the text was deliberately changed.

An especially vivid example of the scribal emendations is in Ezekiel 8:17: *He said to me, Do you see, son of man? Is it too light a thing for the house of Judah to do the abominations they do here, that they should fill the land with violence and further provoke me to anger?* And the verse concludes with the statement, וְהִנָּם שֹׁלְחִים אֶת-הַזְּמוֹרָה אֶל-אַפָּם *Behold, they put the branch to their nose!* The last word, אַפָּם *their nose*, has been emended by the scribes. It originally read אַפִּי *my nose*, and one gets the very vivid picture of rebellious Judah flaunting their sinfulness before Yahveh, just as if they were shaking a branch in his face. The thought was too vivid and unseemly for the pious סוֹפְרִים, and so the emendation was made.

Sometimes explanatory remarks were added to the text. In Isaiah 51:17 and 22 a rare poetic word for a *goblet* is used, קֻבַּעַת

, and in both places the explanatory gloss, כּוֹס (an ordinary word for a *cup*), has been added. In Joshua 1:2 the word לָהֶם *to them* occurs. To make sure the identity of the *them*, the gloss לִבְנֵי יִשְׂרָאֵל *to the children* of *Israel* was added, a phrase interestingly not in the Septuagint. Sometimes the glossator was wrong, as for example in Jeremiah 41:16, where the ordinary word for *men*, גְּבָרִים , was misunderstood to be גִּבֹּרִים *warriors*, with the result that he added wrongly the explanatory gloss אַנְשֵׁי מִלְחָמָה *men of battle*, that is, *warriors*.

Sometimes additions are made to make a passage contemporary, as for example in Micah 4:10, where the prophet has been prophesying about the destruction of Jerusalem and exile at the hands of the Assyrians. When this did not take place, the prophecy was updated to refer to the Babylonian exile, and someone has added the line, וּבָאת עַד-בָּבֶל *and you shall enter Babylon*. Or again, some additions to the text are simply pious observations, like the one that breaks up the poetry in Isaiah 40:7, אָכֵן חָצִיר הָעָם *Surely the people is grass!*

## 47 K$^{e}$ṮÎḆ AND Q$^{e}$RE

When after the first century C. E. the consonantal Hebrew text was pretty much fixed, corrections and emendations were still made, but now without changing the text itself. The changes were made in the margins, so that while a word was written (*k$^{e}$ṯîḇ*) in the text in one way, it was to be read (*q$^{e}$rê*) according to what was in the margin. Isaiah 9:2 provides a good example.

הִרְבִּיתָ הַגּוֹי

לֹא֯ הִגְדַּלְתָּ הַשִּׂמְחָה          לו
ק״

The consonantal text reads, *You have increased the nation* ‖ *you have not made great the joy*. Over the word לֹא֯ *not* is a small circle, a sign that directs the reader to the margin. There in the margin one finds the consonants לו and just below it ק״ , the abbreviation for קְרֵא , an Aramaic word meaning *(to be) read.* This means that the consonants in the margin are to be read instead of those in the text; note that the vowel points in the text are for the consonants in the margin. The translation of Isaiah 9:2, then, according to the *k^e^ṯîḇ* / *q^e^rê* is: *You have increased the nation* ‖ *to/for it you have made great the joy.* Among standard English translations it may be noted that *KJV* follows the *k^e^ṯîḇ* and *NRSV* follows the *q^e^rê.* Actually, while the Masoretes saw that something was wrong with the text and so made the marginal correction, they did not go far enough; a serious problem related to poetic structure remained. Almost certainly the consonants of the words הַגּוֹי *the nation* and לֹא *not* are to be read together: הגוילא and emended to הגילא < הַגִּילָה *the gladness / joy*, so that the line now reads in full consonance with the context: *You have increased the gladness* ‖ *you have made great the joy.*

There are about 1300 cases of *k^e^ṯîḇ* / *q^e^rê* in the present Hebrew text. One of the most numerous is that of the divine name יהוה. For many generations piety had forbidden the pronouncing of the name. When coming upon it in reading, it was customary to substitute אֲדֹנָי *Lord* [lit., *my Lord*] or אֱלֹהִים *God*. This practice continued into the Masoretic Bible. While יהוה was written in the text, אדני was always read, or אלהים (if אדני was already in the text). This substitution of אדני and אלהים for יהוה happened so frequently that although the vowel points were put in the text under the Tetragrammaton, the changed consonants were not put in the margin, but simply assumed. It is known as a *q^e^rê perpetuum*, a perpetual qerê. Incidentally, when one reads the consonants יהוה with the vowels for אדני , which were placed under them, one gets the name, Yehovah > Jehovah.

The Masoretes, who were charged with the care of the biblical text, took great pains in their work. They went into great, nearly unbelievable detail, counting words and letters, the number of verses, individual forms of words. They determined such things as where the middle of a book is; they noted any and all peculiarities of writing. These notes were written in the margins of the manuscripts and so are known as the *Masora marginalis*, with the notes written on the top and bottom margins called the *Masora magna*, and the notes written on the side the *Masora parva*. The notes at the end of the manuscript are called the *Masora finalis*.

## 48 THE ACCENTS

About the sixth century C. E. the Masoretic vowel points began to be set into the text. In addition a complex system of accents, טְעָמִים, was also put into the text. Actually, the term *accents* is somewhat misleading, for the function of the טְעָמִים was not primarily to indicate stress, but to punctuate and put words into phrases and clauses. They have their origin in ancient systems of cantillation, and the various signs still have musical values.

(a) There are two sets of accents: (a) the common accents used for twenty-one of the books of the Hebrew Bible (*accentus communes*) and (b) the accents used for the books of Psalms, Job and Proverbs (*accentus poetici*). The two sets are actually very similar in signs and use.

The accents themselves are of two kinds: *disjunctive* (separating and distinguishing a word from another) and *conjunctive* (showing what words are to go together). In this way the accents preserve the traditional Masoretic understanding of the biblical text, and are themselves an important commentary.

The major *disjunctive accents* are as follows.

*sillûq* Placed in the tone syllable of the last word of a verse, e.g. דָּבָֽר

*'aṯnaḥ* marks the half-verse, the greatest logical division within the verse, e.g. דָּבָ֑ר

*s^e^gôltā* marks the first of two major divisions; it is postpositive, that is, it is written after the word, e.g. דָּבָר֒

*zâqêp̱ qāṭôn* divides the phrases between *sillûq* and *'aṯnāḥ*, or between *'aṯnāḥ* and *s^e^gôltā*, e.g. דָּבָ֔ר

*r^e^ḇîa'* often divides *zāqēp̱* sections, e.g. דָּבָ֗ר

*ṭip̱ḥā* before *'aṯnāḥ* and *sillûq*, e.g. דָּבָ֖ר

These *disjunctive accents* are the same for the three poetical books, except that for these the *'ôlê v^e^yôrēḏ* often marks the chief division within a verse instead of the *'aṯnāḥ*, e.g. דָּבָ֥֫ר

The major *conjunctive accents* are as follows.

*mûnāḥ* often with *'aṯnāḥ* and *zāqēp̱*, e.g. דָּבָ֣ר

*mêr^e^ḵā* often with *sillûq* and *ṭip̱ḥā*, e.g. דָּבָ֥ר

Note that the combinations of disjunctive and conjunctive accents indicate what words go together in a quite graphic manner; e.g. the mûnāḥ - zāqēp̱ in 1 Kings 17:2 בְּנַ֣חַל כְּרִ֔ית *in wady K^e^rît* or again in 1 Kings 17:8 the combination of mêreḵā - ṭipḥā, וַיְהִ֥י דְבַר־יְהוָ֖ה *and the word of Yahveh came.* Familiarity with at least the major accents is very helpful in seeing how words are construed within a sentence, and so facilitates understanding and reading. Note also that the accents are usually placed on the tone, or accented syllable, and so are also helps in pronunciation.

(b) The major disjunctive accents, because they mark the end of a sentence or clause or important phrase within a clause, often affect the pointing of the words by lengthening the vowels of tone syllables, or by restoring reduced vowels, or even by shifting the accent. This is done to give a sense of cadence and finality. Words so affected are said to be *in pause.* These *pausal forms* occur nearly always with sillûq and 'aṯnāḥ, which disjunctive accents mark the end of a sentence and the major division of a verse, and quite frequently with the others noted above.

In pause *the vowels of tone syllables are usually lengthened*; as for example in 1 Kings 18:4 וָמָיִם [instead of וָמַיִם ] *and water*; 1 Kings 17:6 בָּעָרֶב [instead of בָּעֶרֶב ] *in the evening*; 1 Kings 17:20 אֱלֹהָי [instead of אֱלֹהַי ] *my God*; even proper names may be affected as in 1 Kings 18:19 אִיזָבֶל [instead of אִיזֶבֶל ] *Jezebel.*

In pause *original vowels, reduced in inflection, are often restored*; for example, 1 Kings 17:16 כָּלָתָה [instead of כָּלְתָה ] *it comes to an end*; 1 Kings 18:34 וַיְשַׁלֵּשׁוּ [instead of וַיְשַׁלְּשׁוּ ] *and they did it a third time.*

Sometimes with words in pause *the accent is shifted and a vocal šᵉvâ raised to sᵉgôl*; for example, 1 Kings 17:9 לְכַלְכְּלֶךָ [instead of לְכַלְכֶּלְךָ ] *to nourish you*; 1 Kings 18:31 שְׁמֶךָ [instead of שִׁמְךָ ] *your name.*

(c) The Two Tables of Accents.

## ACCENTUS COMMUNES

A. Distinctivi vel domini

1. Sillûq, *end of a verse* דָּבָֽר
2. ’Atnāḥ דָּבָ֑ר
3. Segôltā, *postpositive* דָּבָר֒
4. Šalšelet דָּבָ֓ר ׀
5. Zāqēp qāṭôn דָּבָ֔ר
6. Zāqēp gāḏôl דָּבָ֕ר
7. Reḇîaʻ דָּבָ֗ר
8. Ṭipḥā דָּבָ֖ר
9. Zarqā, *postpositive* דָּבָר֮
10. Paštā, *postpositive* דָּבָר֙
11. Yᵉṯîḇ, *prepositive* דָּ֚בָר
12. Teḇîr דָּבָ֛ר
13. Gereš [Ṭeres] דָּבָ֜ר
14. Garšayim דָּבָ֞ר
15. Pāzēr דָּבָ֡ר
16. Pāzēr gāḏôl [Qarnê pārā] דָּבָ֟ר
17. Telîšā gāḏol, *prepositive* ֠דָּבָר
18. Legarmēh דָּבָ֣ר ׀

B. Conjunctivi vel servi

19. Mûnāḥ דָּבָ֣ר
20. Mahpāḵ [Mehuppāḵ] דָּבָ֤ר
21. Mērekā דָּבָ֥ר
22. Mērekā kepûlā דָּבָ֦ר
23. Dargā דָּבָ֧ר
24. ’Azlā דָּבָ֨ר
25. Telîšā qāṭôn דָּבָר֩
26. Galgal [Yeraḥ] דָּבָ֪ר
27. Mâyelā לְהַחֲלוֹ

## ACCENTUS POETICI

A. Distinctivi vel domini

| | | |
|---|---|---|
| 1. | Sillûq, *end of a verse* | דָבָֽר |
| 2. | ‘Olê veyôrēḏ | דָבָ֥֫ר |
| 3. | ’Aṯnāḥ | דָבָ֑ר |
| 4. | Reḇîa‘ gâḏôl | דָבָ֗ר |
| 5. | Reḇîa‘ mugrāš | דָ֝בָ֗ר |
| 6. | Šalšeleṯ gāḏôl | דָבָ֓ר ׀ |
| 7. | Ṣinnôr [Zarqā], *postpositive* | דָבָר֮ |
| 8. | Reḇîa‘ qāṭôn | דָבָ֗ר |
| 9. | Deḥî [Ṭipḥā], *prepositive* | דָ֭בָר |
| 10. | Pāzēr | דָבָ֡ר |
| 11. | Mehuppāḵ legarmēh | דָבָ֤ר ׀ |
| 12. | ’Azlā legarmēh | דָבָ֨ר ׀ |

B. Conjunctivi vel servi

| | | |
|---|---|---|
| 13. | Mûnāḥ | דָבָ֣ר |
| 14. | Mēreḵā | דָבָ֥ר |
| 15. | ‘Illûy | דָבָ֬ר |
| 16. | Ṭarḥā | דָבָ֖ר |
| 17. | Galgal [Yeraḥ] | דָבָ֪ר |
| 18. | Mehuppāḵ [Mahpāḵ] | דָבָ֤ר |
| 19. | ’Azlā [Qaḏmā] | דָבָ֨ר |
| 20. | Šalšeleṯ qāṭôn | דָבָ֓ר |
| 21. | Ṣinnôrîṯ | דָבָ֘ר |

---

# A GRAMMAR OF BIBLICAL HEBREW

## PART TWO: CONTINUING BIBLICAL HEBREW

### AN INTRODUCTORY NOTE

In *Part One: An Introduction to Biblical Hebrew* students have been given all that is needed to begin reading in the Hebrew Bible, and so to continue the study of Hebrew inductively. With nominal forms virtually nothing additional needs to be done, since all the basic materials of declension, agreement and syntax have been presented and have already been in full use.

The situation with verbal forms, however, is somewhat different. The basic structure of the Hebrew verbal system has been presented: the seven stems, the perfect and imperfect forms, the basic rules for accent and afformatives in conjugating the verb in any stem, participles, and a brief introduction to infinitives. While acquainted with all these things, in actual practice students have really only used the verb in the qal stem. In continuing biblical Hebrew they will need to develop their knowledge of these basic materials. It is suggested that time be taken at the very outset to review and practice the conjugation of the strong verb in all its stems (see II 11, 12-14; cf. I 29-32). A fundamental knowledge of the strong verb is especially important, since it is the basis for dealing with the many variations in verbal forms occasioned by weak letters and gutturals.

Full information concerning the verbal system and all other grammatical forms are found in *A Summary of Hebrew Grammar*. As students read in a connected text, questions of syntax and construction will be raised, and they will be faced with the challenge of understanding Hebrew on its own terms and translating this into their own. This, of course, is one of the chief values and joys of learning Hebrew in the first place--to be able to catch the spirit and flavor of biblical expression, so different from our own. *Notes on Hebrew Syntax*, it is hoped, will assist students in doing this, particularly since it departs somewhat from the traditional approaches to Hebrew syntax.

There are many excellent biblical texts that can be used in an inductive continuation of Hebrew, the books of Ruth and Genesis being among the most popular. The text chosen here, however, is 1 Kings 17-19, the story of Elijah: the drought, the contest on the Carmel and the theophany at Horeb. These chapters not only form an important narrative unity within 1 Kings, but they contain examples of nearly all the grammatical elements of biblical Hebrew, and are short enough, moreover, to be read within a term or even half-semester. All the basic grammar and syntax of biblical Hebrew can be covered in the course of reading them.

In this connection it should be noted that while both *A Summary of Hebrew Grammar* and *Notes on Hebrew Syntax* draw heavily on 1 Kings 17-19 for examples, their scope and contents are not determined by these chapters. They are independent and comprehensive treatments of grammar and syntax, and so are basic references to be used in the reading and study of any passage in the Hebrew Bible.

For study purposes the Elijah narratives have been divided into twelve sections. In each section note is made of points of grammar and syntax raised in the text that could be considered in connection with reading it. Needs of students and the approach of the instructor will of course determine just how and where these items are taken up.

These *Points of Grammar and Syntax* are not intended to be exhaustive. Little or no note, for example, is made of such matters as noun declension, vāv consecutive, prepositional use and the like; nor is any special order suggested for their consideration. Such items are noted only where the text provides good occasion and examples.

However, with verbs, the greatest challenge in learning Hebrew, a more specific and ordered approach is needed. Because verbs with weak letters and gutturals are only variations of the strong verb, it is suggested that they be studied together. In this way, continuing to review the strong verb while studying the variations from it, will not only show the essential unity of the Hebrew verb, but will facilitate the mastery of it.

While of course verbs of all kinds appear throughout the text, one class of verb has been singled out and suggested for special attention in each of the reading sections. Verbs with weak letters are treated first; they are not only the most numerous, but also need the most practice. The order of their consideration is determined by their frequency of occurrence in the various sections.

Finally, although pausal forms are regularly indicated in the *Points of Grammar and Syntax*, the accents themselves, the טְעָמִים , are not mentioned or discussed. It is expected, however, that in the process of reading, the student will become familiar with at least the major accents in the Masoretic text. They not only explain pausal forms, but open up to the student the rich heritage of rabbinical tradition and text interpretation.

In addition to the *Points of Grammar and Syntax* there is a vocabulary for each section, listing the words which are not in the vocabularies of *Part One: An Introduction to Biblical Hebrew.* This has been done to make the student's progress a little easier. The *Glossary* at the end, of course, is complete, including all words for both parts of the *Grammar.*

---

# ELIJAH: YAHVEH AND BA'AL 1 KINGS 17-19

The Elijah story in 1 Kings 17-19 is excellent Hebrew prose and a joy to read simply as literature. In addition, these three chapters contain nearly all the elements of grammar that are needed for a sound knowledge of biblical Hebrew. As they stand now in the Book of Kings, they are a literary unity set within the framework of the Deuteronomic history. At the same time they offer good opportunity for literary criticism: source analysis, form and tradition criticism and narrative approach. Their significance for biblical theology and the history of Israel's faith goes without saying. Elijah is far more important than the slight extent of materials about him would suggest. First met in these chapters, he is already a known and revered figure, as the developing tradition presenting him as a "second Moses" clearly shows.

In these chapters three independent narratives are combined into one: (1) the story of the drought which asks the question, "Who brings the rain? Yahveh or Ba'al?" a story which begins with the announcement of a drought in 1 Kings 17:1 and concludes with the coming of rain and the triumphant run to Jezreel in 18:41-46; (2) the contest on the Carmel, which asks the question, "Who is God?" which is answered by fire and concludes with the slaughter of the prophets of Ba'al in Wadi Qîšôn; and (3) the theophany at Horeb (cf. Exodus 33:12-23), where Yahveh, who has taken over the prerogatives of Ba'al as God and rain-bringer, is disassociated from any natural phenomena whatsoever.

The three stories are closely bound together into one narrative by the theme of persecution and flight with its culmination in the assertion of Yahveh's ultimate supremacy in 1 Kings 19:15-18. The individual stories have been augmented by anecdotes, some of which are probably drawn from the Elisha אִישׁ אֱלֹהִים traditions. A final editing is made by the Deuteronomist, who takes up the narrative and sets it into the framework of the Deuteronomic history. This adaptation is easily seen in 1 Kings 18:18, where the reference to idolatry clearly reflects the Deuteronomic summary of Ahab's reign (1 Kings 16:29-33) and not the issues of the drought and Carmel stories. See the outline and analysis which follow.

It is interesting to note that the traditions around Elijah continue to develop beyond the Kings passages. Already in the Hebrew Bible he comes to have an eschatological role as the messenger sent to prepare for the Day of Yahveh and God's coming, and to bring reconciliation, all in the context of the tôrâ of Moses. The traditions continue to grow beyond the Bible, and Elijah comes to be associated with the resurrection, with deeds of kindness (mostly done anonymously), and with the explication of tôrâ. In Jewish tradition he has become, as James Montgomery observed, "the Haggadic counterpart to the Lawgiver." Of all the great figures in Israel he stands next to Moses in importance. Indeed, it has been said that if Moses is viewed as the founder of the ancient faith, then Elijah is seen as the one who successfully transplants it on new soil.

See the important monograph by Georg Fohrer, *Elia* (Zürich, 1957). Cf. also Odil Hannes Steck, *Überlieferung und Zeitgeschichte in den Elia-Erzählungen* (Neukirchen Verlag, 1968), and the standard commentaries.

-----------------------------

## AN OUTLINE OF 1 KINGS 17-19

| | | |
|---|---|---|
| [1] | 1 Kings 17:1 | Elijah announces a drought |
| | 1 Kings 17:2-7 | Elijah in hiding at Wadi K$^{e}$rîṯ |
| [2] | 1 Kings 17:8-16 | The widow of Ṣar$^{e}$pāṯ and the unending supply of flour and oil |
| [3] | 1 Kings 17:17-24 | The raising of the widow's son |
| [4] | 1 Kings 18:1-6 | Obadiah and Ahab during the drought and the search for water and Elijah |
| [5] | 1 Kings 18:7-18 | The meeting of Elijah with Obadiah and Ahab |
| [6] | 1 Kings 18:19-24 | Elijah's call for a contest on the Carmel |
| [7] | 1 Kings 18:25-29 | The failure of the prophets of Ba'al |
| [8] | 1 Kings 18:30-40 | Elijah's victory and the slaughter of the Ba'al prophets |
| [9] | 1 Kings 18:41-46 | The coming of the rain |
| [10] | 1 Kings 19:1-8 | The flight of Elijah into the wilderness |
| [11] | 1 Kings 19:9-18 | The theophany at Horeb |
| [12] | 1 Kings 19:19-21 | The call of Elisha |

-----------------------------

## AN ANALYSIS OF 1 KINGS 17-19

### THE GREAT DROUGHT

17:1
17:2-6
(17:7) [secondary anecdotes;
—— 17:8-16 cf. Elisha]
17:17-24
18:1ab-2a
—————— 18:3b-4
18:5-9 [editorial story line to combine
—————— 18:10-11 the three narratives]
18:12
—————— 18:13
18:14-15
(18:16)
18:17
[ ] —————— 18:18 [Deuteronomic editorializing about
idolatry; cf. 16:29-33]
18:41-46

### THE CONTEST ON THE CARMEL

[ ? ] —————— 18:19 [editorial story line to combine
18:20-21 the three narratives]
[ ? ] —————— 18:22
18:23-40

### THE THEOPHANY AT HOREB

—————— 19:1-3a [editorial story line to combine
19:3bα the three narratives]
19:3bβ-8a
19:8b-9
[ ] —————— 19:10
19:11-13bα (β)
—————— 19:13b (β)-14
[ ] —————— 19:15-17 [original conclusion of Horeb story lost
or substituted; present conclusion probably by
the editor who combined the three narratives]
—————— 19:18

### THE CALL OF ELISHA

19:19-21

---

# 1

## 1 KINGS 17:1 ELIJAH ANNOUNCES A DROUGHT
## 1 KINGS 17:2-7 ELIJAH IN HIDING AT WADI K$^{e}$RÎṮ

### VOCABULARY

אִם *conj.* if. אִם *is used to introduce a negative oath and* אִם לֹא *a positive oath; note also its use in continuing a question.*

גֶּשֶׁם *n.m.* rain

דָּבַר *vb.* to speak; *usually in the intensive* דִּבֵּר

טַל *n.m.* dew

יָבֵשׁ *vb.* to be dry, be withered

כּוּל *vb.* to contain; *in pilpēl* כִּלְכֵּל to sustain, nourish

מָטָר *n.m.* rain

נַחַל *n.m.* wadi, stream, torrent

סָתַר *vb.* to hide, conceal

עֹרֵב *n.m.* raven

פֶּה *n.m.* mouth; *construct* פִּי

פָּנָה *vb.* to turn

קֶדֶם *n.m.* front, east, aforetime

קֵץ *n.m.* end

שָׁנָה *n.f.* year; *pl.* שָׁנִים / שָׁנוֹת

שָׁתָה *vb.* to drink

תֹּשָׁב / תּוֹשָׁב *n.m.* dweller, sojourner

### POINTS OF GRAMMAR AND SYNTAX

In these chapters of the Elijah cycle verbs with ל״ה are most frequent in occurrence, there being no less than five different roots in this first section alone. It is suggested, therefore, that concentration on the various classes of verbs begin with them. See *A Summary of Hebrew Grammar*, §§ 11-14 for the structure of the strong verb, and § 17 for the discussion of ל״ה verbs. Note also:

| | |
|---|---|
| 17:1 | the oath formula |
| 17:1 | the relative clause with אֲשֶׁר; cf. also 17:3, 5 |
| 17:3 | the use of *hê localē* |
| 17:3 | continuation of the imperative by vāv |

consecutive perfect

17:6 the use of the participle

Note the varying forms of מִן in 17:1, 3, 4, 6, 7

Pausal forms in 17:6 and 7 (twice)

## 2

## 1 KINGS 17:8-16 THE WIDOW OF ṢAR^e^P̱AṮ AND THE UNENDING SUPPLY OF FLOUR AND OIL

### VOCABULARY

אַחֲרוֹן *adj.* coming after, behind
אַךְ *adv.* surely, but
אָכַל *vb.* to eat, devour, destroy
אַלְמָנָה *n.f.* widow
חָסַר *vb.* to lack, need
כַּד *n.f.* jar
כָּלָה *vb.* to be complete, spent, come to an end
כְּלִי *n.m.* article, utensil, vessel, tool
כַּף *n.f.* hand, palm
לָקַח *vb.* to take, capture
מְלֹא *n.m.* fulness, that which fills
מָעוֹג *n.m.* cake
עוּגָה / עֻגָה *n.f.* disc or cake of bread
מְעַט *n.m.* a little, fewness, a few
נָא *enclitic*, not usually to be translated
עֵץ *n.m.* tree, wood
פָּנֶה / פָּנִים *n.m. only in plural* face
פַּת *n.f.* fragment, bit, morsel (of bread)
פֶּתַח *n.m.* opening, doorway, entrance
צַפַּחַת *n.f.* jar, jug
קֶמַח *n.m.* flour, meal
קָרָא 1 *vb.* to call, proclaim. read
קָשַׁשׁ *vb.* to gather stubble
רִאשׁוֹן *adj.* first, former, chief

שֶׁמֶן *n.m.* fatness, oil

שְׁנַיִם / שְׁתַּיִם *n. m. & f., numeral, dual* two

## POINTS OF GRAMMAR AND SYNTAX

Because of their frequent occurrence in this and succeeding sections, verbs with ע״ו and ע״י, as well as ע״ע verbs, are studied here. See *A Summary of Hebrew Grammar*, §§ 11-14 for the basic verb structure, § 19 for Middle Hollow verbs, and § 20 for verbs with Double ʻAyin. Note that a characteristic of these verbs, one that helps to distinguish them from all other verbs with weak letters, is that the vowel between the two or first two consonants of the root can never be reduced to a šᵉvâ. There must always be a full vowel. Note also the pi'ēl stem and the equivalent pilpēl form in 17:9; cf. 17:4.

Note that while the verbs with פ״ו (including הָלַךְ) and פ״י are treated in the next section, they could just as well be treated here. The present order was followed to give students a little "breather" after dealing with the ל״ה verbs. Note also:

17:9, 13 the continuation of the imperative by vāv consecutive perfect
17:9, 10 the use of *hê localē*
17:9, 10 the pointing of the middle hollow verbs
17:10-11 the forms of the verb לָקַח
17:10, 12 the use of הִנֵּה
17:12 the oath formula
17:12 the use of יֵשׁ
17:12 suffixes with verbs
17:13 the negative command with the jussive
17:14, 15 Keṯîḇ and Qerê

Pausal forms in 17:9, 12, 15

# 3

## 1 KINGS 17:17-24 THE RAISING OF THE WIDOW'S SON

### VOCABULARY

בַּעֲלָה *n.f.* mistress, wife
גּוּר *vb.* to sojourn, dwell
גַּם *adv.* also, moreover, even, yea
חָזָק *adj.* strong, mighty
חֵיק *n.m.* bosom
חָלָה *vb.* to be sick, ill
חֳלִי *n.m.* sickness, illness
יֶלֶד *n.m.* child, boy, youth
יָרַד *vb.* to go down, descend
מְאֹד *n.m. & adv.* muchness, abundance, exceedingly, very
מָדַד *vb.* to measure
מִטָּה *n.*f. bed
נְשָׁמָה *n.f.* breath
עָלָה *vb.* to go up, ascend, climb
עֲלִיָּה *n.f.* upper chamber, roof chamber
עִם *prep.* with
עַתָּה *adv.* now
פַּעַם *n.f.* foot, anvil, occurrence, blow
קֶרֶב *n.m.* inward part, midst
רָעַע *vb. denominative* to be unpleasant, harmful, evil
שָׁכַב *vb.* to lie down
שָׁלַח *vb.* to send, extend

### POINTS OF GRAMMAR AND SYNTAX

Verbs with פ״ו (including הָלַךְ) and פ״י have already been met a number of times in the first two reading sections, but now are to be given more detailed attention. See *A Summary of Hebrew Grammar*, §§ 11-14 for the strong verb, § 18 for פ״ו and פ״י verbs. Keep in mind two basic characteristics of verbs with פ״ו: (1) The י is usually assimilated into the prefix of qal imperfect; and (2) the original ו always returns (replacing the י)

in the prefixed stems: nip̄'al, hit̲pa'ēl, hip̄'îl and hop̄'al. Note in this section the number of examples of the hip̄'îl stem: 17:18 (2 times), 19 (2 times), 21 and 23. Note also the hit̲pōlēl (= hit̲pa'ēl) in 17:20 and 21.

The passage also offers a good opportunity to see nouns derived from ל״ה roots: חֳלִי (17:17), עָוֹן (17:18), עֲלִיָּה (17:19, 23), and מִטָּה (17:19) Note also:

| | |
|---|---|
| 17:17 | חָלְיוֹ with the suffix |
| 17:19, 23 | suffixes with verbs (5 times) |
| 17:19, 20 | the relative clause with אֲשֶׁר |
| 17:20 | the interrogative ה |
| 17:21 | the use of numerals (cardinal) |
| 17:21 | the use of the jussive in a positive sense |
| 17:23 | *hê localē* |

Pausal forms in 17:17, 22, and 24

## 4

## 1 KINGS 18:1-6 OBADIAH AND AHAB DURING THE DROUGHT AND THE SEARCH FOR WATER AND ELIJAH

### VOCABULARY

אוּלַי *adv.* perhaps
אֶחָד *adj. & numeral* one, each, a certain one
בַּד *n.m.* separation; *with* ל alone, by itself
בְּהֵמָה *n.f.* animal, cattle, beast
דֶּרֶךְ *n.m. & f.* way, road
חָבָא *vb.* to withdraw, hide
חָלַק *vb.* to divide, share
חֲמִשִּׁים *n. numeral* fifty
חָצִיר *n.m.* grass, herbage
מֵאָה *n.f. numeral* hundred
מַעְיָן *n.m.* spring
מְעָרָה *n.f.* cave

מָצָא *vb.* to come upon, attain, find
סוּס *n.m.* horse
עָבַר *vb.* to pass through, pass over, pass by
פֶּרֶד *n.m.* mule
רַב *adj.* much, many, great
רָעָב *n.m.* famine, hunger
שְׁלִישִׁית *adj. f. numeral* third

## POINTS OF GRAMMAR AND SYNTAX

Thus far only two verbs belonging to the class of verbs with פ״ן have occurred in the readings: נתן and לקח, but there are many more. The basic characteristic of פ״ן verbs is that when the נ has no vowel of its own, it is assimilated by dāgēš fortē into the following consonant. See *A Summary of Hebrew Grammar*, §§ 11-14 for the strong verb, and § 16 for verbs with פ״ן. Note also:

18:1, 4 numerals (cardinal and ordinal); cf. 18: 13
18:1, 2 the nip'al forms; cf. possible textual problem in 18:5
18:3 the use of the participle with הָיָה
18:4 the infinitive construct with ב
18:6 the use of אֶחָד . . . . . אֶחָד
Pausal forms in 18:3 and 4

# 5

## 1 KINGS 18:7-18 THE MEETING OF ELIJAH WITH OBADIAH AND AHAB

### VOCABULARY

בַּעַל *n.m. & P.N.* lord, owner, husband, master; Ba'al
בָּקַשׁ *vb.* to seek
הָרַג *vb.* to kill, slay
מַמְלָכָה *n.f.* kingdom
נָגַד *vb. only in causative* to tell, narrate, declare
נָכַר *vb.* to regard, recognize

נַעַר *n.m.* boy, youth, lad, retainer
נְעֻרִים *n.f. pl.* youth (time of), early life
נָשָׂא *vb.* to lift up, raise, carry, take away, exalt
עָזַב *vb.* to leave, forsake
עָכַר *vb.* to stir up, disturb, trouble
2 קָרָא *vb.* to meet, encounter, befall
שָׁבַע *vb.* to swear

**POINTS OF GRAMMAR AND SYNTAX**

Verbs with gutturals do not lose consonants, but often modify the standard pointing, because (a) they prefer "a" vowels (especially before them), (b) vocal š^e^vâ instead of silent, and (c) cannot take dāgēš fortē. No less than eight verbs with פ guttural occur thirteen times in this reading section. For details see *A Summary of Hebrew Grammar*, §§11-14 on the strong verb and § 21 for verbs with פ guttural.

This section also offers good practice in recognizing verbs with פ״ן; see especially 18:12, 13, and 16. In addition note the use of the participle in 18:9, 11, 12, 14, and 17. Note also:

| | |
|---|---|
| 18:7, 13, 17 | the interrogative ה |
| 18:10, 15 | the oath formula |
| 18:10 | the use of יֵשׁ and אֵין |
| 18:10, 12, 15 | the relative clause with אֲשֶׁר |
| 18:10 | the infinitive construct with suffix |
| 18:10 | the nun energicum with word in pause |
| 18:13, 17, 18 | the infinitive construct with ב and כ |
| 18:13 | numerals (cardinal and distributive use; cf. 18:4 |

Pausal forms in 18:10 (2 times), 12 (3 times), 13 and 14

# 6

## 1 KINGS 18:19-24 ELIJAH'S CHALLENGE FOR A CONTEST ON THE CARMEL

### VOCABULARY

אַרְבָּעָה / אַרְבַּע *n.m. & f., numeral* four
אֵשׁ *n.f.* fire
יָתַר *vb.* to remain over
מָתַי *interrogative adv.* when?
נָגַשׁ *vb.* to draw near, approach
נָתַח *vb.* to cut up, cut in pieces, divide
סָעִיף *n.m.* cleft, branch; *pl.* סְעִפִּים
פָּסַח *vb.* to limp
פַּר *n.m.* bull, steer
קָבַץ *vb.* to gather, collect
שִׂים *vb.* to put, place set
שֻׁלְחָן *n.m.* table

### POINTS OF GRAMMAR AND SYNTAX

With verbs whose second or third radical is a guttural there are often some minor modifications in pointing. See *A Summary of Hebrew Grammar*, §§ 11-14 for the strong verb, and §§ 23 and 24 for verbs with ע guttural and ל guttural respectively. Note also:

| | |
|---|---|
| 18:19, 22 | numerals (cardinal) |
| 18:19 | the use of the article with places and divinities |
| 18:21 | the use of the participle |
| 18:21 | the conditional sentence |
| 18:21, 23 | the pointing of nouns from ע״ע roots when in the plural or with the definite article |
| 18:22, 24 | the nominal sentence |
| 18:23 | the use of the jussive |

Pausal form of the proper name in 18:19

# 7

# 1 KINGS 18:25-29 THE FAILURE OF THE PROPHETS OF BA'AL

## VOCABULARY

גָּדַד *vb.* to cut
דָּם *n.m.* blood
הָתַל *vb.* to deceive, mock
חֶרֶב *n.f.* sword
יָקַץ *vb.* to awake
יָשֵׁן *vb.* to sleep, to be asleep
מִנְחָה *n.f.* offering, gift, tribute
עָפָר *n.m.* dust, earth, dirt
צָהֳרַיִם / צֹהַר *n.m.* noon, midday
קֶשֶׁב *n.m.* attentiveness
רֶמַח *n.m.* spear, lance
שִׂיג *n.m..* a withdrawing, moving away [?]
שִׂיחַ *n.m.* musing, meditation
שָׁפַךְ *vb.* to pour out, pour, shed

## POINTS OF GRAMMAR AND SYNTAX

While two of the five פ״א verbs, אמר and אכל, are used extensively in the Elijah narratives (about 70 times), discussion of them and of the class of verbs with ל״א has been left until now, for they offer little trouble in recognition or reading. For details see *A Summary of Hebrew Grammar*, §§ 11-14 on the strong verb and §§ 22 and 25 for verbs with פ״א and ל״א espectively. Note also:

| | |
|---|---|
| 18:25 | the nominal sentence |
| 18:25 | comparison of adjectives |
| 18:26 | the use of the article with divinities (cf. 18:19) |
| 18:26, 29 | the use of אֵין |
| 18:27 | the uses of כִּי |
| 18:27 | the use of the participle |
| 18:28, 29 | the use of the infinitive construct |

Pausal forms in 18:27 and 29

# 8

## 1 KINGS 18:30-40 ELIJAH'S VICTORY AND THE SLAUGHTER OF THE BA'AL PROPHETS

### VOCABULARY

אֶבֶן *n.f.* stone
בָּנָה *vb.* to build
הָרַס *vb.* to throw down, break down, destroy, ruin
יָצַק *vb.* to pour
לָחַךְ *vb.* to lick
מָלַט *vb.* to escape; in intensive to deliver, rescue
נָפַל *vb.* to fall
סְאָה *n.f.* a measure of flour or grain, one third of an ephah, c. 10.696 quarts
סָבַב *vb.* to turn about, go around, surround
סָבִיב *adv..* & prep. round about, around
עֹלָה *n.f.* burnt offering, whole burnt offering
עָרַךְ *vb.* to arrange, set in order
רָפָא *vb.* to make whole, heal
שֵׁבֶט *n.m.* rod, staff, scepter, tribe
שָׁחַט *vb.* to slaughter
שָׁלוֹשׁ / שְׁלֹשָׁה *n.m. & f.*, numeral three
שָׁלַשׁ *vb. denominative* to do a third time
שָׁנָה *vb.* to repeat, do again
תְּעָלָה *n.f.* water course, trench
תָּפַשׂ *vb.* to lay hold of, wield, handle, use skillfully

### POINTS OF GRAMMAR AND SYNTAX

This reading section offers a good opportunity for reviewing the verb, since all classes of verbs are represented and appear in many different forms, various stems, with and without suffixes, and so on. Note also:

| | |
|---|---|
| 18:31, 32, 34 | numerals (cardinal) |
| 18:31, 38 | the relative clause with אֲשֶׁר |
| 18:34 | dāgēš implicitum |
| 18:36 | the use of the infinitive construct |

| | |
|---|---|
| 18:36, 37, 39 | the nominal sentence |

Pausal forms in 18:31, 34, 35, 38

## 9

## 1 KINGS 18:41-46 THE COMING OF THE RAIN

### VOCABULARY

אָסַר *vb.* to tie, bind, gird, imprison
בֵּין *prep.* between, among
בֶּרֶךְ *n.f.* knee
גָּהַר *vb.* to bend, crouch
הָמוֹן *n.m.* sound, noise, crowd, abundance
מְאוּמָה *indefinite pron.* anything
מֹתֶן *n.m. only in dual* loins
נָבַט *vb.* to look
עָב *n.m.* cloud
עָצַר *vb.* to restrain, retain
עֶשֶׂר / עֲשָׂרָה *n.m. & f.*, numeral ten
קָדַר *vb.* to be dark
רֹאשׁ *n.m.* head, top, summit
רוּץ *vb.* to run
רָכַב *vb.* to ride
רֶכֶב *n.m.* chariot, chariotry
שְׁבִעִית *adj. f.* seventh
שָׁנַס *vb.* to gird up

### POINTS OF GRAMMAR AND SYNTAX

Many examples of ל״ה and Middle Hollow verbs occur in this section. There is also a wide use of the imperative. Note also:

| | |
|---|---|
| 18:41 | the nominal sentence |
| 18:42, 45, 46 | *hê localē* |
| 18:42 | K$^{e}$t̲îb̲ and Qerê |
| 18:43, 44 | numerals (cardinal and ordinal) |
| 18:45 | the use of עַד-כֹּה |

18:46 the infinitive construct
Pausal forms in 18:41 and 44

# 10

## 1 KINGS 19:1-8 THE FLIGHT OF ELIJAH INTO THE WILDERNESS

### VOCABULARY

אֲכִילָה *n.f.* food
אַרְבָּעִים *n. pl., numeral* forty
יָסַף *vb.* to add, increase
כּוֹחַ / כֹּחַ *n.m.* strength, power
מִדְבָּר *n.m.* wilderness
מָחָר *n.m., adv.* morrow, tomorrow
מַלְאָךְ *n.m.* messenger, angel
מְרַאֲשׁוֹת *n.f. pl.* place at the head, head-place
נָגַע *vb.* to touch, strike
נוּחַ *vb.* to rest, settle down, be quiet
עֵת *n.f.* time
רֶצֶף / רִצְפָּה *n.f.* glowing stone, burning coal
שָׁאַל *vb.* to ask, inquire
שֵׁנִית *adj. f.* second

### POINTS OF GRAMMAR AND SYNTAX

This section offers good examples of פ״ו, פ״ן and Middle Hollow verbs, and the opportunity to compare them, noting their distinctive characteristics. A textual problem in 19:3 is an excellent illustration of possible confusion of verb roots because of apocopation and assimilation. Note also:

| | |
|---|---|
| 19:1, 3 | the relative clause with אֲשֶׁר |
| 19:2 | the oath formula |
| 19:2 | nunation with verbs |
| 19:4 | the use of the pronoun |
| 19:4, 6, 7 | the nominal sentence |
| 19:4, 7 | comparison of adjectives |

| | |
|---|---|
| 19:5 | the use of הִנֵּה |
| 19:5 | the use of the participle; cf. 19:7 |
| 19:7, 8 | numerals (cardinal and ordinal) |

Pausal forms in 19:1, 4, 6 (2x), and 7

## 11

## 1 KINGS 19:9-18 THE THEOPHANY AT HOREB

### VOCABULARY

אַדֶּרֶת *n.f.* cloak, mantle
אֶלֶף *n.m., numeral* thousand
דְּמָמָה *n.f.* silence
דַּק *adj.* crushed, pulverized
כָּרַע *vb.* to bow down
לוּט *vb.* to wrap closely, enwrap, envelop
לִין / לוּן *vb.* to lodge, pass the night
נָשַׁק *vb.* to kiss
סֶלַע *n.m.* crag, cliff
פָּרַק *vb.* to tear apart, tear away
קָנָא *vb.* to be zealous, jealous
רַעַשׁ *n.m.* quaking, shaking, earthquake
שָׁאַר *vb.* to remain, be left over
שָׁבַר *vb.* to break, break in pieces, shatter

### POINTS OF GRAMMAR AND SYNTAX

This section offers examples of all classes of verbs except ע״ע, and so also the opportunity for a general review of the verb. Note also:

| | |
|---|---|
| 19:9, 11, 12, 13 | the nominal sentence |
| 19:10, 14 | the use of the infinitive absolute |
| 19:10, 14 | the use of the pronoun |
| 19:11 | the use of dāgēš implicitum |
| 19:13 | the infinitive construct |
| 19:15 | *hê localē* |
| 19:18 | the use of numerals (cardinal) |

19:18 the relative clause with אֲשֶׁר

Pausal forms in 19:10 (2x) and 14 (2x)

# 12

## 1 KINGS 19:19-21 THE CALL OF ELISHA

### VOCABULARY

בָּקָר *n.m.* ox, cattle

בָּשַׁל *vb.* to boil

חָרַשׁ *vb.* to cut in, engrave, plough

צֶמֶד *n.m.* couple, pair

שָׁלַךְ *vb.* to throw, cast away

שָׁרַת *vb.* to serve, minister

### POINTS OF GRAMMAR AND SYNTAX

Again all classes of verbs except ע״ע are represented in this section, affording the opportunity for continued review of the verb. Note also:

19:19 the use of the participle

19:19 numerals (cardinal and ordinal)

19:19 the nominal sentence

19:20 the use of the cohortative

Pausal forms in 19:20 and 21

------------------------------

# THE SEMITIC LANGUAGES

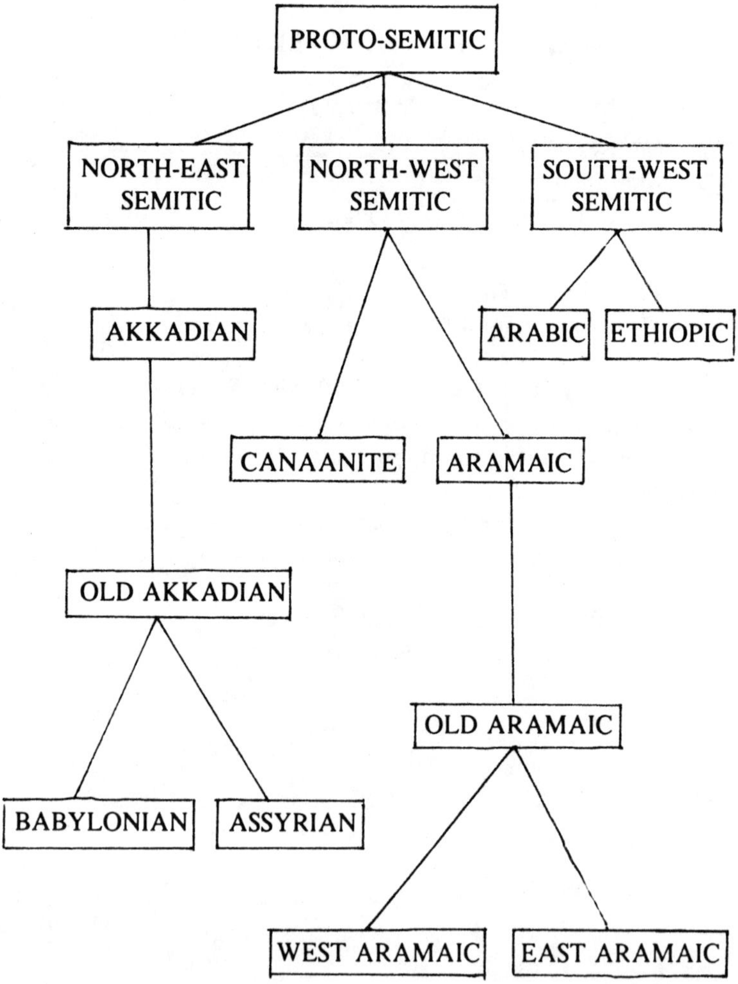

# A SUMMARY OF HEBREW GRAMMAR

## 1 HEBREW AND THE SEMITIC LANGUAGES

(a) The Semitic languages are divided into three major families: (1) North-East Semitic [Akkadian, Babylonian and Assyrian]; (2) North-West Semitic [Canaanite and Aramaic]; and (3) South-West Semitic [Arabic and Ethiopic]. The relationships among these families and their several languages and dialects are governed by strict linguistic laws. As a means of summarizing how these operate scholars have posited a hypothetical language from which, theoretically, all the Semitic languages have sprung. This is known as *Proto-Semitic*, and is an important tool in Semitic philology as well as lexicography, the study of words and their meanings.

A general view of the Semitic "family tree" is shown on the opposite page. Succeeding charts give fuller details of the various families and their dialects and literary materials.

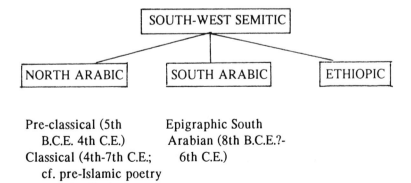

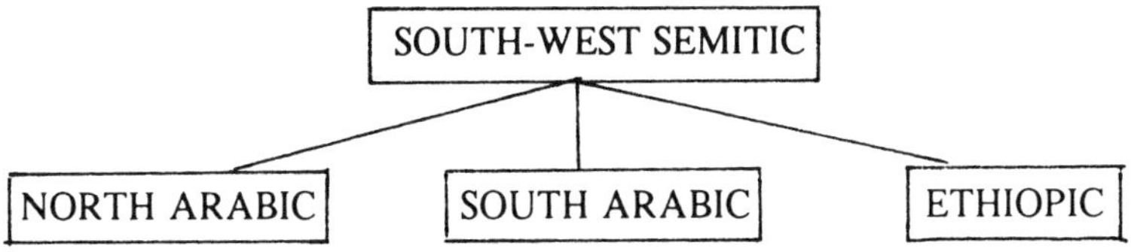


Pre-classical (5th B.C.E. 4th C.E.)
Classical (4th-7th C.E.; cf. pre-Islamic poetry and the Qur'an)

Epigraphic South Arabian (8th B.C.E.?- 6th C.E.)

NORTH-WEST SEMITIC

Byblos (2500-2000)
Proto Sinaitic (1800/1500)
Lachish (1800-1300)

CANAANITE

Ugaritic (14th-13th)
Amarna glosses (14th)
Hebrew (1200-200)
Phoenician & Punic (10th-2nd C.E.)
Moabite (9th: Meša‘)

ARAMAIC

OLD ARAMAIC

Inscriptions from Damascus,
Hama, Arpad, Šam'al, and
Assyria (10th-8th)
Classical or Imperial (7th-4th;
cf. Biblical Aramaic)

WEST ARAMAIC

Nabatean (1st B.C.E.-3rd C.E.)
Palmyrene (1st B.C.E.-3rd C.E.)
Jewish Palestinian (lst-5th C..E.;
cf. targumim)
Samaritan (4th C.E.; cf. targum
to the Pentateuch)
Christian Palestinian (5th-8th C.E.)

EAST ARAMAIC

Syriac (3rd-13th
C.E.)
Babylonian (4th-
6th C.E.; Talmud)
Mandaean (3rd-
8th C.E.)

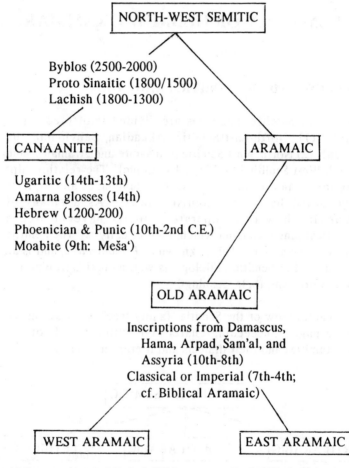

NORTH-EAST SEMITIC

AKKADIAN

OLD AKKADIAN (2500-1950)

BABYLONIAN

ASSYRIAN

Old Babylonian (1950-1530)
Middle Babylonian (1530-1000)
Later Babylonian (*Jungbabylonische*) (1400/1000-500)
New Babylonian (*Neubabylonische*) (1000-600)
Late Babylonian (*Spätbabylonische*) (600-C.E.)

Old Assyrian (1950-1500)
Middle Assyrian (1500-1000)
New Assyrian (1000-600)

(b) The following chart is a synopsis of the Semitic consonantal system, and shows how the Hebrew consonants are related to the other principal Semitic languages: Proto-Semitic, Akkadian, Ugaritic, Aramaic (Syriac), and Arabic. It will be noted that five of the Hebrew consonants combine more than one phoneme. This has significance for lexical relationships. In Ugaritic, for example, the words *'ḏr* and *ǵzr* are completely distinct in spelling and meaning. In Hebrew, however, both words are written in the same way: עזר, a root that occurs frequently in the Hebrew Bible. The interpreter must deal with the problem of two עזר s and how to distinguish between them.

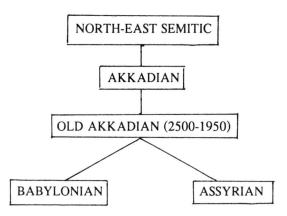

## A SYNOPSIS OF THE SEMITIC CONSONANTAL SYSTEM

| HEB | PROTO | AKKAD | UGAR | ARAM | ARAB |
|---|---|---|---|---|---|
| א | ’ | ’ | ’a<br>’i<br>’u | ’ | ’ |
| ב | b | b | b | b | b |
| ג | g | g | g | g | ǧ |
| ד | d | d | d | d | d |
| ה | h | ’ | h | h | h |
| ו | w | w (m/b) | w (y) | w (y) | w |
| ז | z | z | z | z | z |
| | ḏ | z | d (ḏ) | d | ḏ |
| ח | ḥ | ’ | ḥ | ḥ | ḥ |
| | ḫ | ḫ | ḫ | ḥ | ḫ |
| ט | ṭ | ṭ | ṭ | t | ṭ |
| י | y | y (--) | y (>w) | y | y |
| כ | k | k | k | k | k |
| ל | l | l | l | l | l |
| מ | m | m | m | m | m |
| נ | n | n | n | n | n |
| ס | s | s | s | s | s |
| ע | ‘ | ’ | ‘ | ‘ | ‘ |
| | ǵ | ’ | ǵ | ‘ | ǵ |
| פ | p | p | p | p | f |
| צ | ṣ | ṣ | ṣ | ṣ | ṣ |
| | ṯ | ṣ | ṯ | ṭ | ẓ |
| | ḏ | ṣ | ṣ | ’ | ḍ |
| ק | q | q | q | q | q |
| ר | r | r | r | r | r |
| שׂ | ś | š | š | s | š |
| שׁ | š | š | š | š | s |
| | ṯ | š | ṯ | t | ṯ |
| ת | t | t | t | t | t |

## 2 THE HEBREW ALPHABET

Hebrew has an alphabet of twenty-two characters, all of which are consonants. They have been developed from pictographic writing on an acrophonic principle; see I 2.

| PRINTED | NAME | SOUND | EARLY | VALUE |
|---|---|---|---|---|
| א | 'ālep̱ | ' | 𐤀 | 1 |
| ב | bêṯ | b [ḇ=v] | 𐤁 | 2 |
| ג | gîmel | g [ḡ] | 𐤂 | 3 |
| ד | dāleṯ | d [ḏ] | 𐤃 | 4 |
| ה | hê | h | 𐤄 | 5 |
| ו | vāv | v | 𐤅 | 6 |
| ז | zayin | z | 𐤆 | 7 |
| ח | ḥêṯ | ḥ | 𐤇 | 8 |
| ט | ṭêṯ | ṭ | 𐤈 | 9 |
| י | yôḏ | y | 𐤉 | 10 |
| כ ך | kāp̱ | k [ḵ=ḥ] | 𐤊 | 20 |
| ל | lāmeḏ | l | 𐤋 | 30 |
| מ ם | mêm | m | 𐤌 | 40 |
| נ ן | nûn | n | 𐤍 | 50 |
| ס | sāmeḵ | s | 𐤎 | 60 |
| ע | 'ayin | ' | 𐤏 | 70 |
| פ ף | pē | p [p̄=f] | 𐤐 | 80 |
| צ ץ | ṣāḏê | ṣ | 𐤑 | 90 |
| ק | qôp̱ | q [=ḳ] | 𐤒 | 100 |
| ר | rêš | r | 𐤓 | 200 |
| שׂ | śîn | ś | 𐤔 | |
| שׁ | šîn | š [=sh] | 𐤔 | 300 |
| ת | tāv | t [ṯ] | 𐤕 | 400 |

The twenty-two letters of the Hebrew alphabet may be divided into four groups.

(a) MUTES AND SPIRANTS

[Note: W = weak; M = middle-hard; E = emphatic]

| | W | M | E |
|---|---|---|---|
| Palatal | גּ | כּ | ק |
| Dental | דּ | תּ | ט |
| Labial | בּ | פּ | --- |

The six weak and middle-hard letters of the chart are both mutes and spirants, and so have two sounds: (1) the hard sound of the initial consonant of their names (indicated in a pointed text as above by a dāgēš lēnē, a dot in the letter's bosom) when there is no vowel sound of any kind immediately before them, and (2) as aspirated sound when there is (in which case the dāgēš lēnē cannot stand). These six letters are remembered by the mnemonic device, b$^{e}$gaḏk$^{e}$paṯ. Originally a clear distinction between their hard and soft sounds was made in pronunciation: ב / בּ = b/v; ג / גּ = g/g (as in German *Tage*); ד / דּ = d/th (as in English *the*); כ / כּ = k/ ח ( or as *ch* in German); פ / פּ = p/f; ת/תּ = t/th (as in English *thing*). Modern Israeli pronunciation, however, for all practical purposes observes the soft sounds only of בּ, כּ and פּ.

(b) SIBILANTS

| W | M | E |
|---|---|---|
| ז | שׂ שׁ ס | צ |

(c) SONANTS

| W | M | E |
|---|---|---|
| מ נ | ל ר | ו י |

(d) GUTTURALS

The gutturals, or as they are sometimes described, throat sounds, are א, ה, ע and ח; ר is also often associated with them. The gutturals have the following characteristics.

(i) Gutturals (and ר ) cannot take dāgēš fortē. Usually compensation is made for this by raising the preceding vowel to its tone long. Frequently, however, especially with ח and ה and sometimes with ע, no change is made in the preceding vowel; the dāgēš is said to be implicit (*dāgēš fortē implicitum*). Cf. the pi'ēl of ברך and בער: בֵּרֵךְ and בִּעֵר.

(ii) Gutturals (and ר ) prefer "a" vowels before them and sometimes after them. Cf. מֶלֶךְ, but מֶלַח and בַּעַל.

(a) A final guttural (except א which in final position is quiescent) must be preceded by ◌ַ or ◌ָ.

(b) If a long vowel other than ◌ָ precedes the final guttural, a ◌ַ is inserted between it and the vowel to facilitate the pronunciation of the guttural, e.g. רוּחַ (pronounced *rû-ᵃḥ*). This is called a *furtive paṯaḥ*. It has no accent and it disappears whenever the guttural is no longer final, e.g. רוּחוֹת.

(c) A short ◌ִ before a guttural and sometimes after it is modified to ◌ֶ; cf. יִקְטֹל but אֶקְטֹל.

(iii) When vocal š^e^vâ is required, gutturals must take a ḥaṭep vowel (composite š^e^vâ). The most common is ◌ֲ , although initial א prefers ◌ֱ ; e.g. עֲבָדִים and אֱמוּנָה .

(a) When two vocal š^e^vâs come together and one of them is composite, the first becomes the short vowel of the composite; e.g. בֶּאֱמוּנָה < בְּאֱמוּנָה < אֱמוּנָה + בְּ .

(b) Gutturals often prefer a vocal š^e^vâ to a silent š^e^vâ. Cf. יַחְשֹׁב but also יַחֲשֹׁב .

(e) WEAK CONSONANTS

א, ה, ו and י are weak letters and are frequently called *quiescents.* At the beginning of a syllable they are fully consonantal, but after a full vowel they usually lose their consonantal force and quiesce; e.g. אָב and נָא ; יְמֵי and בִּימֵי ; אֱמוֹר and לֵאמוֹר ; הָיָה .

ה at the end of a word is usually silent. א at the end of a word is always silent, and usually silent also at the end of a syllable which is not final. This has the effect of making the syllable open and so the vowel long; compare קָטַל with שָׁנָה and מָצָא ; קָטַלְתָּ with מָצָאתָ .

א and ה are of such weak character that at the end of a syllable one is sometimes confused with the other; cf. קָרָה *to encounter* and קָרָא *to call.* On some occasions the א is not even written, as in Numbers 11:11 where the regular form מָצָאתִי is written מָצָתִי .

נ is also included with the weak consonants. When it has no vowel of its own, it is usually assimilated into the consonant following it, and the assimilation is marked by dāgēš fortē; cf. fpיִקְטֹל and יִפֹּל < יִנְפֹּל (from the root נפל ).

## 3 THE VOWELS IN HEBREW

The Semitic languages have three primary vowel sounds: *A*, *I* and *U*. These form the basis for three classes of vowels in Hebrew: (1) *A*, (2) *I* and *E*, and (3) *U* and *O*. Each class has four kinds of vowels: (a) *pure short*, vowels which are short by nature and cannot be modified; (b) *pure long*, vowels which are long by nature and cannot be modified; (c) *tone long*, vowels which are long by their relation to the tone (accent); and (d) *indistinct*, or *š$^{e}$vâ*, reductions of tone long vowels to indistinct sounds. Note that there is only one tone long vowel for each class, and it may appear in a closed syllable which has the accent, or in an open syllable just before the accented, or tone syllable.

(a) Spoken Hebrew made use of all these vowels, but written Hebrew was purely consonantal until the ninth century B.C.E. when weak letters began to be used to represent final vowels: ה (and later א) for *â*, י for *î* and *ê*, and ו for *û* and *ô*. This method of representing full vowels developed from *historical writing*, by which is meant that the consonantal element of a dipthong was still written even when the dipthong had been resolved to a long vowel; e.g. the dipthong *-aw* is resolved to *ô* in the word for *day*: *yawm-* > *yôm* (יוֹם < -יַוְם). Because these letters provided a source, or basis, for correct reading, they came to be called *matres lectionis* ("mothers/sources of reading").

At first the *matres* were used only to represent final long vowels. Internal long vowels, except for occasional cases of historical writing, were not indicated by the *matres*. This changed, however, about the sixth century B.C.E. when י and ו came to be used regularly for long vowels within a word; ה, however, was used only at the end of a word. There was a general increase in the use of internal *matres* during the exilic period until the beginning of the Common Era, the fullest development coming in the Maccabean period, as the Dead Sea scrolls abundantly show. At the beginning of the Common Era, as the Masoretes carried through extensive studies to establish a standard consonantal text, the use of the *matres lectionis* was greatly reduced in keeping with earlier manuscript tradition. By the beginning of the second century C.E. the consonantal text as we have it was fairly well fixed.

(b) This was still not sufficient, however, to ensure a correct and standard reading of the text. So it was that from about the sixth century C.E. various attempts were made to indicate the interpretation and pronunciation of the consonantal text by use of signs (נְקוּדִים *points*) written above and below the letters. Three major systems of *pointing* the text developed: the *Babylonian* system in the East, the Palestinian and *Tiberian* systems in the West. Eventually, about the ninth and tenth centuries, the Tiberian system prevailed, and the pointed text as we have it came into being.

The following charts show the Masoretic points for each of the three classes of vowels, and how the points have been combined with the earlier system of *matres lectionis*.

**FIRST CLASS VOWELS**

| | | |
|---|---|---|
| pure short | a ַ | paṯaḥ |
| pure long | â הָ (final) ָ | qāmeṣ |
| tone long | ā ָ | qāmeṣ |
| indistinct (š$^{e}$vâ) | e/a ְ / ֲ | š$^{e}$vâ / ḥaṭep paṯaḥ |

### SECOND CLASS VOWELS

| | | | | | |
|---|---|---|---|---|---|
| pure short | i | ִ | e | ֶ | ḥîreq & segôl |
| pure long | î | יִ / ִ | ê | יֵ / ֵ | ḥîreq & ṣērê |
| tone long | | ē | ֵ | | ṣērê |
| indistinct (š$^{e}$vâ) | | e/e | ְ / ֱ | | š$^{e}$vâ / ḥaṭep segôl |

### THIRD CLASS VOWELS

| | | | | | |
|---|---|---|---|---|---|
| pure short | u | ֻ | o | ָ | qibbûṣ & qāmeṣ ḥāṭûp |
| pure long | û | וּ / ֻ | ô | וֹ / ֹ | šûreq / qibbûṣ & ḥōlem |
| tone long | | ō | ֹ | | ḥōlem |
| indistinct (š$^{e}$vâ) | | e/o | ְ / ֳ | | š$^{e}$vâ/ḥaṭep qāmeṣ |

Note in the above charts how the Masoretic points are combined with the *matres lectionis.* Note also that ָ can represent either a long ā (qāmeṣ) or a short o (qāmeṣ ḥāṭûp). The ָ is a *qāmeṣ* in an open syllable or in a closed syllable that is accented; it is a *qāmeṣ ḥāṭûp* in a closed unaccented syllable.

## 4 Š$^{e}$VÂ, DĀG̱ĒŠ, AND OTHER MASORETIC POINTS

Hebrew has two kinds of syllables: (1) an *open syllable,* which begins with a consonant and ends with a vowel, and (2) a *closed syllable*, which begins and ends with a consonant. Every syllable must have a full vowel (thus excluding vocal šᵉvâ, which is only indistinct). The vowel of an open syllable is long, although it may be short if accented. The vowel of a closed syllable is short, although it may be long if accented.

Every syllable must begin with a consonant. The only exception to this involves the conjunction וְ . Usually pointed with vocal šᵉvâ (וְ), the conjunctioon becomes וּ before labials (ב, מ, פ ) and before another vocal šᵉvâ; e.g. וּבָנִים < בָּנִים + וְ ; וּדְבָרִים < דְּבָרִים + וְ . No more than two consonants may stand at the beginning or the end of a word, and only one consonant may stand at the end of a syllable which is not the final syllable of the word.

(a) The *šᵉvâ* marks the beginning and the end of a syllable. There are two kinds of ševâ: *vocal* ševâ and *silent* ševâ. The *vocal šᵉvâ* is the indistinct sound resulting from the reduction of a tone long vowel; see the vowel charts in *Introduction*, § 3. Except with gutterals, which must take composite šᵉvâs, the signs for vocal šᵉvâ and silent šᵉvâ are the same: ְ . There is little difficulty in distinguishing them, however, since *vocal* šᵉvâ can stand only at the *beginning* of a syllable, and *silent* šᵉvâ only at the *end*.

(i) *Vocal šᵉvâ.* Vocal šᵉvâ is placed under the first of two consonants beginning a syllable. It is frequently the result of the reduction of a tone long vowel, as in דְּבָרִים , the plural of דָּבָר . When in composition two vocal šᵉvâs come together, the following adjustments in vocaliztion are made: (1) if both are *simple* šᵉvâs, the first becomes a short vowel, usually ḥîreq, e.g. דִּבְרֵי < דְּבְרֵי < דְּבָרִים ; (2) if one is a composite šᵉvâ, the first becomes the short vowel of the composite, e.g. בֶּאֱמֶת < בְּאֱמֶת < אֱמֶת + בְּ ; חֲכָמִים < חֲכְמֵי < חַכְמֵי .

(ii) *Silent šᵉvâ.* Silent šᵉvâ is placed (1) under the single sounded consonant ending a syllable if it is not the last syllable of the word, e.g. מַקְטִיל ; or (2) under the two consonants ending a word if both are sounded, e.g. קָטַלְתְּ , but cf. חֵטְא and לִקְרָאת.

If *two simple* šᵉvâs stand together, the first must be *silent* and the second *vocal*, e.g. מַמְלְכוֹת *of kingdoms.*

(b) The *dāgēš* is a dot placed in the middle of a consonant. There are several kinds and uses of dāgēš.

(i) *Dāgēš lēnē.* Dāgēš lēnē is used only with the spirants, בגדכפת , and indicates their hard sound. It is placed in the spirants only when there is no vowel sound of any kind (including vocal šᵉvâ) immediately before them. Without the dāgēš lēnē their sound is aspirated.

(ii) *Dāgēš fortē.* Dāgēš fortē may be used in all letters except gutturals and ר . It indicates a doubled consonant, the first of which ends a syllable, and so can stand only after a full (usually short) vowel, and the second of which begins a new syllable. This means that dāgēš fortē can only stand within a word, because Hebrew cannot write a doubled consonant at the end of a word, as in the English word *hall.* When a dāgēš fortē stands in a spirant, the sound of both consonants is hard; e.g. דִּבֵּר = *dib-bēr.*

Remember that dāgēš lēnē cannot follow a vowel sound, but dāgēš fortē must.

(iii) *Dāgēš fortē implicitum.* Dāgēš fortē is usually not written in the letters ו, י, ל, מ, נ and ק when these letters are pointed with vocal šᵉvâ; e.g. הַלֵּל *praise! (sg)*, but הַלְלוּ *praise! (pl.).* Dāgēš fortē is also omitted with no compensation made in pi'ēl forms of 'ayin guttural verbs, e.g. יְטַהֵר *he purifies*; cf. יְקַטֵּל . In these cases the doubling of the consonant is regarded as *virtual* or *implicit* and so the name *dāgēš fortē implicitum.*

(iv) *Dāgēš fortē conjunctivum.* This use of dāgēš fortē joins two words closely united in pronunciation, especially when they are joined by maqqēp; e.g. מַה-זֶּה *What is this?* and וְזֶה-שְּׁמוֹ *and this is his name* (Jeremiah 23:6).

(c) *Meṯeg (bridle).* The meṯeg is a small perpendicular stroke often placed on the second full syllable before the tone if that syllable is open. It serves as a secondary accent, but also protects a full open vowel distant from the tone; e.g. הָאָדָם = hā'āḏām *the man,* הֶאֱמִין = he'ᵉmîn *he believed,* אָכְלָה = 'āḵᵉlâ *she ate*; cf. אָכְלָה = 'oḵlâ *food.*

(d) *Maqqēp̱.* Maqqēp̱ is a hyphen, joining two or more words. Note that all words before maqqēp̱ lose their accent, and so all closed syllables will have short vowels; cf. אֵת כֹּל הַדָּבָר with אֶת-כָּל-הַדָּבָר.

(e) *Mappîq.* Mappîq is a dot placed in a final ה to indicate that it has full consonantal force and is not simply a mater lectionis, cf. מַלְכָּה = malkâ *queen* with מַלְכָּהּ = malkāh *her king.*

## 5 THE NOUN IN HEBREW

For the basic presentation of the noun in Hebrew see the *Introduction,* §§ 13-17 and 23-25. What is given here is a brief summary of those materials with some additional notes on nominal forms in biblical Hebrew.

(a) *Gender.* There is no gender indicator for masculine nouns. Most feminine nouns end in ָה (from the primitive feminine stem ת- ), but there are many feminine nouns which do not, e.g. יָד *hand* and רוּחַ *wind, spirit.* Note also the feminine participial forms קֹטֶלֶת / קֹטְלָה ; cf. the masculine קֹטֵל .

(b) *Number.* The noun has three numbers: singular, plural and dual. The dual is restricted to the numeral two and to natural pairs, such as eyes and ears. Adjectives have no dual form, and so use the plural with nouns in the dual.

(c) *States.* Nouns have two states: the absolute and the construct.

(i) The *absolute state* is used for the subject, direct and indirect objects, and the last member of a genitival relationship.

| | | | |
|---|---|---|---|
| *Masculine:* | *sing.* | --- | סוּס |
| | *plur.* | ִים | סוּסִים |
| | *dual* | ַיִם | סוּסַיִם |
| *Feminine:* | *sing.* | --- | יָד |
| | *plur.* | וֹת | יָדוֹת |
| | *dual* | ַיִם | יָדַיִם |

OR

| | | | |
|---|---|---|---|
| | *sing.* | ָה | סוּסָה |
| | *plur.* | וֹת | סוּסוֹת |
| | *dual* | ָת + ַיִם | סוּסָתַיִם |

Note that in the dual the original feminine stem ת appears only with feminine nouns ending in ָה.

(ii) The *construct state* is used for the first member of a genitival relationship. The word in construct is reduced to its shortest form by the *reduction of tone long vowels* in open syllables to vocal š$^{e}$vâ and in closed syllables to a short vowel and by the *contraction of endings*: ִים and ַיִם to ֵי and ָה to ַת.

| | | | | |
|---|---|---|---|---|
| *Masculine* | *sg.* | ------ | סוּס | דָּבָר |
| | *pl.* | ֵי < ִים | סוּסֵי | דִּבְרֵי |
| | *du.* | ֵי < ַיִם | סוּסֵי | דִּבְרֵי |

| | | | |
|---|---|---|---|
| *Feminine* | *sg.* | ------ | יָד |
| | *pl.* | וֹת < וֹת | יְדוֹת |
| | *du.* | ֵי < ַיִם | יְדֵי |

OR

| | | | | |
|---|---|---|---|---|
| *Feminine* | *sg.* | ַת < ָה | סוּסַת | שְׂפַת |
| | *pl.* | וֹת < וֹת | סוּסוֹת | שְׂפוֹת |
| | *du.* | ְתֵי < ָתַיִם | סוּסְתֵי | שִׂפְתֵי |

Note that when reducing tone long vowels often two vocal š$^{e}$vâs come together. When this happens (as in the case of דְּבָרִים < דְּבְרֵי ), the first š$^{e}$vâ becomes a ḥîreq (so דְּבְרֵי < דִּבְרֵי ). With a composite š$^{e}$vâ the first š$^{e}$vâ becomes the short vowel of the composite, e.g. חֲכָמִים in the construct: חֲכְמֵי < חַכְמֵי.

A word in construct cannot take the definite article or a pronominal suffix. If the word in absolute is definite the whole expression is definite.

A word in construct immediately precedes the word in the absolute with which it goes. There can be no intervening words or particles.

An adjective modifying any noun in a construct relation follows the whole expression, and, while agreeing in gender and number with whichever noun it modifies, it is in the absolute state. See also §§ 26-27 below.

(d) *Declensions of Nouns.* There are several ways by which nouns in Hebrew may be classified. In Gesenius-Kautzsch-Cowley, *Hebrew Grammar* (Oxford, 1910), there are twelve groupings, based on verbal stems, vocalic patterns, and preformatives and afformatives. Weingreen, *Hebrew Grammar* (Oxford, 1959), gives seven types of masculine nouns, five of feminine nouns ending in *a*, and a list of irregular nouns. Lambdin, *Introduction to Biblical Hebrew* (New York, 1971), on the basis of vocalic patterns has fourteen classifications.

This grammar, following the lead of Davidson-Mauchline, *An Introductory Hebrew Grammar* (Edinburgh, 1966), adopts a simpler approach. Noting that despite all the variations in formation, there are really only three basic patterns in the inflection of nominal forms, the nouns are classified under three declensions. See the *Introduction*, §§ 15-17, for a fuller introductory discussion.

(i) *The First Declension.* The first declension is characterized by words with tone long ָ in the tone or pretone, or in both; e.g. דָּבָר , זָקֵן , נָבִיא , and כּוֹכֵב .. Inflection is characterized by the reduction of distant open tone long vowels; e.g. the plural of דָּבָר is דְּבָרִים , of נָבִיא is נְבִיאִים , but of כּוֹכָב it is כּוֹכָבִים .

Nominal forms with unchangeable vowels, such as סוּס, שִׁיר, צַדִּיק , since they fit the first declension pattern are also included here.

For the construct state nouns of the first declension follow the regular rules of reduction and contraction noted above. Note, however, that words with the pattern ָ ֵ form their construct singular with ַ ; e.g. זָקֵן in the construct is זְקַן .

(ii) *The Second (or, Segholate) Declension.* The second declension is made up of originally monosyllabic nouns; cf. *Introduction*, § 16. It is characterized by having the accent on the first syllable (the original monosyllable) and a s$^{e}$gôl in the last; e.g. מֶלֶךְ (originally *malk-*), סֵפֶר (originally *sipr-*), and בֹּקֶר (originally *buqr-* or *boqr-*). Note that gutturals with their preference for *a* vowels modify this pattern; e.g. מֶלַח (cf. מֶלֶךְ ) and בַּעַל . See § 2 (d) above.

Original monosyllabic forms return in the dual and with pronominal suffixes in the singular; e.g. the dual of רֶגֶל *foot* is רַגְלַיִם , of בֶּרֶךְ *knee* is בִּרְכַּיִם , and of אֹזֶן *ear* is אָזְנַיִם ; מֶלֶךְ *king* with suffixes is מַלְכִּי *my king,* מַלְכְּךָ *your king,* מַלְכֵּנוּ *our king*; cf. בִּרְכִּי *my knee* and אָזְנִי *my ear.*

In the plural second declension nouns appear to follow a first declension analogy; cf. the plural of דָּבָר (דְּבָרִים ) with that of מֶלֶךְ : מְלָכִים . It is possible that these nouns have an internal plural stem ( ָ ָ ) to which are added the usual plural endings; e.g. מְלָכִים < ִים + מָלָךְ [מֶלֶךְ] *kings*; אֲרָצוֹת < וֹת + אָרָץ [אֶרֶץ] *lands;* סְפָרִים < ִים + סָפָר [סֵפֶר] *books*; and בְּקָרִים < ִים + בָּקָר [בֹּקֶר] *mornings.*

The construct singular of second declension nouns is identical with the absolute form. The plural and dual constructs follow the regular rules, contracting endings and reducing tone long vowels, except that when two vocal š$^{e}$vâs come together the first becomes not ḥîreq (see § 5c (ii) above), but the original short (thematic) vowel; e.g. מַלְכֵי < מְלְכֵי < מְלָכִים *kings of,* אַרְצוֹת < אֲרְצוֹת < אֲרָצוֹת *lands of,* סִפְרֵי < סְפְרֵי < סְפָרִים *books of,* בָּקְרֵי < בְּקְרֵי < בְּקָרִים *mornings of.* Note that despite the short vowel the syllable is open and the š$^{e}$vâ following is vocal.

The pointing of Qal infinitive constructs with suffixes reflects the second declension pattern; e.g. עֲמֹד *to stand* with the first person suffix is עָמְדִי *my standing* (the ָ is a short *o* and the $^{e}$vâ is vocal).

There are a few nouns that appear to be first declension feminine nouns ending in ָה , but really belong to the second declension; e.g. מַמְלָכָה *kingdom* and מִלְחָמָה *war.* In the construct singular these nouns take a segholate form, viz. מַמְלֶכֶת and מִלְחֶמֶת . With suffixes they take a monosyllabic form, viz. מַמְלַכְתִּי *my kingdom* and מִלְחַמְתִּי *my war.* Their plural forms are regular, viz. מַמְלָכוֹת and מִלְחָמוֹת .

(iii) *The Third Declension.* The third declension is characterized by words that have an unchangeable vowel in the first syllable and ◌ֵ in the last, e.g. מִסְפֵּד *lamentation* and קוֹטֵל *one who kills* (the Qal participle is often written without the *mater lectionis*: קֹטֵל ). The nouns שֵׁם *name* and בֵּן *son* also belong to this declension. Characteristic of these words is that they reduce the near open ◌ֵ to ◌ְ before vocalic afformatives; e.g. מִסְפְּדִים and קוֹטְלִים ; note that the plural of בֵּן is בָּנִים , but with vocalic suffixes the regular rule is followed, e.g. בְּנִי *my son.* Before consonantal afformatives the ◌ֵ becomes ◌ֶ or occasionally ◌ַ ; e.g. קוֹטֶלְךָ *your killer,* שִׁמְךָ *your name.*

Note that the *third declension reduces the near open vowel,* just the opposite of the *first declension which reduces the distant open.* Because this is characteristic of the conjugation of verbs and the inflection of Qal, Pi'ēl and Hiṯpa'ēl participles, the third declension is often said to follow a *verbal analogy.*

(e) *Nominal forms from* ע״ו *and* ע״י *roots* have unchangeable thematic vowels, and may be said to follow a first declension pattern; e.g. רוּחַ *wind, spirit* (from רוח ), שִׁיר *song,* גֵּר *sojourner* (from גור ), מֵת *dead* (from מות ; note that the noun מָוֶת *death* with its construct form מוֹת also derives from this root).

(f) *Nominal forms from* ע״ע *roots* usually appear as monosyllables, using only the first two consonants, and are often pointed with only a short vowel; e.g. רַע *evil* (from רעע ), עַם

*people* (from עמם ), יָם *sea* (from ימם ), חֹק *statute* (from חקק ), כֹּל *all, whole* (from כלל ), לֵב but also לֵבָב *heart* (from לבב ). With the article nominal forms written with a short vowel sometimes lengthen; e.g. עַם with the article is written הָעָם , but רַע with the article remains unchanged, viz. הָרַע . In the plural and with pronominal suffixes the third consonant reappears by dāgēš fortē; e.g. עַם but עַמִּים and עַמִּי ; לֵב but לִבּוֹת and לִבִּי ; חֹק but חֻקִּים and חֻקּוֹ ; כֹּל but כֻּלּוֹ .

(g) *Nominal forms from ל״ה (originally ל״י ) roots* end either with ה or י . Those ending with ה are analogous to the participles of ל״ה verbs, pointing the final ה with ֶ ; e.g. רֹאֶה *seer,* מִשְׁתֶּה *feast,* שָׂדֶה *field,* עָלֶה *leafage.* In the construct the ֶ becomes ֵ and tone long vowels are reduced to vocal š$^{e}$vâ; e.g. רֹאֵה , מִשְׁתֵּה , שְׂדֵה , עֲלֵה . With plural afformatives and pronominal suffixes the ה is dropped; e.g. שָׂדֶה in the plural is שָׂדִים or שָׂדוֹת *fields;* and with suffixes שָׂדִי *my field,* שָׂדְךָ *your field,* שָׂדֵהוּ *his field,* שָׂדַי *my fields,* שְׂדוֹתֵנוּ *our fields.* Adjectives also resemble the participle, e.g. יָפֶה and יָפִים (masculine) and יָפָה and יָפוֹת *beautiful.*

ל״ה nouns may also end in the original י ; e.g. אֲרִי *lion,* פְּרִי *fruit,* חֲצִי *half,* חֳלִי *sickness.* In their inflection they are related to the second declension, even reflecting the three classes of vowels: a, i, u/o. This can be seen when these nouns have vocalic afformatives, when once again the י has its original consonantal force, creating a closed unaccented syllable; e.g. אַרְיוֹ *his lion,* חֶצְיוֹ *his half,* and חָלְיוֹ *his sickness.*

(h) *Case Endings.* At one time Hebrew, in common with the other Semitic languages, employed case endings: *u* for nominative, *i* for genitive, and *a* for accusative. In biblical Hebrew they are no longer used, although some vestiges remain.

Traces of case endings, for example, may likely be found in ancient proper names; e.g. the nominative וּ in the name

מְתוּשָׁאֵל (Genesis 4:18) and בְּתוּאֵל (Genesis 22:22), and the genitive in the place name פְּנִיאֵל *the face of God* (Genesis 32:31). A trace of the genitive case may also be seen in the construct state of words like אָב *father* and אָח *brother*: אֲבִי (Genesis 4:20) and אֲחִי (Genesis 10:21).

The accusative has commonly been seen as preserved in the unaccented ָה used to express direction toward a place or thing; e.g. צָפוֹן *north*, but צָפוֹנָה *northward*, יְרוּשָׁלַמָה *to Jerusalem*. This locative usage is known as *Hê localē*. Whether this is actually an accusative or simply a ה of direction is debatable. Whichever, *Hê localē* is attached directly to the noun without affecting the accent. It is used with places and objects, occasionally with expressions of time, but never with persons.

## 6 THE DEFINITE ARTICLE

The definite article in Hebrew is הַ ּ , and is attached directly to the noun or adjective; e.g. דָּבָר *a word* and הַדָּבָר *the word*; מַלְכָּה טוֹבָה *a good queen* and הַמַּלְכָּה הַטּוֹבָה *the good queen.*

Gutturals (אהחע) and ר, however, cannot take dāgēš fortē, and so variations are made in the pointing of the article with nominal forms beginning with them. These are summarized in the following chart.

הַ ּ Before all consonants except gutturals and ר

הַ Before ה and ח (except with ָ )*

הָ Before א, ר, ע (except unaccented עָ) and accented הָ **

הֶ Before חָ, חֳ and unaccented הָ and עָ ***

*Examples: הַחֵטְא *the sin*; הַהֵיכָל הַהוּא *that palace*. Note the small mark under the first ה; this is called a *meteg* (bridle), and is placed on the second (counting vocal š$^e$vâ) full syllable before the tone if that syllable is open. It serves to protect a full vowel in an open syllable distant from the tone. It also serves to indicate a secondary accent within a word.

**Examples: הָאָב *the father*; הָאִישׁ *the man*; הָרָשָׁע *the wicked (one)*; הָעִיר *the city*; הָהָר *the mountain.*

***Examples: הֶחָג *the festival*; הֶחָבֵר *the friend, companion*; הֶחֳלִי *the sickness*; הֶעָפָר *the ground, dust.*

**7 PREPOSITIONS**

(a) Prepositions are originally nouns, and are related to their objects much as nouns in a construct relationship. Some prepositions continue to function both as nouns and prepositions, e.g. אַחַר and its plural אַחֲרֵי *after, behind*. אַחַר is a noun which means *that which is behind, the hinder part*, and it appears as a noun with adverbial force in Genesis 10:18 with the meaning *afterwards*; so also in Psalm 68:26 and many other places. It occurs as a regular noun in plural construct in 2 Samuel 2:23, where Abner kills Asahel by striking him in the stomach with the butt of his spear (בְּאַחֲרֵי הַחֲנִית). Cf. also the difficult phrase in Exodus 3:1: אַחַר הַמִּדְבָּר *the hinder part of the wilderness*, or *behind the wilderness.*

פָּנִים *face* is another word which functions both as noun and preposition. It well illustrates the nominal character of prepositions and can give some insight into how they operate. Apart from its basic meaning of *face*, the noun has an adverbial use to express *place*, as in 1 Chronicles 19:10, where Joab sees that the battle is set against him פָּנִים וְאָחוֹר *front and rear*. A similar use is seen in Genesis 33:18, וַיִּחַן אֶת-פְּנֵי הָעִיר *and he camped before* (lit. *at the face of*) *the city*. פָּנִים combined with לְ forms one of the most frequently used prepositions in the Bible, לִפְנֵי *before* (lit. *to the face of*). Like אַחַר and אַחֲרֵי it is properly a construct form.

Like all nominal forms, prepositions may take pronominal suffixes. Prepositions such as אַחֲרֵי and לִפְנֵי, because they are plural, will of course take the plural form of the suffixes. Several prepositions, however, such as אֶל , עַד , and עַל , while singular when standing alone have a plural form with pronominal suffixes; e.g. אֶל-הָעִיר to the city, but אֵלֶיהָ to it. It is interesting in this connection to note that while אַחַר and אַחֲרֵי are both frequently used as prepositions, it is only the plural form that takes suffixes. See *Introduction*, § 28, and § 10 below for tables of prepositions and particles with pronominal suffixes.

Many common prepositions, as noted above in the case of לִפְנֵי , are really combination forms; e.g. בַּעֲבוּר *on account of* (בְּ + עֲבוּר); לְמַעַן *for the sake of, in order that* (מַעַן + לְ ; cf. יַעַן , both from the root ענה ); בִּלְעֲדֵי *beside, apart from* (עֲדֵי + בַּל ); מִלְמַעְלָה *from above* (מַעְלָה + לְ + מִן).

(b) *Inseparable Prepositions.* Prepositions as nominal forms have been described as "worn-down" or "fragmentary" nouns. Indeed, three of the most common prepositions have been so reduced that they are only single letters pointed with vocal š^e^vâ. Not being able to stand alone they are prefixed to the nouns with which they go, and so are known as inseparable prepositions. They are בְּ *in, by, with, at, from*; כְּ *like, according to, as*; לְ *to, for*.

The usual pointing of these prepositions is with simple vocal š^e^vâ; e.g. בְּשָׁלוֹם *in peace*, or כְּאֵל *like a god.* If the noun begins with a vocal š^e^vâ, the pointing of the inseparable preposition is ḥîreq before a simple š^e^vâ, and before a composite š^e^vâ the corresponding short vowel; e.g. < מְלָכִים + לְ לִמְלָכִים *for kings*; בֶּאֱמוּנָה < אֱמוּנָה + בְּ *in faithfulness.* When placed on words accented on the first syllable, the inseparable preposition is automatically set in an open pretone, and so often is pointed with ָ ; e.g. בָּזֶה < זֶה + בְּ *by this*; כָּאֵלֶּה < אֵלֶּה + כְּ

*like these*; לָהֶם < הֵם + לְ *to them*; לָעַד < עַד + לְ *forever*; + לְ לָבֶטַח < בֶּטַח *in security*; לָלֶכֶת < לֶכֶת + לְ *to go*; לָתֵת < תֵּת + לְ *to give.*

When an inseparable preposition is placed on a word with the definite article, it replaces the weak ה of the article, but keeps the pointing of the article; e.g. בַּדָּבָר < הַדָּבָר + בְּ *by the word*; לֶעָפָר < הֶעָפָר + לְ *to the ground, dust.*

The common preposition, מִן *from, out of, at*, is usually joined to its object by maqqēp̄, e.g. מִן־הָאָרֶץ *from the earth.* Frequently, however, like the inseparable prepositions, it is also attached directly to its object. When this happens, the נ having no vowel of its own is assimilated by dāgēš fortē into the first consonant of the noun, e.g. מִסֵּפֶר < סֵפֶר + מִן *from a book.* If the first consonant of the noun is a guttural or ר, which cannot take dāgēš fortē, the נ is dropped, and compensation is made by raising the ִ to its tone long ֵ ; e.g. מֵהַסֵּפֶר < הַסֵּפֶר + מִן *from the book.*

## 8 THE CONJUNCTION VAV

Like the inseparable prepositions, the conjunction ו is pointed with vocal š$^{e}$vâ ( וְ ) and is attached directly to the word with which it goes, e.g. וְרוּחַ *and a wind.* Before simple vocal š$^{e}$vâ, מ, ו, and the labials ב and פ the usual pointing וְ is modified to וּ, thus becoming the only exception to the rule that every syllable must begin with a consonant; e.g. דְּבָרִים + וְ וּדְבָרִים < *and words*; וּמֶלֶךְ < מֶלֶךְ + וְ *and a king.* Before a composite š$^{e}$vâ, however, the usual rules are followed, and ו is pointed with the short vowel of the composite, e.g. וֶאֱמֶת *and truth.* With words accented on the first syllable ו is often pointed with ָ. This occurs especially with such common expressions as יוֹם וָלַיְלָה *day and night*, טוֹב וָרָע *good and evil*, סוּס וָרֶכֶב *horse and chariot*, and זָהָב וָכֶסֶף *gold and silver.*

Note that the conjunction ו does not replace the ה of the article.

## 9 PRONOUNS IN HEBREW

(a) *Personal Pronouns.* The personal pronouns in Hebrew are used only in the nominative case. To indicate direct and indirect objects, objects of prepositions, and possession one must use the pronominal suffixes; see below in § 10. The pronominal suffixes as well as the personal endings for the verb in the perfect are largely adaptations of elements of the personal pronouns.

| | | |
|---|---|---|
| 1c sg | אָנֹכִי, אֲנִי | *I* |
| 2m sg | אַתָּה | *you (masc.)* |
| 2f sg | אַתְּ | *you (fem.)* |
| 3m sg | הוּא | *he* |
| 3f sg | הִיא | *she* |
| 1c pl | אֲנַחְנוּ | *we* |
| 2m pl | אַתֶּם | *you (masc.)* |
| 2f pl | אַתֵּן, אַתֵּנָה | *you (fem.)* |
| 3m pl | הֵם, הֵמָּה | *they (masc.)* |
| 3f pl | הֵנָּה | *they (fem.)* |

It may be noted that אָנֹכִי is used much less than אֲנִי in the Hebrew Bible, and predominantly in the earlier books. There is also a tendency, especially in the later books to simplify the language by using the masculine plural pronouns for both masculine and feminine antecedents, for example in Zechariah 5:10 and Song of Solomon 6:8.

(b) *Demonstrative Pronouns.*

| | | | |
|---|---|---|---|
| זֶה | *this (masc.)* | הוּא | *that (masc.)* |
| זֹאת | *this (fem.)* | הִיא | *that (fem.)* |
| אֵ֫לֶּה | *these (com.)* | הֵם (הֵ֫מָּה) | *those (masc.)* |
| | | הֵ֫נָּה | *those (fem.)* |

It will be noticed that the demonstrative, *that/those*, is simply the third person pronoun. As in the case of the pronouns themselves, there is a tendency to use the third masculine plural form as a common gender form.

When used as the subject, the demonstrative stands first in the sentence and agrees in gender and number with the predicate.

| | |
|---|---|
| זֶה הָאִישׁ׃ | *This [is] the man.* |
| זֹאת הָאָ֫רֶץ׃ | *This [is] the land.* |
| אֵ֫לֶּה הַדְּבָרִים׃ | *These [are] the words.* |

When used as a qualifying adjective, the demonstrative can only modify a definite noun, because as a demonstrative it points to what is definite. Like the adjective it follows the noun, agrees in number and gender, and takes the definite article.

| | | | |
|---|---|---|---|
| הָאִישׁ הַזֶּה | *this man* | הָאָ֫רֶץ הַהִיא | *that land* |
| הָאִישׁ הַהוּא | *that man* | הַדְּבָרִים הָאֵ֫לֶּה | *these words* |
| הָאָ֫רֶץ הַזֹּאת | *this land* | הַדְּבָרִים הַהֵם | *those words* |

With other words modifying the same noun, the demonstrative stands last, e.g. הָאָ֫רֶץ הַטּוֹבָה הַזֹּאת *this good land.*

(c) *Interrogative Pronouns.*

| | |
|---|---|
| מִי | *who? whoever* |
| מַה | *what? how! whatever* |

Both interrogative pronouns are indeclinable. The pointing of מַה is similar to that of the article, often connected to the next word by maqqēp̄ and dāgēš (*dāgēš fortē conjunctivum*), e.g. מַה־טּוֹב *How good!* Before א and ר it has the pointing מָה, e.g. מָה אֵלֶּה *What are these?* Before gutturals with ָ the pointing is מֶה, e.g. מֶה עָשָׂה *What did he do?* Elsewhere the pointing is simply מַה.

Although indeclinable the interrogative may be used with prepositions; e.g. לְמִי *to whom?*; בַּמָּה *by what?*; עַד־מָה *until when, how long?* Both מִי and מַה can also have an indefinite meaning; מִי־יָרֵא *whoever is afraid* (Judges 7:3); וִיהִי־מָה *whatever happens* (2 Samuel 18:22).

(d) *Relative Pronouns.* אֲשֶׁר is the principal relative pronoun. Its abbreviated form, שֶׁ, which is directly attached to the first word of the relation, occurs only rarely and in late writings. Similarly, זוּ, a secondary form from the demonstrative זֶה, is occasionally found in later books.

The relative pronouns were originally demonstrative forms. Like the interrogatives, they are indeclinable, although they may be combined with prepositions. They do not really correspond at all to the relative pronouns of western languages, *who, whose, whom* and so on. They are only indicators of relationship.

אֲשֶׁר is a particle that simply indicates that there is a relationship between what has gone before and what follows. Precisely what is related and what the relationship is can be known only from the full context. In translating, then, it is best to use as neutral a word as possible, such as that, until the signalled relationship is clear. See *Introduction*, § 39, and the notes on syntax below in § 41.

## 10 PRONOMINAL SUFFIXES

Afformatives in Hebrew may be described as *vocalic*, i.e. an ending which is simply a vowel, e.g. ִי and וֹ, and as *consonantal*, i.e. an ending which begins with a consonant, e.g. ךָ and נוּ. They may also be decribed as *heavy*, i.e. an ending which begins and ends with a consonant, e.g. כֶם and הֶם, and as *light*, i.e. all other endings, whether vocalic or consonantal. These distinctions are helpful in seeing how words with pronominal suffixes are pointed.

A noun and its pronominal suffix express a genitive relationship: דְּבָרִי *the word of me*, that is, *my word*. The noun, therefore, is technically in a construct state. In biblical Hebrew, however, this original construct form is preserved only with the heavy endings, e.g. דְּבַרְכֶם *your (pl.) word*, דִּבְרֵיהֶם *their words*. With the light suffixes the regular patterns of the three declensions are followed, e.g. דְּבָרִי *my word*, סִפְרָהּ *her book*, and מַקְלֵנוּ *our staff*. See § 5d above and the tables below.

(a) *Pronominal Suffixes with Nouns.* The following tables show the suffixes on singular and plural nouns with examples for all three declensions. In the table of suffixes for plural nouns note that the pronominal endings include the contractions of the nouns' plural and dual forms. Note also that monosyllabic and heavy endings take the accent; dyssyllabic (except heavy) endings have the accent on the penult, e.g. ֵנוּ or ֶיהָ.

Because of the pronominal suffix the noun is considered definite, and so no article is used; cf. הַדָּבָר הַטּוֹב לַמֶּלֶךְ *the good word belongs to the king* and דְּבָרוֹ הַטּוֹב *his good word*. With coordinate nouns the suffix is repeated with each noun, e.g. to say *my God and king* in Hebrew, one must write אֱלֹהַי וּמַלְכִּי *my God and my king*.

(i) Suffixes on Singular Nouns

| | | | | | |
|---|---|---|---|---|---|
| 1c sg | ִי | *my* | דְּבָרִי | בִּרְכָתִי | חַסְדִּי |
| 2m sg | ְךָ | *your* | דְּבָרְךָ | בִּרְכָתְךָ | חַסְדְּךָ |
| 2f sg | ֵךְ | *your* | דְּבָרֵךְ | בִּרְכָתֵךְ | חַסְדֵּךְ |
| 3m sg | וֹ | *his* | דְּבָרוֹ | בִּרְכָתוֹ | חַסְדּוֹ |
| 3f sg | ָהּ | *her* | דְּבָרָהּ | בִּרְכָתָהּ | חַסְדָּהּ |
| 1c pl | ֵנוּ | *our* | דְּבָרֵנוּ | בִּרְכָתֵנוּ | חַסְדֵּנוּ |
| 2m pl | ְכֶם | *your* | דְּבַרְכֶם | בִּרְכַתְכֶם | חַסְדְּכֶם |
| 2f pl | ְכֶן | *your* | דְּבַרְכֶן | בִּרְכַתְכֶן | חַסְדְּכֶן |
| 3m pl | ָם | *their* | דְּבָרָם | בִּרְכָתָם | חַסְדָּם |
| 3f pl | ָן | *their* | דְּבָרָן | בִּרְכָתָן | חַסְדָּן |

(ii) Suffixes on Plural Nouns

Note that the following suffixes include the contraction of the noun's plural and/or dual endings as in the following example: דִּבְרֵיכֶם < כֶם + דְּבָרִים .

| | | | | | |
|---|---|---|---|---|---|
| 1c sg | ַי | *my* | דְּבָרַי | בִּרְכוֹתַי | חֲסָדַי |
| 2m sg | ֶיךָ | *your* | דְּבָרֶיךָ | בִּרְכוֹתֶךָ | חֲסָדֶיךָ |
| 2f sg | ַיִךְ | *your* | דְּבָרַיִךְ | בִּרְכוֹתַיִךְ: | חֲסָדַיִךְ |
| 3m sg | ָיו | *his* | דְּבָרָיו | בִּרְכוֹתָיו | חֲסָדָיו |
| 3f sg | ֶיהָ | *her* | דְּבָרֶיהָ | בִּרְכוֹתֶיהָ | חֲסָדֶיהָ |
| 1c pl | ֵינוּ | *our* | דְּבָרֵינוּ | בִּרְכוֹתֵינוּ | חֲסָדֵינוּ |
| 2m pl | ֵיכֶם | *your* | דִּבְרֵיכֶם | בִּרְכוֹתֵיכֶם | חַסְדֵיכֶם |
| 2f pl | ֵיכֶן | *your* | דִּבְרֵיכֶן | בִּרְכוֹתֵיכֶם | חַסְדֵיכֶן |
| 3m pl | ֵיהֶם | *their* | דִּבְרֵיהֶם | בִּרְכוֹתֵיכֶן | חַסְדֵיהֶם |
| 3f pl | ֵיהֶן | *their* | דִּבְרֵיהֶן | בִּרְכוֹתֵיכֶן | חַסְדֵיהֶן |

(b) *Pronominal Suffixes with the Inseparable Prepositions*

| | | | | |
|---|---|---|---|---|
| 1c sg | בִּי | כָּמוֹנִי | לִי | מִמֶּנִּי |
| 2m sg | בְּךָ | כָּמוֹךָ | לְךָ | מִמְּךָ |
| 2f sg | בָּךְ | ----- | לָךְ | מִמֵּךְ |
| 3m sg | בּוֹ | כָּמוֹהוּ | לוֹ | מִמֶּנּוּ |
| 3f sg | בָּהּ | כָּמוֹהָ | לָהּ | מִמֶּנָּה |
| 1c pl | בָּנוּ | כָּמוֹנוּ | לָנוּ | מִמֶּנּוּ |
| 2m pl | בָּכֶם | כָּכֶם | לָכֶם | מִכֶּם |
| 2f pl | בָּכֶן | ----- | לָכֶן | מִכֶּן |
| 3m pl | בָּהֶם / בָּם | כָּהֶם | לָהֶם | מֵהֶם |
| 3f pl | בָּהֶן | כָּהֵנָּה | לָהֶן | מֵהֶן |

(c) *Pronominal Suffixes with Prepositions and the Accusative Particle*

| | [אֶל] | [עַל] | [אֵת] | [אֵת / אֶת-] |
|---|---|---|---|---|
| 1c sg | אֵלַי | עָלַי | אִתִּי | אֹתִי |
| 2m sg | אֵלֶיךָ | עָלֶיךָ | אִתְּךָ | אֹתְךָ |
| 2f sg | אֵלַיִךְ | עָלַיִךְ | אִתָּךְ | אֹתָךְ |
| 3m sg | אֵלָיו | עָלָיו | אִתּוֹ | אֹתוֹ |
| 3f sg | אֵלֶיהָ | עָלֶיהָ | אִתָּהּ | אֹתָהּ |
| 1c pl | אֵלֵינוּ | עָלֵינוּ | אִתָּנוּ | אֹתָנוּ |
| 2m pl | אֲלֵיכֶם | עֲלֵיכֶם | אִתְּכֶם | אֹתְכֶם |
| 2f pl | אֲלֵיכֶן | עֲלֵיכֶן | אִתְּכֶן | אֹתְכֶן |
| 3m pl | אֲלֵיהֶם | עֲלֵיהֶם | אִתָּם | אֹתָם |
| 3f pl | אֲלֵיהֶן | עֲלֵיהֶן | אִתָּן | אֶתְהֶן |

(d) *Pronominal Suffixes with Verbs.*

(i) The pronominal suffixes for verbs are the same as those for nouns and prepositions except for the following.

(a) The suffix for the first person singular is נִי (nominal ִי ); compare כְּבוֹדִי *my glory* with כִּבְּדוּנִי *they glorified me* (Isaiah 29:13) and וּתְכַבְּדֵנִי *and you will glorify me* (Psalm 50:15).

(b) With verbs in the imperfect and related forms the suffix for the third masculine singular is הוּ (nominal וֹ ) and for the third feminine singular is הָ (nominal ָהּ ); e.g. וַיַּשְׁכִּבֵהוּ *and he laid him down* (1 Kings 17:19); וַיַּצִּילֶהָ *and he delivered her [= the plot of ground]* (2 Samuel 23:12); וְכִבְשֻׁהָ *and subdue her [the earth]* (Genesis 1:28).

(ii) When a connecting vowel is needed between the verb form and the suffix, the perfect uses *a* vowels and the imperfect and related forms use *e* vowels; e.g. הִצִּילַנִי *he delivered me* (Psalm 34:5); יַצִּילֵנִי *he delivers me* (Psalm 18:18). See also the examples above.

(iii) With suffixes original verbal forms reappear in the following.

(a) The third feminine singular perfect afformative ָה [קָטְלָה] becomes ַת [-קָטַלַת], e.g. אֲכָלַתְהוּ < הוּ + אָכְלָה *she [a wild beast] devoured him* (Genesis 37:20).

(b) The second feminine singular perfect afformative תְּ [קָטַלְתְּ] becomes תִּ / תִּי [(קְטַלְתִּ(י]; e.g. > הוּ + הִכְרַעַתְּ הִכְרַעְתִּנִי *you (fem.) have bowed me down* (Judges 11:35). With this shift the verbal form becomes identical with the first common singular perfect; context, however, removes any ambiguity.

Note also that in three places the second person masculine plural afformative תֶּם becomes תּוּ / תְּ ; e.g. הֶעֱלִתָנוּ < נוּ + הֶעֱלִיתֶם *you have brought us up* (Numbers 20:5 and 21:5); צַמְתֻּנִי *you fasted (for) me* (Zechariah 7:5).

(iv) Verbs with suffixes are pointed according to the following patterns.

(a) Qal perfect and all imperfects and imperatives in a follow a first declension pattern; e.g. קְטָלוֹ < וֹ + קָטַל *he killed him*; שָׁלְחֵנִי < נִי + שְׁלַח *send me!* .

(b) Pi'ēl perfect and all imperfects and imperatives in a and o follow a third declension pattern; e.g. < ָם + קִבֵּץ קִבְּצָם *he gathered them*; יִשְׁמְרֵנִי < נִי + יִשְׁמֹר *he guards me.*

(c) Qal imperative in *o* and infinitive constructs in *o* follow a second declension patterm; e.g. < נִי + שְׁמֹר שָׁמְרֵנִי *Keep me!*; שָׁמְרוֹ < וֹ + שְׁמֹר *his keeping.*

(v) With imperfect and imperative forms of the verb, especially in pause, a נ is sometimes placed before the singular suffixes to give the form more weight or body, perhaps even emphasis. This נ , called a *nûn energicum*, is usually assimilated by dāgēš fortē into the first consonant of the first and second person suffixes; e.g. תְּבַעֲתַנִּי *you terrify me* (Job 7:14); וִיבָרְכֶךָּ *and he will bless you* (Genesis 49:25). With the third person suffix the ה appears to be assimilated into the נ ; e.g. לֹא תְבָרְכֶנּוּ *you shall not bless him* (Numbers 23:25); cf. יְבָרְכֵנוּ *he will bless us* (Psalm 67:7); לֹא־יַצִּילֶנָּה *he will not deliver her* (Hosea 2:12). Note that with *nûn energicum* the accent is always on the connecting vowel.

## 11 THE VERB IN HEBREW: THE BASIC STRUCTURE

The basic structure and inflection of the verb in biblical Hebrew are best seen in verbs whose radicals (root letters) are neither weak letters (אהוי) nor gutturals (אהחע), and so in verbs such as קטל , the standard paradigm word, or מֹשׁל or שׁמר . These verbs are traditionally called "strong" or "regular," while other verbs are referred to as "weak" and even sometimes as "irregular." The distinction is valid, but the terminology is misleading, for verbs with weak letters and gutturals are neither weak nor irregular. They follow the normal pattern of verbal inflection, modified, however, by the characteristics of the weak letters and gutturals. They are simply "regular variations," as it were, of the basic pattern of the Hebrew verb. Accordingly, the following presentation of the verb begins with the so-called strong or regular verb to lay down the basic pattern, and then on the basis of this to go on to consider verbs with weak letters and verbs with gutturals. See also the *Introduction*, §§ 29-38.

(a) *The Stems of the Verb.* In its basic structure the Hebrew verb has *three voices* (active, passive and reflexive) and *seven stems* (*Simple* active and reflexive; *Intensive*-Repetitive active, passive and reflexive; and *Causative* active and passive).

The names of the stems are their simplest form, the third masculine singular perfect of פעל , the old paradigm word. The structure of the verb is summarized in the following charts, which give not only the names of the stems, but also the third masculine singular perfect and imperfect forms of each stem using the common paradigm word קטל. It is essential to know these forms, both perfect and imperfect, for they provide the pattern for each stem and are always the starting point for conjugating the verb in any of its stems.

| | Active | Passive | Reflexive |
|---|---|---|---|
| Simple | qal קָטַל | ---------- | nip'al נִקְטַל |
| Intensive | pi'ēl קִטֵּל | pu'al קֻטַּל | hiṯpa'ēl הִתְקַטֵּל |
| Causative | hip'îl הִקְטִיל | hop'al הָקְטַל | ---------- |

| | | | Perfect | Imperfect |
|---|---|---|---|---|
| Simple | Active<br>Reflexive | qal<br>nip'al | קָטַל<br>נִקְטַל | יִקְטֹל<br>יִקָּטֵל* |
| Intensive | Active<br>Passive<br>Reflexive | pi'ēl<br>pu'al<br>hiṯpa'ēl | קִטֵּל<br>קֻטַּל<br>הִתְקַטֵּל | יְקַטֵּל<br>יְקֻטַּל<br>יִתְקַטֵּל |
| Causative | Active<br>Passive | hip'îl<br>hop'al | הִקְטִיל<br>הָקְטַל | יַקְטִיל<br>יָקְטַל |

* The נ of the nip'al is assimilated into the first radical by dāgēš fortē.

(b) *The Personal Afformatives and Preformatives* The personal subject of the verb is indicated by additions and modifications made to the basic third masculine singular form of the stem. In the *perfect* the personal subject is indicated by *afformatives*, and in the *imperfect* the personal subject is indicated primarily by *preformatives* which exchange the י of the basic third masculine singular form for the appropriate personal prefix. There is only one set each, one for the perfect and one for the imperfect, and they serve all the stems. See the following chart.

| | Perfect | Imperfect |
|---|---|---|
| 3m sg | ------ | ------ י |
| 3f sg | ָה ------ | ------תּ |
| 2m sg | תָּ ------ | ------תּ |
| 2f sg | תְּ ------ | ִי. ----תּ |
| 1c sg | תִּי ------ | ------א |
| 3m pl | וּ -------- | וּ ----- י |
| 3f pl | וּ -------- | נָה ----תּ |
| 2m pl | תֶּם ------ | וּ ------תּ |
| 2f pl | תֶּן ------ | נָה ----תּ |
| 1c pl | נוּ ------- | ------- נ |

Note that instead of the simple afformative וּ for imperfect plurals, many times a fuller ending with nûn is used: וּן (called *nûn paragogicum*). This occurs mostly in older books, and usually at the end of a sentence or clause, and so with pausal forms; e.g. תִּשְׁמָעוּן *you hear* (Deuteronomy 1:17); cf. תִּשְׁמְעוּ. The reason for such nunation may be for emphasis or cadence, perhaps also for euphony in cases where a final וּ is followed by א or ע; cf. 1 Kings 19:2, where both reasons may be evidenced: כֹּה-יַעֲשׂוּן אֱלֹהִים וְכֹה יוֹסִפוּן *Thus may God do and thus may he add.*

(c) *The Two Statements Governing Conjugation.* To conjugate the verb in any of its stems, one begins with the basic perfect or imperfect form (the third masculine singular), and simply adds to it the personal afformatives for the perfect, and for the imperfect makes the appropriate changes in the personal prefixes, adding any endings that go with them.

When placing afformatives on the basic stem, however, the pointing may be affected: (1) *vocalic and heavy afformatives* usually take the accent and so modify the original pointing of the basic stem, and (2) *consonantal afformatives* affect the vowels ִי and ֵ . These modifications follow regular rules, and are summarized in the following two statements.

(1) *The accent remains where it is on the basic form,*[1] *except*

*(a) with vocalic endings (except hip̄'îl) when the accent shifts to the ultima and the penult becomes* ְ ;[2]
*(b) and with heavy endings, when the accent shifts to the ultima and the distant open is reduced to* ְ .[3]

[1] קָטַל, קָטַלְתָּ, קָטַלְתְּ, קָטַלְתִּי, קָטַלְנוּ

[2] קָטַל + ָה > קָטָלָה > קָטְלָה *she killed*
יִקְטֹל + וּ > יִקְטֹלוּ > יִקְטְלוּ *they kill*

(but in the hip'îl there is no change of accent or pointing: הִקְטִיל + ָה > הִקְטִילָה *she caused to kill*)

[3] קָטַל + תֶּם > קָטַלְתֶּם > קְטַלְתֶּם *you (pl.) killed*

(2) *Before consonantal endings* ִי *and* ֵ *become* ַ,[1] *except*

*(a) with hip̄'îl imperfect, where* ִי *becomes* ֵ ,[2]
*(b) and with pi'ēl imperfect, where the* ֵ *remains unchanged.*[3]

[1] הִקְטִיל + תִּי > הִקְטִילְתִּי > הִקְטַלְתִּי *I caused to kill*
קִטֵּל + תִּי > קִטֵּלְתִּי > קִטַּלְתִּי *I killed*

[2] יַקְטִיל + תִּי > יַקְטִילְתִּי > יַקְטֵלְתִּי *I cause to kill*

[3] תְּקַטֵּל + נָה > תְּקַטֵּלְנָה *they/you (f.pl) kill*

In summary, to conjugate the verb one needs to know three things:

*(1) the basic third masculine singular stems in the perfect and imperfect,*
*(2) the personal preformatives and afformatives for the perfect and imperfect,*
*(3) the two statements concerning accent and consonantal afformatives.*

On the basis of these three elements the strong verb can be conjugated in all its stems.

## 12 THE SIMPLE STEMS: QAL AND NIP̱'AL

The simple stems of the verb express the plain, basic meaning of the verbal root. Originally the simple stems appeared in all three voices, but now in the Hebrew Bible they occur only in the active and reflexive voices with only a few traces of the passive. The nip'al doubles for both reflexive and passive.

The active voice of the simple stems is called *qal*, a name deriving from the root קלל which mean *to be slight, light, quick.* It is called this because it is the verb in its simplest, lightest, most unadorned form.

The *qal participle* is קוֹטֵל / קֹטֵל and it belongs to the third declension, reducing the ֵ to ְ before vocalic afformatives and to ֶ before consonantal afformatives. Note that although the ḥōlem is pure long, and so unchangeable, it is frequently written without the vāv (*dēfectīvē*). The feminine participle may be formed simply by adding הָ , as in קֹטְלָה ; more frequently, however, it has the form קֹטֶלֶת, and follows a second declension pattern in inflection. Although there is no longer a passive voice in the simple stems (its function being taken over largely by the nip'al) a passive participle is regularly found. It has the form קָטוּל *(m.)* and קְטוּלָה *(f.)*; it follows the first declension in inflection.

Most verbs in qal have the pattern ◌ָ◌ַ, as in קָטַל. There are some verbs, however, that have the pattern ◌ָ◌ֵ or ◌ָ◌ֹ, such as כָּבֵד *to be heavy* and קָטֹן *to be small.* These verbs (sometimes called, although not very accurately, *stative* or *intransitive*) show a slight variation from the regular pattern of the qal.

(a) In the perfect tense verbs of the ◌ָ◌ֵ type (except for the third masculine singular) follow the normal rules, the ◌ֵ becoming ◌ְ with vocalic afformatives and ◌ַ before consonantal afformatives; e.g. כָּבֵד, כָּבְדָה, כָּבַדְתָּ. Verbs of the ◌ָ◌ֹ type reduce the ḥōlem to ševâ before vocalic afformatives, but elsewhere retain the ḥōlem; e.g. קָטֹן, קָטְנָה, קָטֹנְתָּ.

(b) Both types form their imperfects with ◌ַ; e.g. יִכְבַּד and יִקְטַן.

(c) The masculine qal participle is identical with the third masculine singular perfect form; e.g. כָּבֵד and קָטֹן. The feminine participle is formed by the addition of ◌ָה; e.g. כְּבֵדָה and קְטַנָּה. Both follow a first declension pattern.

As the basic third masculine singular imperfect stem indicates, the usual pointing of the second syllable of qal imperfect is with ◌ֹ. However, as noted in the verbs of the types ◌ָ◌ֵ and ◌ָ◌ֹ, some verbs (especially intransitives) form their imperfects in ◌ַ. Other variations also occur, usually due to the nature of the last letter of the verb root. Verbs ending in ע or ח, for example, often form the qal imperfect in ◌ַ, because gutturals prefer a vowels especially before them; e.g. יִשְׁמַע *he hears* and יִשְׂמַח *he rejoices.* Again, the regular pointing of qal imperfect for verbs ending in א is with ◌ָ, e.g. יִמְצָא *he finds*; and for verbs ending in ה with ◌ֶ, e.g. יִשְׁתֶּה *he drinks.* Despite these variations. however, the basic structure of the qal imperfect is easily recognizable.

The *imperative* is based on the second person imperfect. It is formed by dropping the personal prefixes and making any necessary pointing modifications.

| | |
|---|---|
| masculine singular | קְטֹל < תִּקְטֹל |
| feminine singular | קִטְלִי < קְטְלִי < תִּקְטְלִי |
| masculine plural | קִטְלוּ < קְטְלוּ < תִּקְטְלוּ |
| feminine plural | קְטֹלְנָה < תִּקְטֹלְנָה |

The second person singular masculine imperative is sometimes augmented by the addition of הָ ; e.g. שָׁמְרָה נַפְשִׁי *Guard my being* (Psalm 86:2); שִׁמְעָה תְפִלָּתִי *Hear my prayer* (Psalm 39:13). It will be noted that with the addition of הָ the pointing follows a second declension pattern. This augmented form is sometimes called an "emphatic imperative," but in reality there is little if any difference in meaning between the longer and shorter forms.

The imperative form cannot be used with a negative. For negative commands one must use either (1) the imperfect with לֹא, used especially in more formal contexts, e.g. לֹא תִּגְנֹב *You shall not steal = Do not steal* (Exodus 20:15); or (2) the jussive (see below) with אַל, which is the more common usage, e.g. אַל-תִּירָא *Let you not fear = Do not fear* (1 Kings 17:13).

The *jussive*, used only in the second and third persons, is related to the imperative. In form, however, it closely resembles the second and third person imperfect. Indeed, in the strong verb the jussive and imperfect forms are identical except in the hip'îl (see below, § 14). They can be distinguished only by the context and the interpreter's understanding. To translate the jussive, phrases with *let* or *may* are commonly used; e.g. תִּקְרַב *let you draw near*; אַל-תִּקְרַב הֲלֹם *let you not draw near here* (Exodus 3:5); אָז יִקְרַב *then let him draw near* (Exodus 12:48).

The *cohortative*, used only in the first person, is also related to the imperative. In meaning it expresses intentionality and wish, and like the jussive may be translated by *let* and *may*. It is formed by adding ָה to the first person imperfect form, and (following the rule about vocalic afformatives on verbs) reducing the near open syllable to š$^{e}$vâ.

| | |
|---|---|
| Let me kill | אֶקְטֹל + ָה > אֶקְטֹלָה > אֶקְטְלָה |
| Let us kill | נִקְטֹל + ָה > נִקְטֹלָה > נִקְטְלָה |

The reflexive stem, *nip̄ʻal*, is characterized by a prefixed נ to the verb root. The נ regularly appears in the perfect, but in the imperfect it is assimilated into the following consonant because it has no vowel of its own; e.g. יִנְמָלֵט > יִמָּלֵט *he escapes* (cf. 1 Kings 18:40). With the *imperatives and infinitives*, which are regularly formed by dropping the imperfect preformatives, the nipʻal prefixes a ה in order to preserve the assimilated נ of the stem; e.g. מַהֵר הִמָּלֵט שָׁמָּה *quickly escape thither* (Genesis 19:22); לְהִמָּלֵט הָהָרָה *to escape to the mountain* (Genesis 19:19). The participle of the nipʻal is based on the perfect stem, lenthening the ַ to ָ to make it a nominal form; e.g. נִקְטַל > נִקְטָל, as in הַנִּמְלָט *the one escaping* (1 Kings 19:17). The participle is inflected as a first declension noun; cf. the plural הַנִּמְלָטִים *the ones escaping.*

The meaning of nipʻal is properly reflexive; e.g. וְנִסְתַּרְתָּ *and hide yourself* (1 Kings 17:3). It may also express reciprocal action, as in נִלְחַם *he fought* (cf. the Greek middle and the Latin deponent verbs). The most common use, however, is as a passive; e.g. קָבַר *he buried,* but נִקְבַּר *he was buried*; יִוָּדַע *it will be known* (1 Kings 18:36).

## 12 THE SIMPLE STEMS

| | | QAL | NIP‘AL |
|---|---|---|---|
| Perfect | 3 m.s. | קָטַל | נִקְטַל |
| | 3 f.s. | קָטְלָה | נִקְטְלָה |
| | 2 m.s. | קָטַלְתָּ | נִקְטַלְתָּ |
| | 2 f.s. | קָטַלְתְּ | נִקְטַלְתְּ |
| | 1 c.s. | קָטַלְתִּי | נִקְטַלְתִּי |
| | 3 c.p. | קָטְלוּ | נִקְטְלוּ |
| | 2 m.p. | קְטַלְתֶּם | נִקְטַלְתֶּם |
| | 2 f.p. | קְטַלְתֶּן | נִקְטַלְתֶּן |
| | 1 c.p. | קָטַלְנוּ | נִקְטַלְנוּ |
| Imperfect | 3 m.s. | יִקְטֹל | יִקָּטֵל |
| | 3 f.s. | תִּקְטֹל | תִּקָּטֵל |
| | 2 m.s. | תִּקְטֹל | תִּקָּטֵל |
| | 2 f.s. | תִּקְטְלִי | תִּקָּטְלִי |
| | 1 c.s. | אֶקְטֹל | אֶקָּטֵל |
| | 3 m.p. | יִקְטְלוּ | יִקָּטְלוּ |
| | 3 f.p. | תִּקְטֹלְנָה | תִּקָּטַלְנָה |
| | 2 m.p | תִּקְטְלוּ | תִּקָּטְלוּ |
| | 2 f.p. | תִּקְטֹלְנָה | תִּקָּטַלְנָה |
| | 1 c.p | נִקְטֹל | נִקָּטֵל |
| Imperative | m.s. | קְטֹל | הִקָּטֵל |
| | f.s. | קִטְלִי | הִקָּטְלִי |
| | m.p. | קִטְלוּ | הִקָּטְלוּ |
| | f.p. | קְטֹלְנָה | הִקָּטַלְנָה |
| Infinitive const. | | קְטֹל | הִקָּטֵל |
| Infinitive absol. | | קָטֹל | קָטֹל |
| Participle | | קֹטֵל | נִקְטָל |
| (passive) | | קָטוּל | |

## 13 THE INTENSIVE-REPETITIVE STEMS

| | | PI‘ĒL | PU‘AL | HIṮPA‘ĒL |
|---|---|---|---|---|
| Perfect | 3 m.s | קִטֵּל | קֻטַּל | הִתְקַטֵּל |
| | 3 f.s. | קִטְּלָה | קֻטְּלָה | הִתְקַטְּלָה |
| | 2 m.s. | קִטַּלְתָּ | קֻטַּלְתָּ | הִתְקַטַּלְתָּ |
| | 2 f.s. | קִטַּלְתְּ | קֻטַּלְתְּ | הִתְקַטַּלְתְּ |
| | 1 c.s. | קִטַּלְתִּי | קֻטַּלְתִּי | הִתְקַטַּלְתִּי |
| | 3 c.p. | קִטְּלוּ | קֻטְּלוּ | הִתְקַטְּלוּ |
| | 2.m.p. | קִטַּלְתֶּם | קֻטַּלְתֶּם | הִתְקַטַּלְתֶּם |
| | 2 f.p. | קִטַּלְתֶּן | קֻטַּלְתֶּן | הִתְקַטַּלְתֶּן |
| | 1 c.p. | קִטַּלְנוּ | קֻטַּלְנוּ | הִתְקַטַּלְנוּ |
| Imperfect | 3 m.s. | יְקַטֵּל | יְקֻטַּל | יִתְקַטֵּל |
| | 3 f.s. | תְּקַטֵּל | תְּקֻטַּל | תִּתְקַטֵּל |
| | 2 m.s. | תְּקַטֵּל | תְּקֻטַּל | תִּתְקַטֵּל |
| | 2 f.s. | תְּקַטְּלִי | תְּקֻטְּלִי | תִּתְקַטְּלִי |
| | 1 c.s. | אֲקַטֵּל | אֲקֻטַּל | אֶתְקַטֵּל |
| | 3 m.p. | יְקַטְּלוּ | יְקֻטְּלוּ | יִתְקַטְּלוּ |
| | 2 f.p. | תְּקַטֵּלְנָה | תְּקֻטַּלְנָה | תִּתְקַטַּלְנָה |
| | 2 m.p. | תְּקַטְּלוּ | תְּקֻטְּלוּ | תִּתְקַטְּלוּ |
| | 2 f.p. | תְּקַטֵּלְנָה | תְּקֻטַּלְנָה | תִּתְקַטַּלְנָה |
| | 1 c.p. | נְקַטֵּל | נְקֻטַּל | נִתְקַטֵּל |
| Imperative | m.s. | קַטֵּל | | הִתְקַטֵּל |
| | f.s. | קַטְּלִי | | הִתְקַטְּלִי |
| | m.p. | קַטְּלוּ | | הִתְקַטְּלוּ |
| | f.p. | קַטֵּלְנָה | | הִתְקַטַּלְנָה |
| Infinitive const. | | קַטֵּל | קֻטַּל | הִתְקַטֵּל |
| Infinitive absol. | | קַטֹּל/קַטֵּל | קֻטֹּל | הִתְקַטֵּל |
| Participle | | מְקַטֵּל | מְקֻטָּל | מִתְקַטֵּל |

*A Summary of Hebrew Grammar*

## 14 THE CAUSATIVE STEMS

| | | HIP̱‘ÎL | HOP̱‘AL |
|---|---|---|---|
| Perfect | 3 m.s. | הִקְטִיל | הָקְטַל |
| | 3 f.s. | הִקְטִילָה | הָקְטְלָה |
| | 2 m.s. | הִקְטַלְתָּ | הָקְטַלְתָּ |
| | 2 f.s. | הִקְטַלְתְּ | הָקְטַלְתְּ |
| | 1 c.s. | הִקְטַלְתִּי | הָקְטַלְתִּי |
| | 3 c.p. | הִקְטִילוּ | הָקְטְלוּ |
| | 2 m.p. | הִקְטַלְתֶּם | הָקְטַלְתֶּם |
| | 2 f.p. | הִקְטַלְתֶּן | הָקְטַלְתֶּן |
| | 1 c.p. | הִקְטַלְנוּ | הָקְטַלְנוּ |
| Imperfect | 3 m.s. | יַקְטִיל | יָקְטַל |
| | 3 f.s. | תַּקְטִיל | תָּקְטַל |
| | 2 m.s. | תַּקְטִיל | תָּקְטַל |
| | 2 f.s. | תַּקְטִילִי | תָּקְטְלִי |
| | 1 c.s. | אַקְטִיל | אָקְטַל |
| | 3 m.p. | יַקְטִילוּ | יָקְטְלוּ |
| | 3 f.p. | תַּקְטֵלְנָה | תָּקְטַלְנָה |
| | 2 m.p. | תַּקְטִילוּ | תָּקְטְלוּ |
| | 2 f.p. | תַּקְטֵלְנָה | תָּקְטַלְנָה |
| | 1 c.p. | נַקְטִיל | נָקְטַל |
| Imperative | m.s. | הַקְטֵל | |
| | f.s. | הַקְטִילִי | |
| | m.p. | הַקְטִילוּ | |
| | f.p. | הַקְטֵלְנָה | |
| Infinitive const. | | הַקְטִיל | הָקְטַל |
| Infinitive absol. | | הַקְטֵל | הָקְטֵל |
| Participle | | מַקְטִיל | מָקְטָל |

## 13 THE INTENSIVE-REPETITIVE STEMS: PI'ĒL, PU'AL, AND HIṮPA'ĒL

The intensive-repetitive stems of the verb are characterized by the doubling of the middle radical by dāgēš fortē. When gutturals and ר, which cannot take dāgēš fortē, appear as the middle radical, compensation may be made by raising the previous vowel to its tone long. This is always done for ר, occasionally for א, but hardly ever for ה, ח, or ע; e.g. from ברך: בֵּרֵךְ < בִּרֵּךְ *he blessed,* יְבָרֵךְ < יְבַרֵּךְ *he blesses*, and בֻּרַּךְ בֹּרַךְ < *he was blessed*; and similarly פֵּאֵר and יְפָאֵר (from פאר *to beautify*); but also without compensation נִאֵץ and יְנַאֵץ (from נאץ *to spurn*); מִהֵר and יְמַהֵר (from מהר *to hurry*); נִחַם and יְנַחֵם (from נחם *to comfort*); בִּאֵר and יְבַאֵר (from באר *to burn*). Even when the dāgēš is not written and no compensation is made, the basic patterns of the intensive-repetitive stems are clearly evident.

In addition to the doubling of the middle radical the reflexive voice of the intensive repetitive stems has the prefix - הִתְ in the perfect and - יִתְ ( - תִתְ and so on) in the imperfect.; e.g. הִתְקַטֵּל and יִתְקַטֵּל .

Note that the ת of these reflexive prefixes may change place and character under the following circumstances.

(a) Before the sibilants, ס צ שׂ שׁ , the ת changes place (metathesis) with the sibilant without, however, changing the pointing; e.g. הִשְׁתַּמֵּר < הִתְשַׁמֵּר *he watched himself*.

(b) Before the strong sibilant צ the ת not only changes places, but itself becomes ט; e.g. הִתְצַדֵּק הִצְטַדֵּק < הִצְתַּדֵּק < *he justified himself*.

(c) Before the dentals, ת ט ד , the ת is assimilated by dāgēš fortē; so instead of הִתְטַהֵר , the form is הִטַּהֵר *he purified himself.*

The *participles* for the intensive-repetitive stems are based on the third masculine singular forms of the imperfect, a מ replacing the personal prefix, and the final ַ of the pu‘al becoming a nominal ָ ; e.g. מְקַדֵּשׁ > יְקַדֵּשׁ , מְקֻדָּשׁ > יְקֻדַּשׁ , and מִתְקַדֵּשׁ > יִתְקַדֵּשׁ from the root קדשׁ *to be holy.* The pi‘ēl and hiṯpa‘ēl participles belong to the third declension, and the pu‘al participle to the first; cf. the plural forms מְקַדְּשִׁים , מִתְקַדְּשִׁים and מְקֻדָּשִׁים .

The *imperative* is regularly formed from the second person of the imperfect by dropping the personal preformatives, e.g. קַטֵּל > תְּקַטֵּל , קַטְּלִי > תְּקַטְּלִי , and so on. The cohortative is regularly formed by adding the afformative ָה- to the first person imperfects; e.g. אֲקַטְּלָה > ָה + אֲקַטֵּל and > ָה + נְקַטֵּל נְקַטְּלָה . As usual in the strong verb the *jussive* forms coincide with the imperfect of the second and third persons.

The *infinitive construct* is identical with the masculine singular imperative, קַטֵּל , קֻטַּל and הִתְקַטֵּל . The *infinitive absolute* for pi‘ēl and hiṯpa‘ēl usually has the same form as the infinitive construct, although occasionally the pi‘ēl infinitive absolute will appear with a ḥolem, e.g. קַטֹּל . The pu‘al infinitive construct is regularly with ḥolem, קֻטֹּל .

In meaning these stems either (a) *intensify the simple meaning of the verb root*, e.g. סָפַר *he counted*, but סִפֵּר *he recounted, told*; וַיֶּחִי *and he lived* (1 Kings 17:22), but וּנְחַיֶּה *and we will keep alive* (1 Kings 18:5); or (b) *indicate what is habitual or customary*, e.g. עִוֵּר *he is blind*; וַיְפַסְּחוּ *and they limped (danced) [about the altar]* (1 Kings 18:26; cf. 1 Kings 18:21). Occasionally these stems take on a causative sense, as in 1 Kings 18:35: וְגַם אֶת-הַתְּעָלָה מִלֵּא-מָיִם *and even the trench it filled with water.* The pu'al and hiṯpa'ēl are simply the passive and reflexive voices for these meanings.

Some verbs occur only (or almost exclusively) in the intensive-repetitive stems, but with no special emphasis or intensity implied; e.g. בקשׁ *to seek* (cf. 1 Kings 19:10, 14) and צוה *to command* (cf. 1 Kings 17:4, 12). Note also in this connection that there is sometimes little or no difference between the meaning of a verb in the simple stem and the same verb in the intensive-repetitive stem. Compare, for example, the nip'al of the root נבא *to be a prophet* with the hiṯpa'ēl in 1 Kings 18:29 and the mixed usage in 1 Samuel 10:5-13; both stems are used with the same meaning. This is especially true in poetry, where after the manner of Canaanite poetry, alternation of stems in parallel lines is employed to achieve variety of expression and not difference in meaning.

## 14 THE CAUSATIVE STEMS: HIP̱'IL AND HOP̱'AL

The causative stems of the verb, of which only the active and passive remain, are characterized by a prefixed הַ , which is refined in the perfect hip'îl to ḥîreq (הִקְטִיל ) and elided into qāmēṣ ḥaṭûp and qibbûṣ in the hop'al (הָקְטַל or הֻקְטַל ). In addition to the prefixed ה the hip'îl also has ִי as a thematic vowel in both the perfect and imperfect: הִקְטִיל and יַקְטִיל. In this connection note the exceptions made with regard to the hip'îl in the *Two Statements* concerning accent and consonantal afformatives; see above in § 11c.

The *imperative*, as always, is based on the second person imperfect forms; the personal prefix, ת , is simply replaced by the characteristic ה of the hip'îl; e.g. הַשְׁמִיעִי < תַּשְׁמִיעִי *proclaim! (f.s.) [lit. cause to hear]*; הַשְׁמִיעוּ < תַּשְׁמִיעוּ *proclaim! (m. pl.)* The masculine singular imperative follows the same pattern, but has a further modification; it not only replaces the ת with ה, but modifies the ִי to ֵ ; < תַּשְׁלִיךְ הַשְׁלֵךְ < הַשְׁלִיךְ *throw!*

The *infinitive absolute* takes the same form as the masculine singular imperative, הַקְטֵל , but the *infinitive construct* follows the usual pattern, הַקְטִיל .

The *jussive* forms, which in the strong verb are usually identical to the imperfect, take a form similar to that of the masculine singular imperative, namely, יַשְׁלֵךְ *may he throw* and תַּשְׁלֵךְ *may you throw.* The *cohortative* follows the normal rules for the hip'îl, e.g. אַשְׁלִיכָה *let me throw.*

The *participles* are based on the third masculine singular imperfect forms of the stems, a מ replacing the personal prefix, and in hop'al the _ becoming a nominal ָ ; e.g. מַקְטִיל and מָקְטָל . They are inflected as first declension nouns; cf. the plurals מַקְטִילִים and מָקְטָלִים .

In meaning, the causative stems are just that; so, for example, the qal לָמוּת *to die* (1 Kings 19:4), but the hip'îl לְהָמִית *to cause to die, i.e. to kill* (1 Kings 17:20); similarly, compare וָמָתְנוּ *and we shall die* (1 Kings 17:12) with יָמִית *he will kill* (1 Kings 19:17).

## 15 UNUSUAL STEMS: ŠAP̱'ĒL AND HIŠTAP̱'ĒL

The šap'ēl ( = Š) and hištap'ēl ( = Št) stems, well-known in Akkadian, Aramaic and Syriac, are also present in Northwest Semitic, clearly in Ugaritic and with traces in Hebrew. Šap'ēl generally carries a causative meaning; cf. hip'îl. In Ugaritic, which has no clearly attested hip'îl, it is the regular causative form. With an infixed t the šap'ēl has a reflexive or reciprocal meaning; cf. the hit̲pa'ēl. Note that in biblical Hebrew the reflexive of the causative has fallen out.

While not frequent in biblical Hebrew these stems are clearly present. The šap'ēl, for example. lies behind the noun שַׁלְהֶבֶת *flame* (Ezekiel 21:3, Job 15:30; Song of Songs 8:6); cf. the usual nouns meaning *flame*: לַהַב and לֶהָבָה .

The most striking example of the Št form is a verb that occurs 172 times in the Bible and means *to prostrate oneself, bow down*: לְהִשְׁתַּחֲוֹת (Genesis 18:12); cf. also הִשְׁתַּחֲוָה *he bowed down*, הִשְׁתַּחֲוִיתָ *you bowed down* (perfect forms), and יִשְׁתַּחֲוֶה *he bows down*, יִשְׁתַּחֲווּ *they bow down* (imperfect forms). The verb is well-attested in Ugaritic, *tšthwy*, a Št form of the root *ḥwy*, which would appear in Hebrew as חוה, a ל״ה (originally ל״י) verb.

Traditionally, however, the Hebrew lexica have analyzed the verb as a hit̲pa'ēl of the root שחה (with metathesis of the שׁ and ת). This may work in some few apocopated forms, but it does not explain the consonantal vav, unless one sees the word as a combination of ל״ה and ל״ו roots. Recognizing the closeness of Ugaritic and Hebrew in the Northwest Semitic family, it is better to see the verb as a Št form of the root חוה.

## 16 VERBS WITH PĒ NŪN [פ״ן]

Verbs of this class (which includes לקח) begin with a nûn, which in inflection is frequently assimilated and often dropped. Operative here is the general principle that when nûn does not have a full vowel of its own, it is usually assimilated into the following consonant by dāgēš fortē. The phenomenon is familiar in English, where, for example, the *n* of the negative particle, *in*-, when combined with another word is assimilated into the first letter of that word, as in "illogical" (*in* + *logical*) and "immobile" (*in* + *mobile*). Note the following characteristics of פ״ן verbs.

(a) When nûn has no vowel of its own, it is assimilated by dāgēš fortē into the next letter. This happens throughout the qal imperfect, e.g. וַתִּפֹּל < וַתִּנְפֹּל *and it (fire) fell* (1 Kings 18:38); וַיִּגַּשׁ < וַיִּנְגַּשׁ *and he drew near* (1 Kings 18:21; וַיִּקַּח < וַיִּלְקַח *and he took* (1 Kings 17:23).

It will be noted from the above examples that פ״ן verbs may form their qal imperfects either with the usual ˙ or with _ . See also the note on נתן below at (d).

This same process of assimilation also takes place in the nip‘al perfect and in both the perfect and imperfect of hip‘îl and hop‘al; e.g. נִבְּאוּ < נִנְבְּאוּ *they prophesied* (Jeremiah 2:8); הִנְגִּיד הִגִּיד < *he has told* (Micah 6:8); וַיַּבֵּט < וַיִּנְבֵּט *and he looked* (1 Kings 18:43); הֻגַּד < הֻנְגַּד *it was told* (1 Kings 18:13); < וַיִּנְגַּד וַיֻּגַּד *and it was told* (1 Kings 1:51).

(b) The *qal imperative*, as always, is based on the second person imperfect forms. In the case of imperfects in ˙ the assimilated nûn reappears in the imperative; so the imperative of נפל, based on תִּפֹּל *you fall*, is the quite regular form נְפֹל *fall!* For פ״ן verbs forming their imperfect in _ the assimilated nûn is usually dropped. So for נגשׁ the imperative masculine singular is גַּשׁ, based on תִּגַּשׁ *you draw near*; similarly from the plural form תִּגְּשׁוּ the imperative is גְּשׁוּ, as in 1 Kings 18:30. Cf. the imperative of לקח: קַח < תִּקַּח *take (m.s.)!*; קְחִי < תִּקְחִי *take (f.s.)!* (1 Kings 17:10), but note also the full form לִקְחִי in 1 Kings 17:11.

(c) The *qal infinitive construct*, which often reflects imperfect forms, makes a similar distinction between verbs forming their imperfects in ˙ or _ . Verbs forming their imperfect in ˙ follow the regular pattern of the strong verb; so נְפֹל / לִנְפֹּל from נפל *to fall.* Verbs forming their imperfect in _ and dropping the nûn in the imperative do the same here. Having dropped the nûn a ת is then added to the end of the two remaining consonants, and the form is pointed as a second declension noun; e.g. from נגשׁ: גֶּשֶׁת < גַּשְׁתְּ < ת + גַּשׁ *to draw near, a drawing near*, as in Numbers 8:19. With ל the infinitive appears as לָגֶשֶׁת, the ל pointed with ָ since it stands in an open pretone. Cf. also לָקַחַת *to take* (1 Kings 17:11); note that the pointing of the infinitive with ַ is dictated by the medial guttural ח. Cf. the infinitive construct of פ״ן verbs.

(d) Among the פ״ן verbs special note needs to be made of נתן *to give, set, appoint*, which having two nûns is doubly weak. In qal perfect the second nûn is assimilated into the afformatives; e.g. וְנָתַתִּי < וְנָתַנְתִּי *and I will place* (1 Kings 18:23). נתן, alone among the פ״ן verbs, forms its imperfect in ֵ : וַיִּתֵּן *and he gave* (1 Kings 19:21). In its imperative נתן drops the initial nûn: תֵּן *(m.s.)* and תְּנוּ *(m.pl.)*. The infinitive construct, however, is not תֶּנֶת but תֵּת, again because of the weakness of the nûn.

## 17 VERBS WITH LĀMED̲ HÊ [ל״ה]

While the verbs in this classification now end in ה (ל״ה), they originally ended in י (ל״י), and in some few cases in ו ( ל״ו ). Characteristic of these verbs is that in the course of inflection the ה is often replaced by the original י, and sometimes, depending on its position or accent, dropped altogether. These characteristics may be summarized as follows.

(a) When ה *is final*, the vowel preceding it is:

(i) ָה for all perfects; e.g. לא-הָיָה *there shall not be* (1 Kings 17:7) and חָלָה *he was sick* (1 Kings 17:17)

(ii) ֶה for all imperfects and participles in the absolute state; e.g. אִם-יִהְיֶה *if there shall be* (1 Kings 17:1); יִשְׁתֶּה *he will drink* and תִּשְׁתֶּה *you shall drink* (1 Kings 17:6 and 4); or the participle עֹנֶה *one (m.) answering* (1 Kings 18:26); note the feminine form of the participle, as in 1 Kings 18:44, עֹלָה *one (f.) going up.*

(iii) הֵ for all imperatives and participles in the construct state; e.g. עֲלֵה אֱכֹל וּשְׁתֵה *go up, eat and drink* (1 Kings 18:41); עֹשֵׂה שָׁמַיִם וָאָרֶץ *maker of heaven and earth* (Psalm 115:15), but cf. Psalm 146:6, עֹשֶׂה שָׁמַיִם וָאָרֶץ *the one making heaven and earth.*

(b) When ה *is not final:*

(i) *It drops out before vocalic afformatives*, except before the 3 f. s. perfect, where it is replaced by ת; e.g. the 3 m. pl. perfect of ענה is עָנוּ (cf. קָטְלוּ) *they answered* (1 Kings 18:21). Note also the imperatives עֲשִׂי do, make! (f. s.) and שְׁנוּ repeat! (1 Kings 17:13 and 18:34).

In the 3 f. s. perfect the ה is replaced by ת before the personal afformative הָ in order to distinguish it from the 3 m. s.; e.g. כָּלָה *it (m.) is spent*, but כָּלְתָה *it (f.) is spent* (as in 1 Kings 17:16, where the form occurs in pause).

(ii) *It becomes* י *before consonantal afformatives*, and is pointed:

- ִי in perfect active and hiṯpa'ēl forms,
- ֶי before נָה- in imperfect and imperative forms,
- ֵי in perfect nip'al and hop'al forms.

Note the following perfect forms: (qal) פָּנִיתָ *you turned* and עָשִׂיתִי *I did* (1 Kings 17:3 and 18:13); (pi'ēl) צִוִּיתִי *I commanded* (1 Kings 17:4); (nip'al) נִגְלֵיתִי *I was revealed, I revealed myself* (1 Samuel 2:27). Note the imperfect form with נָה- : תִּבְכֶּינָה *they weep* (Psalm 78:64).

(c) The *infinitive construct* replaces the final ה with וֹת; e.g. in qal: וַיַּעֲלֶה אַחְאָב לֶאֱכֹל וְלִשְׁתּוֹת *and Ahab went up to eat and to drink* (1 Kings 18:42); so also in nip'al: הֵרָאוֹת *to show himself, to appear* (1 Kings 18:2). The *infinitive absolute* usually follows the regular pattern of the strong verb (קָטֹל), although sometimes the final ה is not written; e.g. בָּכֹה or בכוֹ *weeping* (Psalm 126:6, Isaiah 30:19); שָׁתֹה or שָׁתוֹ *drinking* (Isaiah 21:5, Jeremiah 25:28), but once it appears as שָׁתוֹת in Isaiah 22:13, אָכֹל בָּשָׂר וְשָׁתוֹת יָיִן *eating flesh and drinking wine.*

(d) Because of the weakness of ה, especially in a final position, it sometimes disappears when the accent is shifted to the beginning of the word. When this happens there is also usually a modification in pointing as well. Such apocopation, or shortening, occurs chiefly with the jussive and vāv consecutive forms. For example, the regular qal imperfect of שׁתה occurs in 1 Kings 17:6, יִשְׁתֶּה *he drinks*; but in 1 Kings 19:6 the accent is drawn back because of the vāv consecutive, the ה is dropped, and the pointing modified: וַיֵּשְׁתְּ < וַיִּשְׁתְּ < וַיִּשְׁתֶּה < וַיִּשְׁתֶּה *and he drank.* Compare, however, 1 Kings 19:8 where וַיִּשְׁתֶּה remains unchanged despite the vāv consecutive, because the word is in pause with the accent on the last syllable. Note also יִהְיֶה *it happens* (1 Kings 17:1) and וַיְהִי *and it happened* (1 Kings 18:43); וַיַּעֲלֶה and וַיַּעַל *and he went up* (1 Kings 18:42 and 18:43); compare יִרְאֶה *he sees* with וַיַּרְא *and he saw* (1 Kings 19:3).

(e) The original י reappears in the qal passive participle, where it takes on its full consonantal force; so from עשׂה to do, make the qal passive participles are עָשׂוּי it (m.) is made and עֲשׂוּיָה it (f.) is made and in the plural, עֲשׂוּיִם and עֲשׂוּיוֹת; cf. קָטוּל and קְטוּלָה.

> In this connection note the nouns from ל״ה roots, such as פְּרִי fruit (from פרה) and חֳלִי sickness (from חלה). With afformatives the י regains its consonantal force; e.g. פִּרְיָהּ her fruit; חָלְיוֹ his sickness (1 Kings 17:17).

## 18 VERBS WITH PĒ YOḎ AND PĒ VĀV [פ״י and פ״ו]

Yôḏ appears as the first letter of many verb roots, but in only eight of these is it original; all the other verbs beginning in yôḏ originally began with vāv.

I. PĒ YOḎ VERBS [פ״י]. The eight פ״י verbs in biblical Hebrew are יבשׁ *to be dry,* יטב *to be pleasing, good,* ילל *to wail* (only in hip̄ʿîl), ימן *to go to the right* (only in hip̄ʿîl), ינק *to suck,* יצר *to form,* יקץ *to wake up,* and ישׁר *to be straight, upright.* These original פ״י verbs cause little difficulty, since most of the variations from the pattern of the strong verb result from the tendency of the yôḏ simply to quiesce with second class vowels.

(a) So it is that in the *qal imperfect*, which these verbs form with paṯaḥ, the yôḏ of the root quiesces with the ḥîreq of the preformatives; e.g. וַיִּיבַשׁ *and it dried up* 1 Kings 17:7). Note that while quiescent, the י is still written; occasionally, however, with the preformative of the 3 m. s. and pl. the two yôḏs are elided and written as one; e.g. וְיִקָץ (for the usual וְיִיקָץ) *and he will wake up* (1 Kings 18:27).

(b) Similarly, in the *hip̄ʿîl perfect and imperfect* the yôḏ quiesces with the preformatives, and the normal pointing is modified to ◌ֵ .

| | | |
|---|---|---|
| hip̄ʿîl perfect | הִיְנִיק > הֵינִיק | (cf. הִקְטִיל) |
| hip̄ʿîl imperfect | יַיְנִיק > יֵינִיק | (cf. יַקְטִיל) |

Note that יבשׁ *to be dry,* although a פ״י verb, follows a פ״ו analogy in the hip̄ʿîl, and appears as הוֹבִישׁ.

II. PĒ VĀV VERBS [פ״ו]. Most verbs beginning in yôḏ began originally in vāv. This original ו reappears in the prefixing stems: nip̄ʿal, hiṯpaʿēl, hip̄ʿîl and hop̄ʿal. The verb הלך *to go, walk* also belongs to this class. The characteristics of the

פ״ו verbs are summarized in the following.

(a) *Qal perfect and its participle* follow the regular pattern of the strong verb; e.g. יָדַעְתִּי *I know* (1 Kings 17:24) and וְיָשַׁבְתָּ *and you shall dwell* (1 Kings 17:9); יֹשֵׁב *one (who is) dwelling* (1 Kings 17:19) and יָרֵא *one fearing* (1 Kings 18:3).

(b) *Qal imperfect* takes two forms: one preserving the yôḏ and one dropping it.

(i) When the yôḏ is preserved, the verb is treated as a פ״י, and the initial י quiesces with the vowel of the preformative; e.g. וַיִּישַׁן *and he slept* (1 Kings 19:5) and אַל-תִּירְאִי *and be not afraid* (1 Kings 17:13).

(ii) When the initial yôḏ is dropped, the preformatives are pointed by compensation with ◌ֵ and the imperfect is formed with ◌ֵ (with ◌ַ before gutturals); e.g. (from הלך) אֵלֵךְ *I shall go* (1 Kings 18:12), וַיֵּצֵא *and he went out* (1 Kings 19:13); (from ידע) אֵדָע *I know* (a pausal form) (1 Kings 18:12), וְיֵדְעוּ *and they shall know* (1 Kings 18:37). Note that with vāv consecutive the accent is frequently pulled back to the beginning of the word with the result that the vowel of the last syllable, now closed and unaccented, is shortened; e.g. אֵלֵךְ *I shall go* (1 Kings 18:12), but with vav consecutive וַתֵּלֶךְ *and you went* (1 Kings 18:18).

(c) If the yôḏ is dropped in qal imperfect, it is also dropped in *qal imperative*; e.g. צֵא (from תֵּצֵא) *go out!* (1 Kings 19:11), וְרֵד (from תֵּרֵד) *and go down!* (1 Kings 18:44), לֵךְ (from תֵּלֵךְ) *go!* (1 Kings 17:39), לְכוּ (from תֵּלְכוּ) *go! (pl.)*. Often the masculine imperative singular is given more weight by the addition of ◌ָה; cf. שֵׁב and שְׁבָה *sit!*; רֵד and רְדָה *go down!*.

(d) If the yôḏ is dropped in the qal imperfect, it is also dropped in the *infinitive construct*. ת is added to the end of the two remaining consonants, and the form is pointed and treated as a second declension noun; cf. the infinitive construct of the פ״ן verbs. Note the following examples: לֶכֶת < לֵךְ (from הלך) *going, to go*; שֶׁבֶת < שֵׁב (from ישב) *dwelling, to dwell*; < דַּע דַּעַת (from ידע) *knowing, to know.* The ל prefix, if used, stands in a near open syllable, and so is pointed with ָ ; e.g. לָלֶכֶת *to go.*

(e) The original vāv reappears in stems formed by prefixed elements.

| | | |
|---|---|---|
| Nip'al perfect | נוֹתַרְתִּי | *I am left* (1 Kings 18:22) (cf. נִקְטַלְתִּי) |
| Nip'al imperfect | יִוָּדַע | *it will be known* (1 Kings 18:36) (cf. יִקָּטֵל) |
| Hiṯpa'ēl perfect | הִתְוַדַּע | *he made himself known* (Genesis 45:1) (cf. הִתְקַטֵּל) |
| Hip'îl perfect | הוֹשִׁיב | *he made to dwell* (Ezekiel 254) (cf. הִקְטִיל) |
| Hip'îl imperfect | יוֹשִׁיב | *he makes to dwell* (Genesis 47:11) (cf. יַקְטִיל) |
| Hop'al perfect | וְהוּשַׁבְתֶּם | *and you will make to dwell* (Isaiah 5:8) (cf. הָקְטַלְתֶּם) |
| Hop'al imperfect | תּוּשָׁב | *she shall be inhabited* (Isaiah 44:26) (cf. תָּקְטַל) |

(f) There are a few verbs beginning with yôḏ (and usually with צ as the second root letter) that act like פ״ן verbs, assimilating the yôḏ into the second letter by dāgēš fortē; e.g. (from יצת) וַתִּצַּת *and it [wickedness] kindled* (Isaiah 9:17). See also יצע *to spread*, יצק *to pour*, and יצר *to form.* Cf. יצב and נצב *to stand.*

## 19 VERBS WITH ‘AYIN VĀV AND ‘AYIN YOḎ [ע״ו and ע״י] (MIDDLE HOLLOW VERBS)

Verbs of this class are monosyllabic, having for their second letter a vocalic vāv or yōḏ. Because they have only two consonants instead of the usual three, only their first and third as it were, they are frequently called "middle hollow" verbs. Instead of the usual third masculine singular qal perfect form, the form cited as the root for these verbs is the actual infinitive construct; e.g. קוּם *to rise*, בּוֹא *to enter*, and שִׂים *to place, set.*

Because verbs with ע״ו and ע״י have only two consonants there are differences from the strong verb. These differences, however, are basically only adaptations of the patterns and forms of the strong verb. An outline of these variations follows.

(a) The *qal perfect* is usually pointed with *a vowels*: ָ when alone and with vocalic afformatives, and ַ with consonantal afformatives; e.g. קָם , קָמָה , קַמְתָּ , קַמְתְּ , קַמְתִּי , קָמוּ , קַמְתֶּם , קַמְתֶּן , and קַמְנוּ (from קוּם *to rise*); שָׂם , שָׂמָה , שַׂמְתָּ , etc. (from שִׂים *to set*); בָּא , בָּאָה , but בָּאתָ because of the quiescent א (from בּוֹא *to enter*). It will be noted that whatever the thematic vowel of the infinitive construct may be, the standard pointing for the qal perfect is with an *a vowel.* Occasionally, however, the qal perfect is formed with ֵ or ֹ ; e.g. מֵת *he died* (from מוּת ), but see 1 Kings 17:12, וָמָתְנוּ *and we shall die*; and בּוֹשׁ , בּוֹשָׁה , בֹּשְׁתָּ , etc. (from בּוֹשׁ *to be ashamed*).

(b) The qal participle masculine singular is identical with the qal third singular perfect form: בָּא *he entered*, or *one entering*. The feminine singular participle, בָּאָה *one (f.) entering*, is distinguishable from the qal third feminine singular only by the accent, בָּאָה *she entered*, since the tendency in these verbs is to retain the accent on the basic qal perfect form except for heavy endings and consecutive forms.

(c) The *qal imperfect* is formed with the thematic vowel of the infinitive construct. Thus the qal imperfect of קוּם *to rise*: יָקוּם , תָּקוּם , תָּקוּמִי , אָקוּם , יָקוּמוּ , etc.; or of בּוֹא *to enter*: יָבוֹא , תָּבוֹא , etc. Cf. אָשִׂים *I shall set* (1 Kings 18:23), יָשִׂימוּ *they will set* (1 Kings 18:23), and תָּשִׂימוּ *you (pl) will set* (1 Kings 18:25). Note that the preformative stands in an open pretone, and so is usually pointed with a tone long ָ (although sometimes with ֵ as in the case of יֵבוֹשׁ *he is ashamed*) It is important to remember that the thematic vowel of middle hollow verbs can be shortened, but never reduced to š$^{e}$vâ.

The *imperative* is regular, formed by dropping the second person personal prefixes; e.g. קוּם לֵךְ צָרְפַתָה *Rise, go to Ṣarep̱aṯ* (1 Kings 17:9); בֹּאִי עֲשִׂי כִדְבָרֵךְ *Go in, do according to your word* (1 Kings 17:13).

(d) In the *nip̱'al* middle hollow verbs have the thematic vowel וֹ .

> (i) The prefixed נ of the perfect is pointed with tone long ָ , as in נָקוֹם *it was raised* (cf. נִקְטַל ).
>
> (ii) The imperfect uses the regular pointing of the preformatives and assimilates the נ into the first radical by dāḡēš fortē, as in יִקּוֹם < יִנְקוֹם *it is raised* (cf. יִקָּטֵל ).

(e) The *hip̱'îl* has the regular thematic vowel ִי with the preformatives pointed with the tone long values of the strong verb form.

| | | |
|---|---|---|
| Hip̱'îl perfect | הֵמִית < הֵמִית *he killed* | (cf. הִקְטִיל ) |
| Hip̱'îl imperfect | יָמִית < יַמִית *he kills* | (cf. יַקְטִיל ) |

The *hop̱'al* follows a similar pattern, having its regular thematic vowel ַ with the preformatives pointed with šûreq, reflecting its usual third class vowel.

Hop'al perfect הוּקַם < הָקַם *it was established* (cf. הָקְטַל )

Hop'al imperfect יוּקַם < יָקַם *it is established* (cf. יָקְטַל )

The *causative participles* are based on the third masculine singular perfect forms with a prefixed מ: for hip'îl מֵקִים *(m.)* and מְקִימָה *(f.)*; for hop̱'al מוּקָם *(m.)* and מוּקָמָה *(f.)*. Inflection follows the first declension pattern.

(f) Frequently with vāv consecutive imperfect the accent is pulled back to the penult, thus leaving the last syllable closed and unaccented. Consequently, the long (thematic) vowel is shortened; e.g. אָשִׂים *I shall set* (1 Kings 18:23), but וַיָּשֶׂם *and he set* (1 Kings 18:33); יָשׁוּב *he returns*, but וַיָּשָׁב *and he returned* (1 Kings 19:6); יָרוּץ *he runs*, but וַיָּרָץ *and he ran* (1 Kings 18:46); יָלִיט (hip'îl of לוּט ) *he hides*, but וַיָּלֶט *and he hid* (1 Kings 19:13). Note that while the thematic vowel of a middle hollow verb may be shortened, it can never be reduced to š$^{e}$vâ.

(g) Since middle hollow verbs have no middle radical to double, they form their intensive-repetitive stems either by doubling the second radical, or less frequently by doubling both radicals.

Pôlēl (= pi'ēl) שׁוֹבֵב *he restored*; יְשׁוֹבֵב *he restores* (Psalm 23:3); [from שׁוּב].

Pôlal (= pu'al) שׁוֹבַב *he was restored*; [from שׁוּב].

Hiṯpôlēl (= hiṯpa'ēl) מִתְגּוֹר *one sojourning* (1 Kings 17:20); [a participle from גּוּר ].

Pilpēl (= pi'ēl) כִּלְכֵּל *he sustained*; יְכַלְכֵּל *he sustains* (cf. יְקַטֵּל ). See 1 Kings 18:4, וְכִלְכְּלָם *and he sustained them*, also 1 Kings 18:13, וָאֲכַלְכְּלֵם *and I sustained them*; [from כּוּל ].

**20 VERBS WITH ‘AYIN ‘AYIN [ע״ע] (DOUBLE ‘AYIN VERBS)**

The second and third radicals of this class of verbs are identical, and when possible are often written with only one letter (especially when there are no afformatives), or as one letter with dāgēš fortē; e.g. רַב *it was great, many* and רַבּוּ *they were great, many* (from רבב); but also סָבַב *he turned about* (from סבב). All three radicals are used when required, as in the intensive-repetitive stems, and often in the qal perfect third feminine singular and third common plural forms; e.g. סָבְבָה *she turned about* and סָבְבוּ *they turned about.*

(a) *Qal perfect* is pointed with ַ; e.g. רַב *it is many. Qal imperfect* is formed with ֹ and the preformative, standing in the near open syllable, is pointed with ָ; e.g. יָסֹב *he turns about* and יָסֹבּוּ *they turn about.* Note that the accent tends to remain on the basic form of the verb; cf. the middle hollow verbs. The qal imperfect of stative, or intransitive, verbs is formed with ַ and the preformatives are pointed with ֵ; e.g. יֵרַךְ *it is soft* (from רכך); cf. the strong verb יִכְבַּד *he is heavy.* The *imperative* is formed in the usual fashion, by dropping the second person prefix of the imperfect. [Note that sometimes in the qal imperfect of ע״ע verbs the preformative may be pointed with the usual ִ in which case the first radical, rather than the second is doubled; thus, the usual form is יָסֹב, but forms such as יִסֹּב occasionally occur.]

(b) *Connecting vowels* are used before consonantal afformatives. In perfect forms the connective is וֹ (or written dēfectīvē ֹ), as in 1 Samuel 22:22 סַבֹּתִי *I turned around.* In imperfect forms the connecting vowel is ֶי, as in תְּסֻבֶּינָה *they (f. pl.) turn around.*

(c) The *nip̄‘al perfect* is formed with the usual ַ, but the nûn of the stem, standing in the open pretone, is pointed with ָ

; e.g. נָסַב < נִסַּב *it was turned around* (cf. נִקְטַל). The *nip̄'al imperfect* is also formed with ַ, but the assimilation of the nûn of the stem and the pointing of the personal preformatives follow the usual pattern; e.g. יִסַּב < יִנְסַב *it is turned around* (cf. יִקָּטֵל).

(d) The *hip̄'îl perfect* is pointed with ֵ in the third person singular forms, but with the usual ִ and ַ elsewhere; the ה of the stem is pointed with a tone long ֵ, which is reduced to ֲ when distant open; e.g. הֵסֵב *he made to turn* (2 Kings 16:18) and הֵסַבּוּ *they made to turn* (1 Samuel 5:9); הֲרֵעוֹתָ *you have caused harm* (1 Kings 17:20). The *hip̄'îl imperfect* is formed with ֵ or ִ, and the preformatives are pointed with a tone long ָ, as in יָסֵב *he causes to turn* (cf. 1 Kings 21:4) and יָסֵבּוּ *they cause to turn* (cf. Judges 18:23).

(e) The *hop̄'al* reflects the regular hop'al pattern: הוּסַב *he was caused to turn* in the perfect and יוּסַב *he is caused to turn* in the imperfect.

(f) The *intensive-repetitive forms* follow the regular patterns of the strong verb. Frequently, however, alternative intensive forms are used, such as pô'ēl and hiṯpô'ēl (see under ע״ו and ע״י verbs, § 19); e.g. וַיִּתְמֹדֵד *and he stretched himself out* (1 Kings 17:21) and וַיִּתְגֹּדְדוּ *and they cut themselves* (1 Kings 18:28).

## 21 VERBS WITH PĒ GUTTURAL

*A preliminary note.* The forms of verbs with gutturals are simply modifications of the regular forms of the strong verb occasioned by the nature of the gutturals themselves. See § 2d above for a full discussion of their characteristics.. How gutturals affect the conjugation of the verb may be seen by comparing the third masculine singular and plural qal imperfect of the verb עמד *to stand* with קטל.

יַעֲמֹד[2] < יַעְמֹד[1] < יִעְמֹד = יִקְטֹל

יַעַמְדוּ[3] < יַעֲמְדוּ[2] < יַעְמְדוּ[1] < יִעְמְדוּ = יִקְטְלוּ

1 Gutturals prefer a vowels before them.
2 Gutturals prefer vocal š^e^vâ.
3 When two vocal š^e^vâs come together and one is a composite, the first becomes the short vowel of the composite.

(a) The *qal perfect* and all the *intensive-repetitive stems* of verbs with Pē Guttural follow the regular strong verb, there being no modification necessary, because in these stems the initial guttural carries a full vowel; e.g. עָבַר *he passed through*, הֲרַגְתָּ *you killed*, חָדְלוּ *they desisted*, חִשֵּׁב *he considered*, עֻבַּד *it was worked*, הִתְחַדֵּשׁ *he renewed himself*, and so on.

In all the other stems (except nip'al imperfect, see below), namely *qal imperfect*, *nip̱'al perfect*, and both the *perfect and imperfect of hip̱'îl and hop̱'al*, wherever the initial root letter is pointed with silent š^e^vâ, the gutteural's preference for vocal instead of silent š^e^vâ as well as the tendency to modify a short ◌ִ to ◌ֶ are fully at work; e.g. אֶעֱבֹר (cf. אֶקְטֹל) *I pass through*, נֶעֱבַדְתֶּם (cf. נִקְטַלְתֶּם) *you are tilled*, הֶחֱרִיב (cf. הִקְטִיל) *he laid waste*, יַעֲמִיד (cf. יַקְטִיל) *he makes to stand up*, יָעֳמַד (cf. יָקְטַל) *it is made to stand up*. Note, however, that even here ח often retains the usual silent š^e^vâ; e.g. לֹא תֶחְסַר *it will not lack* (1 Kings 17:14) and וָאַחְבִּא *and I hid* (1 Kings 18:13).

(b) In *qal imperfect* verbs that form their imperfect in ◌ֹ (usually transitive) point the preformatives with ◌ַ; e.g. וַיַּעֲמֹד *and he stood* (1 Kings 19:13). Verbs that form their imperfects in ◌ַ (usually intransitive) point the preformatives with ◌ֶ (originally ◌ִ); e.g. לֹא תֶחְסַר *it will not lack* (1 Kings 17:14).

(c) In the *nip̱'al imperfect, imperative and infinitive*, because gutturals and ר cannot take dāgēš fortē, the preceding short vowel is raised to its tone long; e.g. יֵהָבֵא < יִחָבֵא (cf. יִקָּטֵל ) *he is hidden*; see also the imperative of ראה in 1 Kings 18:1, הֵרָאֵה *show yourself! / appear!*

## 22 VERBS WITH PĒ 'ĀLEP̱ [פ״א]

A sub-class of the Pe Gutturals, there are only five Pē 'Ālep verbs in biblical Hebrew: אבד *to perish*, אבה *to be willing*, אכל *to eat*, אמר *to say*, and אפה *to bake*. These verbs are exactly the same as the Pē Guttural verbs except in the *qal imperfect*.

(a) The א after the preformative is quiescent, and the imperfect preformatives are pointed with ˙ ; e.g. יֹאמַר *he says*. Note that in the first common singular only one א is written: אֹמַר *I say*

(b) The *imperfect* is formed with _ , which often in pause becomes .. ; e.g. וַתֹּאכַל *and she ate* (1 Kings 17:15), וַיֹּאכֵלוּ *and they ate* (1 Kings 19:21), וַיֹּאמֶר *and he said* (1 Kings 17:1).

(c) Although the imperfect is with _ , the *imperative and infinitive construct* are with the usual ˙ ; e.g. אֱכֹל *eat!* (1 Kings 18:8) and לֶאֱכֹל *to eat* (1 Kings 18:42); אֱמֹר *say!* (1 Kings 18:8) and לֵאמֹר *to say, saying* (1 Kings 17:2).

## 23 VERBS WITH 'AYIN GUTTURAL

(a) The gutturals' preference for a vowels can be seen in the *qal imperfects*, which are usually formed with _ ; e.g. יִבְחַר *he chooses*. Similarly, the *pi'ēl perfect* often has _ instead of the usual .. ; e.g. נִחַם (cf. קִטֵּל ) *he comforted*, בֵּרַךְ and בֵּרֵךְ *he blessed*.

(b) When vocal šᵉvâ is required, gutturals must use a composite šᵉvâ; e.g. וְיִבְחֲרוּ *and they choose* (1 Kings 18:23).

(c) Gutturals and ר cannot take dāgēš fortē, and so in the *intensive-repetitive stems* compensation (by raising the preceding short vowel to its tone long) is always made for ר , and occasionally for א , but hardly ever for ה , ח , and ע , for which the pointing remains unchanged, the dāgēš fortē's being understood as implicit (*dāgēš fortē implicitum*). Note the following examples: בֵּרַךְ and יְבָרֵךְ *he blessed* and *he blesses*; מֵאֵן and יְמָאֵן *he refused* and *he refuses*; but בִּעֵר and יְבַעֵר *he burned* and *he burns* (cf. קִטֵּל and יְקַטֵּל ). See § 13 above.

**24 VERBS WITH LĀMED̲ GUTTURAL**

The governing principle for these verbs is that a final guttural requires an *a* vowel; cf. Lāmed̲ 'Ālep̲ below.

(a) The ˙ of the *qal imperfect* and the .. of the *nip̄'al imperfect, the pi'ēl and hit̲pa'ēl perfect and imperfect* stems are all usually modified to _ . Only in the infinitive absolute, the qal infinitive construct, the participles, and some pausal forms do the usual ˙ and .. appear. Thus, the qal imperfect vav consecutive of שמע *to hear* is וַיִּשְׁמַע *and he heard* (1 Kings 17:22), but the infinitive construct is כְּשְׁמֹעַ *when [Elijah] heard* (1 Kings 19:13). Cf. also תִּמְשַׁח *you will anoint* (1 Kings 19:16); וַיִּשְׁלַח *and he sent* (1 Kings 18:20); שְׁלַח *send!* (1 Kings 19:5); note also the participle שֹׁלֵחַ *one sending.*

(b) Final gutturals preceded by unchangeable long vowels of the second or third class require a *furtive pat̲ah̩*; e.g. וְהִשְׁבִּיעַ *and I make to swear* (1 Kings 18:10); נֹגֵעַ *one touching* (1 Kings 19:5); and כְּשְׁמֹעַ *while hearing* (1 Kings 19:13).

(c) An extension of this principle applies to the second person feminine singular perfect forms, where a helping _ is placed before the ת afformative without, however, affecting the accent or the rest of the pointing; e.g. שָׁלַחַת < שָׁלַחְתְּ (cf. קָטַלְתְּ ) *you (f.) send.*

## 25 VERBS WITH LĀMED ʼALEP [ל״א]

(a) Because א at the end of a syllable is quiescent, the preceding vowel is lengthened; e.g. מָצָא instead of מָצַא (cf. קָטַל).

(b) *Qal perfect active and qal imperfect active and stative* are formed with ָ throughout; e.g. חָטָאתִי *I have sinned* (1 Kings 18:9); וּקְרָאתֶם *and you shall call* (1 Kings 18:24); וַיִּמְצָא *and he found* (1 Kings 19:19); נִמְצָא *we found* (1 Kings 18:5); וַיִּקְרָא and he called (1 Kings 17:10).

(c) *Qal perfect statives and all other perfect stems* are formed with ֵ; e.g. מָלֵאתָ *you are full*; מִלֵּא *he filled* (1 Kings 18:35); קִנֵּאתִי *I have been zealous* (1 Kings 19:10); מֻצֵּאתָ *you have been found*, the puʻal of מצא.

(d) All *imperfects and imperatives* have ֶ before the feminine plural afformative, -נָה ; e.g. תִּמְצֶאנָה *you (f. pl.) find.*

(e) Occasionally a quiescent א is not written; so, for example, מָצָתִי for מָצָאתִי in לֹא-מָצָתִי חֵן בְּעֵינֶיךָ *I have not found favor in your eyes* (Numbers 11:11).

---

Note that many verbs are a combination of weak letters and gutturals. This is seen primarily in the first and third radicals of the root, especially with פ״ן , פ״ו and Pē Guttural verbs in combination with ל״ה and ל״א; e.g. נכה and נשׂא , יצא and 2סוֹ , ענה and חבא . Such verbs show the characteristics of both classes of variations from the strong verb. A knowledge, however, of the basic structure of the stems and the general characteristics of weak letters and gutturals will guide one through these more complex forms.

---

# NOTES ON HEBREW SYNTAX

While the following *Notes on Hebrew Syntax* are a systematic presentation of the basics of Hebrew expression--how nouns and verbs and sentences operate, they are not intended to cover all aspects of the subject, but are designed to provide students with the kind of knowledge and approach that will help them deal with the biblical text on its own terms.

It is with this concern in view, that the traditional categories and terms used in standard treatments of Hebrew syntax have as much as possible been avoided, especially in the discussion of clauses and sentences. This has been done because these traditional terms and categories are derived primarily from the study of Greek, Latin and English; and while they reflect a language structure appropriate for these languages, it is one that is essentially foreign to Hebrew. Consequently, to use such terms and categories in the study of biblical Hebrew can only hamper students in catching the feel of Hebrew expression, and deprive them of the challenge and excitement of understanding the Hebrew writers in the way they expressed themselves.

For details and concerns which go beyond these Notes, students are referred to Gesenius-Kautzsch-Cowley, *Gesenius' Hebrew Grammar* (Oxford, $1910^2$), which despite its age still remains the basic reference grammar for biblical Hebrew. Its strength, as James Barr has observed (*Encyclopedia Judaica*, XVI, 1396), is "its genius for detail and comprehensive empirical observation; his [Gesenius'] approach was sober and avoided speculation." "Yet," Barr also notes, "the empirical accuracy of Gesenius' work does not conceal the fact that his conceptual terminology was often unsuited to the subject." This difficulty, as noted above, is found in most grammars and treatments of Hebrew, and allowances must be made when using them.

Less exhaustive than Gesenius, but of the same character, is A. B. Davidson, *Hebrew Syntax* (London, 1901[3]). Very helpful, especially to beginning students is Ronald J. Williams, *Hebrew Syntax: An Outline* (Toronto, 1976[2]), a work which reflects the same linguistic tradition, but makes some important modifications in understandings and terminology.

Pertinent references to these works and to this grammar are made at the beginning of each of the sections of *Notes on Hebrew Syntax.*

---------------------

## 26 THE NOUN AND THE DEFINITE ARTICLE

For general matters of gender and number, construct, apposition and the like see *An Introduction to Biblical Hebrew*, §§ 13-14, 23-24, and *A Summary of Hebrew Grammar*, § 5; Gesenius-Kautzsch, §§ 122-124, 128-131; Davidson, §§ 12-18; and Williams §§ 1-72. The notes here deal primarily with the noun as definite and its use with the article. Further details are in Gesenius-Kautzsch, §§ 125-127; Davidson, §§ 19-22; and Williams, 82-93. Note that *An Introduction*, § 19, and *A Summary*, § 6, deal only with the ה of the article and its pointing.

(a) There is no indefinite article, "a" and "an," in Hebrew. A noun without the definite article, therefore, is usually considered indefinite.

(b) Some nominal forms, however, are definite even without the article, because of being definite in themselves, such as pronouns and proper names, or because of composition. Proper names are, of course, definite because they refer to specific persons, places, or groups. Some proper names, it may be noted, were originally appellatives with the article and even as proper names retain the article; e.g. הַגָּלִיל *the Galilee* [= the circuit/district]; הָעַי the Ai [= the ruin]; הַכַּרְמֶל *the Carmel* [= the fertile land; cf. כֶּרֶם ]; הַיַּרְדֵּן *the Jordan* [= the river]. It is interesting to note that Job 40:23 is the only place that יַרְדֵּן appears without the article, and standing in parallel to נָהָר, also without an article, probably means simply *river*. In this connection note that נָהָר and יְאֹר both mean *a river*, but with the definite article they denote specific rivers, namely, the Euphrates and the Nile, respectively.

Pronouns are also definite in themselves, pointing as they do to specific persons and things. Consequently, nouns with pronominal suffixes are also definite, and so do not take a definite article; e.g. הַדָּבָר *the word*, but דְּבָרִי *my word* (1 Kings 17:1); cf. מֵחֵיקָהּ *from her bosom* (1 Kings 17:19).

Nouns in construct cannot take a definite article. If the final member of the construct relation is definite, the whole construction is definite; so, for example, דְּבַר יהוה is not *a word of Yahveh*, but *the word of Yahveh*; or again, בֶּן-הָאִשָּׁה is not *a son of the woman*, but the *son of the woman* (1 Kings 17:17). To say *a son of the woman* one must use a construction such as בֵּן לָאִשָּׁה *(lit.) a son to the woman.*

(c) The use of the article in Hebrew is generally the same as in English: to make a noun definite and specific. At the same time, Hebrew often uses the article where English does not.

(i) Hebrew uses the definite article in a number of stock phrases or idioms, where English would use a demonstrative or adverbial form; e.g. הַיּוֹם *today (lit. the day)* (1 Kings 18:15). Cf also הַלַּיְלָה *tonight* (Genesis 19:34); הַשָּׁנָה *this year* (Isaiah 37:30); and הַפַּעַם *this time* (Genesis 18:32).

(ii) The article is often used with persons and things thought of as specific and definite, although not yet introduced as known in the text. This happens especially in the course of narrative, as in 1 Kings 17:12: כַּף-קֶמַח בַּכַּד וּמְעַט-שֶׁמֶן בַּצַּפַּחַת *a handful of flour in the jar and a bit of oil in the flask*, where English would usually say simply "in a jar" and "in a flask."

(iii) There is frequent use of the definite article with classes of persons or things, and even of abstract ideas, where English would use no article at all. Note the following examples: בָּאֵשׁ *with fire* (Joshua 11:9); בַּשֶּׁמֶן *with oil* (Psalm 23:5); הָעֹרְבִים *ravens* (1 Kings 17:4); הָאֲרִי . . . הַדֹּב *a lion . . .a bear* (Amos 5:19); כַּשָּׁנִים כַּשֶּׁלֶג *like scarlet, like snow* (Isaiah 1:18); וְהָאֱמוּנָה *and faithfulness* (Isaiah 11:5; no doubt צֶדֶק in the half-line before should also have the article, its having been lost through haplography).

(iv) A distinctive use of the article is its possible function as a vocative; e.g. הוֹשִׁעָה הַמֶּלֶךְ *Save, [O] king!* (2 Samuel 14:4). Cf. also 1 Kings 18:26, where the prophets of Ba'al call out, הַבַּעַל עֲנֵנוּ *[O] Ba'al, answer us!*, although it should be noted that the article is used with אֱלֹהִים and בַּעַל elsewhere in the immediate context where clearly no vocative is intended.

(d) Despite the wide use of the article in Hebrew, it is often omitted where one would expect it. This is especially the case in poetry; e.g. אַפְסֵי-אָרֶץ *[the] ends of [the] earth* (Psalm 2:8); עִם-שָׁמֶשׁ *with [the] sun* and לִפְנֵי יָרֵחַ *before [the] moon* (Psalm 72:5). It is also sometimes omitted when a noun or an adjective has virtually become a proper name, as with אֱלֹהִים *God (= Yahveh)* or קָדוֹשׁ, as in Isaiah 40:25, where it clearly means the Holy One.

## 27 THE ADJECTIVE

See also *An Introduction*, § 21; Gesenius-Kautzsch, §§ 132-133; Davidson, §§ 30-34; and Williams, §§ 73-81.

(a) Adjectives in Hebrew may be used in two ways: as a qualifying adjective and as a predicate adjective. The *qualifying adjective* always follows the noun it modifies, and agrees with it in gender and number. Because the adjective has no dual form, a plural form is used with dual nouns. If the noun is definite, the adjective must also be definite, and have an article. If more than one adjective is used with a definite noun, each adjective must also be definite and each have an article. Note the following examples: הַנָּהָר הַגָּדוֹל *the great river* (Deuteronomy 1:7); לִפְקֹחַ עֵינַיִם עִוְרוֹת *to open blind eyes* (Isaiah 42:7); אֵל רַחוּם וְחַנּוּן *a gracious and merciful God* (Exodus 34:6); מֵי הַנָּהָר הָעֲצוּמִים וְהָרַבִּים *the mighty and plenteous waters of the River (= the Euphrates)* (Isaiah 8:7).

When the demonstratives, *this* and *that*, are used in a qualifying position, they also take the article, follow the noun, and in a series stand last. Note the following examples: בָּהָר הַזֶּה *at this mountain* (Deuteronomy 1:6); בַּיָּמִים הָהֵם *in those days* (Isaiah 38:1); כָּל-הַמִּדְבָּר הַגָּדוֹל וְהַנּוֹרָא הַהוּא *all that great and terrible wilderness* (Deuteronomy 1:19).

An adjective modifying a noun in construct follows the whole expression and, while agreeing in gender and number with the noun it modifies, is in the absolute state; e.g. וְלַהַב אֵשׁ אוֹכֵלָה *and a flame of devouring fire* (Isaiah 29:6); וַעֲטֶרֶת זָהָב גְּדוֹלָה *and a great crown of gold* (Esther 8:15). If the final noun in the construct is definite, the whole expression is definite, and so any adjective modifying any noun in the expression must take the article; e.g. יוֹם יהוה הַגָּדוֹל וְהַנּוֹרָא *the great and terrible day of Yahveh* (Malachi 3:23); בַּת-בָּבֶל הַשְּׁדוּדָה *the devastated daughter of Babylon* (Psalm 137:8).

(b) *Predicate adjectives*, like qualifying adjectives, agree in gender and number with the subject; e.g. גָּדוֹל יהוה *great is Yahveh* (Psalm 48:1); טוֹב הַדָּבָר *the word is good* (1 Kings 18:24); תּוֹרַת יהוה תְּמִימָה *the instruction of Yahveh is perfect* (Psalm 19:8); פִּקּוּדֵי יהוה יְשָׁרִים *the precepts of Yahveh are upright* (Psalm 19:9); כִּי טֹבֹת הֵנָּה *that they are fair* (Genesis 6:2). Upon occasion, however, especially when the adjective comes first, this agreement is not always maintained, e.g. יָשָׁר מִשְׁפָּטֶיךָ *upright are your judgments* (Psalm 119:137), unless the ם of the plural has been lost by haplography.

The predicate adjective is normally without the article, even when the subject is definite. The usual position of the predicate adjective is before the subject, but in this, as elsewhere in matters of word order, there is considerable variation; cf. thc examples above.

(c) There is no *comparison of adjectives* in Hebrew as in English: "great, greater, greatest." The comparative degree may be implied from the context, as in Genesis 1:16, where God makes אֶת-שְׁנֵי הַמְּאֹרֹת הַגְּדֹלִים *the two great lights*, and then they are spoken of as הַמָּאוֹר הַגָּדֹל *the great kight* [NRSV: *the greater light*] and הַמָּאוֹר הַקָּטֹן *the small light* [NRSV: *the lesser light*]. Usually, however, the comparative degree is expressed by the adjective followed by the preposition מִן ; e.g. כִּי-לֹא טוֹב אָנֹכִי מֵאֲבֹתָי *(lit.) for not good (am) I from my fathers, that is, I am not better than my fathers* (1 Kings 19:5); גּוֹיִם גְּדֹלִים וַעֲצֻמִים מִכֶּם *nations great[er] and [more] powerful than you* (Deuteronomy 11:23).

The superlative degree may be expressed in a variety of ways. Most simply it is expressed by the adjective and the article; e.g. דָּוִד הוּא הַקָּטָן *David was the small one* [NRSV: *the youngest*] (1 Samuel 17:14). Note the combination of the comparative and superlative degrees in Deuteronomy 7:7: לֹא מֵרֻבְּכֶם מִכָּל-הָעַמִּים *(lit.) not from your being numerous from all the peoples, that is, not because you are more numerous than all the peoples*, and then at the end of the verse, כִּי-אַתֶּם הַמְעַט מִכָּל-הָעַמִּים *(lit.) for you are the few from all the peoples*, that is, *for you are the fewest of all the peoples.* The superlative may also be expressed by the repetition of the word in a construct relation; e.g. שִׁיר הַשִּׁירִים *the song of songs*, that is, the song *par excellence*; בֵּין הַקֹּדֶשׁ וּבֵין קֹדֶשׁ הַקֳּדָשִׁים *between the holy (place) and the holy of holies*, that is, *the holiest* (Exodus 26:33). Simple repetition may also express the superlative, e.g. קָדוֹשׁ קָדוֹשׁ קָדוֹשׁ *holy, holy, holy*, that is, the thrice Holy One, the absolutely Holy One (Isaiah 6:3).

Note also the use of מְאֹד *very (lit., muchness)* and its intensification by the preposition עַד *unto, to*; e.g. וַיְהִי חָלְיוֹ חָזָק מְאֹד *and his sickness was very strong* (1 Kings 17:17); כִּי-יָפָה הִיא מְאֹד *for she was very beautiful* (Genesis 12:14); וְהַנַּעֲרָה יָפָה עַד-מְאֹד *and the maiden was very beautiful* (1 Kings 1:4).

A similar intensification of degree, expressing what is extraordinary, is achieved by using אֵל and אֱלֹהִים in construct with what is being described; e.g. אַרְזֵי אֵל *(lit.) cedars of God*, that is, *mighty cedars* (Psalm 80:11); כְּהַרְרֵי-אֵל ‖ תְּהוֹם רַבָּה *(lit.) mountains of God ‖ (the) great deep*, expressing the extremes of height and depth (Psalm 36:7); cf. הַר-אֱלֹהִים ‖ הַר גַּבְנֻנִּים *mountain of God ‖ mountain of many peaks* (Psalm 68:16).

(d) Adjectives are often used as nouns; e.g. וְצַדִּיק בֶּאֱמוּנָתוֹ יִחְיֶה *and a righteous one by his faithfulness lives* (Habakkuk 2:4); דֶּרֶךְ צַדִּיקִים ‖ דֶּרֶךְ רְשָׁעִים *way of righteous ones ‖ way of wicked ones* (Psalm 1:6). Note also the description of Yahveh as "the Holy One," e.g. the very frequent epithet קְדוֹשׁ יִשְׂרָאֵל *the Holy One of Israel* (Isaiah 1:4); cf. also קְדוֹשׁ יַעֲקֹב *the Holy One of Jacob* (Isaiah 29:23) and אֲנִי יהוה קְדוֹשְׁכֶם *I am Yahveh, your Holy One* (Isaiah 43:15). קָדוֹשׁ alone and without the article stands as a designation for God in Isaiah 40:25, יֹאמַר קָדוֹשׁ *says [the] Holy One.*

## 28 NUMERALS

See also Gesenius-Kautzsch, §§ 97-98, 134; Davidson, §§ 35-38; and Williams, §§ 94-105.

Numerals 1 and 2 are nominal forms, both adjective and noun, and agree in gender and number with the noun enumerated. Numerals 3 to 10 are nouns with both a masculine and feminine form, which in appearance, however, seem not to agree with the noun enumerated.

| | Masculine Absolute | Masculine Construct | Feminine Absolute | Feminine Construct |
|---|---|---|---|---|
| 1 | אֶחָד | אַחַד | אַהַת | אַחַת |
| 2 | שְׁנַיִם | שְׁנֵי | שְׁתַּיִם | שְׁתֵּי |
| 3 | שְׁלֹשָׁה | שְׁלֹשֶׁת | שָׁלֹשׁ | שְׁלֹשׁ |
| 4 | אַרְבָּעָה | אַרְבַּעַת | אַרְבַּע | אַרְבַּע |
| 5 | חֲמִשָּׁה | חֲמֵשֶׁת | חָמֵשׁ | חֲמֵשׁ |
| 6 | שִׁשָּׁה | שֵׁשֶׁת | שֵׁשׁ | שֵׁשׁ |
| 7 | שִׁבְה | שִׁבְעַת | שֶׁבַע | שְׁבַע |
| 8 | שְׁמֹנָה | שְׁמֹנַת | שְׁמֹנֶה | שְׁמֹנֶה |
| 9 | תִּשְׁעָה | תִּשְׁעַת | תֵּשַׁע | תְּשַׁע |
| 10 | עֲשָׂרָ | עֲשֶׂרֶת | עֶשֶׂר | עֶשֶׂר |

Numbers 11 to 19 are compounds, combining the units 1 to 9 with 10, עָשָׂר for masculine and עֶשְׂרֵה for feminine. See the following chart, noting the variations for 11 and 12.

| | Masculine | Feminine |
|---|---|---|
| 11 | אַחַד עָשָׂר | אַחַת עֶשְׂרֵה |
| | עַשְׁתֵּי עָשָׂר | עַשְׁתֵּי עֶשְׂרֵה |
| 12 | שְׁנֵים עָשָׂר | שְׁתֵּים עֶשְׂרֵה |
| | שְׁנֵי עָשָׂר | שְׁתֵּי עֶשְׂרֵה |
| 13 | שְׁלֹשָׁה עָשָׂר | שְׁלֹשׁ עֶשְׂרֵה |
| 14 | אַרְבָּעָה עָשָׂר | אַרְבַּע עֶשְׂרֵה |
| 15 | חֲמִשָּׁה עָשָׂר | חֲמֵשׁ עֶשְׂרֵה |
| 16 | שִׁשָּׁה עָשָׂר | שֵׁשׁ עֶשְׂרֵה |
| 17 | שִׁבְעָה עָשָׂר | שְׁבַע עֶשְׂרֵה |
| 18 | שְׁמֹנָת עָשָׂר | שְׁמֹנֶה עֶשְׂרֵה |
| 19 | תִּשְׁעָה עָשָׂר | תְּשַׁע עֶשְׂרֵה |

The numbers 20 to 99 are combinations of tens and the units 1 to 9. The tens are simply the plural forms of the units: עֶשְׂרִים = 20, שְׁלֹשִׁים = 30, and so on. The individual units are connected to the tens by וְ. The indiviudal unit may stand either before or after the ten, e.g. either חָמֵשׁ וּשְׁלֹשִׁים or שְׁלֹשִׁים וְחָמֵשׁ = 35.

For 100 to 900 forms of מֵאָה are used: מֵאָה = 100; מָאתַיִם (dual) = 200; שְׁלוֹשׁ מֵאוֹת = 300, and so on. A similar pattern is followed for the thousands: אֶלֶף = 1000; אַלְפַּיִם (dual) = 200; שְׁלֹשֶׁת אֲלָפִים = 3000, and so on; cf. שִׁבְעַת אֲלָפִים 7000 (1 Kings 19:18). In the same way רְבָבָה = 10,000; רִבּוֹתַיִם (dual) = 20,000; שְׁלֹשׁ רְבָבוֹת = 30,000, and so on.

The numeral 1 is an adjective and usually stands after its noun; e.g. הַפָּר הָאֶחָד *one bull* (1 Kings 18:23); כְּאִישׁ אֶחָד *as one man* (Judges 20:8); שָׁנָה אַחַת *one year* (2 Kings 8:26; but cf. שְׁנַיִם עֵצִים *two sticks* (1 Kings 17:12); שְׁנַיִם פָּרִים *two bulls* (1 Kings 18:23); שְׁנֵי בָנִים *two sons* (Genesis 10:25); שְׁתַּיִם נָשִׁים *two women* (Zechariah 5:9); שְׁתֵּי בָנוֹת *two daughters* (Genesis 19:8). Note that both the numerals, 1 and 2, agree in gender and number with the noun enumerated.

All numerals from 3 to 10 may stand in the construct before the noun enumerated, or they may stand in the absolute either before or after the word enumerated as words in apposition. In Job 1:2, for example, the enumeration of Job's children, שִׁבְעָה בָנִים וְשָׁלוֹשׁ בָּנוֹת, could also be written with no difference in meaning, בָּנִים שִׁבעָה וּבָנוֹת שָׁלוֹשׁ, or in a construct relation, שִׁבְעַת בָּנִים וּשְׁלוֹשׁ בָּנוֹת. Cf. אַרְבָּעָה כַדִּים *4 pots* (1 Kings 18:34).

From 11 to 19 the numerals usually stand before the noun, and (except for some common nouns like יוֹם, שָׁנָה, אִישׁ, and נֶפֶשׁ) the noun is usually in the plural; e.g. שְׁתֵּים עֶשְׂרֵה אֲבָנִים *twelve stones* (1 Kings 18:34); שְׁנֵים-עָשָׂר צְמָדִים *twelve yokes* (1 Kings 19:19); but אַרְבָּעָה יוֹם *14 days* (1 Kings 8:65); וְשֵׁשׁ-עֶשְׂרֵה שָׁנָה *and 16 years* (2 Kings 16:2). For 20 and on, if the object numbered stands before the number, it is in the plural, but if it stands after the number, it is usually in the singular.

(a) Numerals are given a *distributive* meaning by simple repetition, occasionally joined by ו ; e.g. שְׁנַיִם שְׁנַיִם *by twos* (Genesis 7:9); חֲמִשִּׁים חֲמִשִּׁים *by fifties* (1 Kings 18:13; cf. v. 4); שֵׁשׁ כְּנָפַיִם שֵׁשׁ כְּנָפַיִם לְאֶחָד *six wings to each* (Isaiah 6:2); שֵׁשׁ וָשֵׁשׁ *six each* (2 Samuel 21:20).

(b) A *multiplicative* use (to indicate the number of times somethiong occurs) may be expressed simply by the numeral; e.g. כִּי שֶׁבַע יִפּוֹל צַדִּיק וָקָם *for seven [times] a righteous one will fall and rise* (Proverbs 24:16). More often, however, the number is combined with פַּעַם *beat, foot, occurrence*; e.g. שָׁלוֹשׁ פְּעָמִים *three times* (1 Kings 17:21); שֶׁבַע פְּעָמִים *seven times* (1 Kings 18:43).

(c) Special forms for the *ordinals* are used only for 1 to 10, that is for the first to the tenth. The ordinal for 1 is רִאשׁוֹן and רִאשׁוֹנָה for masculine and feminine respectively. The ordinals for 2 to 10 are based on the cardinals to which are added ִי for the masculine and ִית (occasionally ִיָּה ) for feminine, with the insertion of י between the second and third radicals of the cardinal; e.g. שֵׁנִי and שֵׁנִית *second (m. and f.)*; שְׁלִישִׁי and שְׁלִישִׁית *third (m. and f.)*. The ordinals are used as regular adjectives; e.g. בַּשָּׁנָה הַשְּׁלִישִׁית *in the third year* (1 Kings 18:1), often with the noun understood as in בַּשְּׁבִעִית *at the seventh [time]* (1 Kings 18:44). For ordinals of numbers higher than 10 the regular cardinal numerals are used; e.g. בְּאַרְבָּעִים שָׁנָה *in the fortieth year* (Deuteronomy 1:3); וְהוּא בִּשְׁנֵים הֶעָשָׂר *and he was with the twelfth* (1 Kings 19:19).

(d) A Note on Writing Numbers. Symbols for representing numbers are known from the very beginning of writing in the ancient Near East, and these were used throughout the biblical times. Considerably later, when the alphabet was fixed in number and order, numerical values were given to the individual letters, so that these, too, could be used to represent numerals. This apparently happened about the second century B. C. E. during the Hasmonean rule.

So it was that א to י came to = 1 to 10; and then כ came to = 20, ל = 30, and so on. See the chart of the alphabet in *An Introduction*, § 2, and *A Summary*, § 2. For the intervening numbers the tens are combined with the individual units; e.g. 11 = יא , 12 = יב , 33 = לג , and so on. Note, however, that following this procedure the numbers 15 and 16 would form parts of the Divine Name, יה and יו ; to avoid this 15 is written טו (9+6) and 16 is טז (9+7). An abbreviation sign is often used after a single letter or before the last lettert of a compound numerical form to indicate the letters are being used as numbers; e.g. ו״ *6*; כ״ד *24*.

For numbers above 100, the appropriate hundred letter beginning with ק = 100 is used; e.g. 145 = קמ״ה; 415 = ת״טו . With ת (= 400) the end of the alphabet is reached, and so for numbers above the 400s combinations must be used; e.g. 746 = תשמ״ו (400+300+40+6); 1074 = תתרע״ד (400+400+200+70+4). To simplify the writing of dates, the thousands are generally omitted. So the year in which this grammar was completed, 1993, would be written תתקץ״ג (400+400+100+90+3 = [1]993). Traditional Jewish chronology begins with the creation of the world. Rabbinical tradition sets this as 3760 B.C.E, and so the year 1993 would be 5753 in Jewish tradition and written תשן״ג.

Giving numerical values to the letters of the alphabet forms the basis for the very popular exegetical method known as *gematria*, by which a secret meaning of a text is sought through the numerical values of the words. Hence it is said among some that there are 611 commandments in the Tôrâ, this being the sum of the letters, תורה (400+6+200+5 = 611). Or, again, the number of 318 men born in the house of Abraham (Genesis 14:14) is derived from the name of Eliezer, Abraham's steward and heir (Genesis 15:2), which adds up to 318. The numerical value of הַשָּׂטָן *the satan, accuser* is 364, which is said to mean that there is one day of the year in which the Satan has no power, namely Yom Kippur. Whether engaged in seriously or playfully, gematria was a challenge to piety and imagination. Of course, it could lead to various and often conflicting results, as the discussions among the rabbis abundantly show. It was a method, however, very common throughout the Hellenistic world (perhaps even begun by the Greeks), and also popular among the early Christians. No doubt the most famous and debated biblical example is the number 666 in the book of Revelation.

## 29 THE PERFECT AND IMPERFECT FORMS OF THE VERB

See also *An Introduction*, § 29 (b); Gesenius-Kautzsch, §§106-107; Davidson, 39-45; and Williams, §§ 161-177 (see pages 4-5 for his comments on terminology).

Traditionally the perfect and imperfect forms of the verb have been called "tenses," the perfect being described as past action and the imperfect as future. The terms, perfect and imperfect, however, do not describe the time of an action (when it took place), but its quality (whether it is complete or incomplete). Rather than calling them "tenses," which is misleading, it is better to speak of them as "forms" or "aspects" of the verb.

The *perfect form or aspect of the verb* is a suffixing form, and describes an action as completed, finished; and this may be in the past, present, or future. The *imperfect form or aspect of the verb* is primarily a prefixing form, and describes an action as incomplete, still in progress; and this, too, may be in the past, present, or future.

How one translates these verbal forms into English depends upon the context and the interpreter's own understanding of the text. In that a completed (perfect) action is usually associated with what has happened, and so the past, and an incomplete (imperfect) action is usually associated with what is happening now or will happen and be finished, and so the present or future, it is suggested that until the context makes the thought clear, one provisionally translate *a perfect in the past tense* and an *imperfect in the present tense.*

This, however, can only be provisional, for a perfect and imperfect may refer to the same action or event. This aspect of *time-lessness* in verbal forms is well-illustrated by the alternation of perfect and imperfect forms of the same verb in synonymous parallelism, a well-known device in Canaanite as well as Hebrew poetry. See, for example, Psalm 38:12, where *NRSV* rightly translates the imperfect and perfect forms of the verb by the same tense: *My friends and companions stand* ( יַעֲמֹדוּ ) *aloof from my affliction,* ǁ *and my neighbors stand* ( עָמָדוּ ) *far off.* Note that the next verse has a similar *qṭl* ǁ *yqṭl* sequence, but with different verbs: דִּבְּרוּ *they speak* and the parallel יֶהְגּוּ *they meditate.*

See also Psalm 93:3, where the same device is used in the description of God's victory over the primordial ocean:

נָשְׂאוּ נְהָרוֹת יהוה
נָשְׂאוּ נְהָרוֹת קוֹלָם
יִשְׂאוּ נְהָרוֹת דָּכְיָם

*The floods lifted up, Yahveh,* ǁ *the floods lifted up their thunder,* ǁ *the floods lifted up their crashing.* Whether the verbs are translated in the past tense as here, or put into the present tense, all three forms of the verb must be in the same tense, as they are in all modern translations except the *NRSV*.

## 30 IMPERATIVE, JUSSIVE AND COHORTATIVE

The imperative, jussive and cohortative are all related to the imperfect and in part derived from it. For their formation, see *A Summary of Hebrew Grammar*, §§ 12-14, for the strong verb, and §§ 16 ff. for verbs with weak letters and gutterals. See also *An Introduction*, §§ 33-35; Gesenius-Kautzsch, §§ 108-110; Davidson, §§ 60-65; and Williams, §§ 183-191.

(a) *The Imperative.* The imperative is used only for the second person, and only for positive commands; e.g. לֵךְ מִזֶּה *Go from here!* (1 Kings 17:3); תִּפְשׂוּ אֶת-נְבִיאֵי הַבַּעַל *Sieze the prophets of Ba'al!* (1 Kings 18:40). For negative commands the jussive with אַל or the imperfect with לֹא must be used; e.g. אַל תִּירָאִי *Do not be afraid!* (1 Kings 17:13); לֹא-תִּגְנֹב *Do not steal!* (Exodus 20:15).

Very frequently the particle נָא is added to the imperative and also to the jussive and cohortative. Although variously translated as *pray, please, now,* it is really only an enclitic with no specific meaning, and probably should not be translated at all. Perhaps its function is to soften the abruptness of a command, perhaps to strengthen it, perhaps to give some weight or cadence to the short imperative form. Note the following examples: קְחִי-נָא לִי *bring to me* (1 Kings 17:10); עֲלֵה-נָא הַבֵּט *go up, look* (1 Kings 18:43); תָּשָׁב נָא נֶפֶשׁ-הַיֶּלֶד הַזֶּה *let the life of this boy return* (1 Kings 17:21); אֶשְּׁקָה-נָּא לְאָבִי וּלְאִמִּי *let me kiss my father and my mother* (1 Kings 19:20).

What has been said about the particle נָא may also be said of the so-called "emphatic imperative," the masculine singular imperative with the termination ָה . There is really no discernible difference in meaning between the simple imperative and its augmented form. Cf. for example אֱסֹר וָרֵד *harness and go down* (1 Kings 18:44) and מְהֵרָה רֵדָה *hurry, go down* (2 Kings 1:11); רְדָה אֵלַי *go down to me* (Genesis 45:9).

Two imperatives often appear together with or without a ו ; e.g. קוּם לֵךְ *rise, go* (1 Kings 17:9); זֹאת עֲשׂוּ וִחְיוּ *this do and live* (Genesis 42:18). Such combinations, especially with ו , are frequently said to express purpose or condition, and that passages like the examples above should be translated as, *Rise to go!* or, *Rise that you may go!*; and *This do that you may live!*; and even, *If you do this you shall live.* To deal with the text this way is to miss the flavor and character of the language. Purpose or condition may be one's ultimate interpretation of the words in combination, but neither is what is explicitly or grammatically expressed! See the discussion below at § 40 dealing with compound sentences.

(b) *The Jussive.* The jussive is used only for the second and third persons. It expresses a command, an exhortation, or a wish, and may be translated in the second person as a command, *you shall*, and in the second and third persons with the help of words like *let* or *may*. Examples: שִׁבְעַת יָמִים תּוֹחֵל *seven days you shall wait* (1 Samuel 10:8); יְהִי אוֹר *let there be light!* (Genesis 1:3); וְיֵרְדְּ מִיָּם עַד-יָם *and may he have dominion from sea to sea* (Psalm 72:8); תֵּרֶד אֵשׁ מִן-הַשָּׁמַיִם *let fire come down from heaven* (2 Kings 1:10). Note also that the jussive with אַל is used as the regular negative imperative; see (a) above.

With the jussive there is a tendency to draw the accent back towards the beginning of the word, reflecting perhaps the peremptoriness of a command. While the jussive resembles and is often identical with the imperfect, verbs with weak letters usually show a marked difference in form between the two: the shift in accent, for example, may result in the shortening of tone long vowels in ע״ו and ע״י verbs, and apocopation in verbs with ל״ה. On this see the appropriate sections in *A Summary of Hebrew Grammar*. One advantage of such variations, of course, is that they make a jussive easily recognizable. With the strong verb, however, except for the hip'îl, the imperfect and jussive forms are the same.

This identity in form can lead to ambiguities which can only be resolved by the context and ultimately by the interpreter's overall understanding of a passage. In Psalm 149:2, for example, the verbs in form and accent could be either imperfects or jussives: יִשְׂמַח יִשְׂרָאֵל בְּעֹשָׂיו ‖ בְּנֵי-צִיּוֹן יָגִילוּ בְמַלְכָּם. The verbs are regularly taken as jussives and so translated as in *NRSV*, *Let Israel be glad in its Maker* ‖ *let the children of Zion rejoice in their King*; and this is because of their immediate context, the two imperatives of verse 1, הַלְלוּ יָהּ *Praise Yah!* and שִׁירוּ *Sing!*

More difficult is a case like Psalm 29:11: יהוה עֹז לְעַמּוֹ יִתֵּן ‖ יהוה יְבָרֵךְ אֶת-עַמּוֹ בַשָּׁלוֹם. The verse may be translated either in the indicative, *Yahveh gives strength to his people* ‖ *Yahveh blesses his people with peace*, or it may be translated as a wish or blessing, *May Yahveh give strength to his people* || *may Yahveh bless his people with peace.* The choice between the two depends on whether one understands verse 11 as the climax of a cultic liturgy, or as a pious wish appended to a description of a powerful God.

(c) *The Cohortative.* The cohortative, characterized by the termination ָה , is used only with the first person. It may be translated as the jussive by *let me/us* or *may I/we.* It is generally said that the cohortative tends to show intentionality; however, as in the case of the so-called "emphatic imperative," this should not be pressed. Note the following examples: אֶשְּׁקָה-נָּא לְאָבִי וּלְאִמִּי וְאֵלְכָה אַחֲרֶיךָ *let me kiss my father and my mother and I shall go after you* (1 Kings 19:20); אָשִׁירָה לְיהוה *I will sing to Yahveh* or *Let me sing to Yahveh* (Exodus 15:1), but cf. וַאֲנִי אָשִׁיר עֻזֶּךָ *and I, I shall sing your might* (Psalm 59:17); נֵלְכָה-נָּא עַד-הַיַּרְדֵּן *let us go to the Jordan* (2 Kings 6:2), but cf. שָׂמַחְתִּי בְּאֹמְרִים לִי בֵּית יהוה נֵלֵךְ *I was glad with those saying to me, To the house of Yahveh we shall go,* or as most translations read, *I was glad when they said to me, Let us go to the house of the Lord!* (Psalm 122:1).

## 31 VĀV CONSECUTIVE

See also *An Introduction*, § 40; Gesenius-Kautzsch §§ 111-112; Davidson, §§ 46-57; and Williams, §§ 176-179.

(a) The narrative device known as vāv consecutive is described in *An Introduction to Biblical Hebrew*, § 40, as follows:

> For *consecutive narrative in the past* the first verb is in the perfect [completed action] or its equivalent, and all following verbs are in the imperfect prefixed with .וַ , or before א with וָ .....

> For *consecutive narrative in the present or future* the process is simply reversed. The first verb is in the imperfect [incomplete action] or its equivalent (including the imperative) and all succeeding verbs are in the perfect prefixed with ו pointed exactly like the simple conjunctive וְ .....
>
> With vāv consecutive the verb must stand first in the clause with no intervening word however small. When such a word is necessary, for example לֹא or כִּי, the consecutive narrative is broken, and one must start all over.

Because this narrative device seems to reverse the usual meaning of perfect and imperfect, it is sometimes referred to as *vāv conversive.* In actuality one should probably refer to it as *vāv conservational*, since it no doubt preserves more ancient usages as in Akkadian, the permansive *qaṭil* (with ו and the perfect) and the preterite *iqtul* (with ו and the imperfect). Rather than dealing with the historical development of the phenomenon, or introducing new terminology, this grammar prefers to keep the old name, *vāv consecutive*, and simply describe what it does.

When one begins with a perfect form, expressed or implied, the actions which follow are represented by the imperfect form of the verbs with .וַ . Similarly, after an imperfect form, or a form related to the imperfect (imperative, jussive, cohortative, infinitive, participle), the actions following are represented by the perfect form of the verbs with simple וְ . In other words, vāv consecutive is a way of continuing what has preceded. Consequently, it is used mostly in narrative, setting forth the chronological succession of actions and events. Note the following examples: (i) vāv consecutive imperfect: וַיֵּלֶךְ וַיַּעַשׂ כִּדְבַר יהוה וַיֵּלֶךְ וַיֵּשֶׁב בְּנַחַל כְּרִית *and he went and he did according to the word of Yahveh, and he went and he dwelt at Wadi Kerîṯ* (1 Kings 17:5); (ii) vāv consecutive perfect (following an imperative): לֵךְ מִזֶּה וּפָנִיתָ לְּךָ קֵדְמָה וְנִסְתַּרְתָּ בְּנַחַל כְּרִית *go from here and turn yourself eastward and hide yourself at Wadi Kerîṯ* (1 Kings 17:3); (c) vāv consecutive perfect following an imperfect, interrupted and resumed: וַאֲנִי אֶעֱשֶׂה אֶת-הַפָּר הָאֶחָד וְנָתַתִּי עַל-הָעֵצִים וְאֵשׁ לֹא אָשִׂים וּקְרָאתֶם בְּשֵׁם אֱלֹהֵיכֶם וַאֲנִי אֶקְרָא בְשֵׁם-יהוה וְהָיָה . . . . . *and I, I shall prepare one bull and place (it) upon the wood, and fire I shall not set, and you will call in the name of your God, and I, I shall call on the name of Yahveh, and it shall be* . . . . . (1 Kings 18:23-24).

(b) Because vāv consecutive sets forth the chronological succession of actions, it may also express the logical consequence of a previous action. In this sense it may even serve to express result and purpose. So in 1 Kings 17:3, for example, Elijah is told to go eastward in order to hide. A vāv consecutive may even appear in an apodosis (the conclusion of a conditional sentence), e.g. אִם-אָמַרְנוּ נָבוֹא הָעִיר וְהָרָעָב בָּעִיר וָמַתְנוּ שָׁם וְאִם-יָשַׁבְנוּ פֹה וָמָתְנוּ *(literally) If we say, Let us enter the city, and the famine [is] in the city, and we shall die there; and if we dwell here, and we shall die* (1 Kings 7:4). *NRSV* gives a much smoother translation: *If we say, "Let us enter the city," the famine is in the city, and we shall die there; but if we sit here, we shall also die.* In all of this, however, it is important to remember that while we may interpret the final meaning in terms of purpose and result, these notions are not explicitly expressed in the Hebrew text, where all the actions are connected simply by ו . See the remarks below at § 40 concerning compound sentences.

(c) The vāv consecutive imperfect has virtually an independent use, frequently standing at the beginning of a narrative, even whole books. The Elijah narratives begin, וַיֹּאמֶר אֵלִיָּהוּ *And Elijah said* (1 Kings 17:1); cf. Isaiah 7:1, וַיְהִי בִּימֵי אָחָז בֶּן-יוֹתָם *And it happened in the days of Ahaz son of Jotham.* The books of Leviticua, Numbers, Joshua, Judges, 1 and 2 Samuel, 2 Kings, Ezekiel, Jonah, Ruth and Esther all begin with a vāv consecutive imperfect form, often simply with וַיְהִי *And it happened*, or as some have translated, *Once upon a time.*

The vāv consecutive perfect may also have an almost independent use. It frequently introduces an oracle about the future, as in Isaiah 7:18, וְהָיָה בַּיּוֹם הַהוּא *And it will happen in that day.* Again, in Deuteronomy 10:16 the vāv consecutive perfect is clearly used as an imperative, but it stands virtually independent, not immediately following an actual or implied imperative form: וּמַלְתֶּם אֵת עָרְלַת לְבַבְכֶם *and you shall circumcise the foreskin of your heart,* an exhortation that follows two verses of description of God's love and choice of the patriarchs and their seed (verses 14-15). Cf. also Deuteronomy 10:19 and 11:1.

## 32 THE INFINITIVES

See also *An Introduction*, § 38; Gesenius-Kautzsch, §§ 113-115; Davidson, §§84-96, and Williams, §§ 192-212.

Infinitives are *verbal nouns* expressing the basic meaning or action of their verbal roots. In Latin terminology they are even called *nomina actionis* (nouns of action). They are most easily translated as nouns ending in *-ing*, thereby maintaining both their nominal and verbal character; e.g. וְהִנֵּה שָׂשׂוֹן וְשִׂמְחָה הָרֹג בָּקָר וְשָׁחֹט צֹאן אָכֹל בָּשָׂר וְשָׁתוֹת יָיִן *And behold, joy and gladness, slaying cattle and slaughtering sheep, eating meat and drinking wine* (Isaiah 22:13).

Hebrew has two infinitives: the *infinitive absolute* (as in the above verse from Isaiah) and the *infinitive construct*.

(a) *The Infinitive Construct.* As a verbal noun the infinitive construct has the characteristics both of a noun and a verb. *As a noun* it may be the subject of a sentence, the direct object, the object of a preposition, and part of a construct relation; it may also take pronominal suffixes and be inflected. *As a verb* it may take a subject and an object. In Genesis 2:18 the infinitive in a construct relationship is the subject of the sentence: לֹא-טוֹב הֱיוֹת הָאָדָם לְבַדּוֹ *The man's being alone [is] not good.* In Genesis 2:4 the infinitive is in a construct relationship as part of a prepositional phrase and has both a subject and direct object: בְּיוֹם עֲשׂוֹת יהוה אֱלֹהִים אֶרֶץ וְשָׁמָיִם *in the day of Yahveh God's making earth and heaven.* The infinitive appears as a direct object with pronominal suffixes in Psalm 139:2: יָדַעְתָּ שִׁבְתִּי וְקוּמִי *you know my sitting and my rising.* Note that with pronominal suffixes the inflection of the infinitive follows a second declension pattern, as for example in Psalm 139:2 above: שֶׁבֶת + ִי > שִׁבְתִּי (the infinitive construct of ישׁב).

The infinitive construct, since it is a nominal form, frequently appears with prepositions; e.g. בְּשָׁמְרָם עֵקֶב רָב *in keeping them [is] great reward* (Psalm 19:12); הִנֵּה הָעָם חֹטְאִים לַיהוה לֶאֱכֹל עַל-הַדָּם *Behold, the people are sinning against Yahveh by/with regard to eating with the blood* (1 Samuel 14:33); עַד-שְׁפָךְ-דָּם עֲלֵיהֶם *until the gushing of blood on them* (1 Kings 18:28); עַד לַעֲלוֹת הַמִּנְחָה *until the offering up of the minḥâ* (1 Kings 18:29). Very often the infinitive construct with ל yields a meaning similar to the ordinary English infinitive; e.g. כִּי בָא לִשְׁפֹּט הָאָרֶץ *yea, he comes to judge (literally, he comes with regard to/for judging) the earth* (Psalm 98:9); לַעֲשֹׂתָם *to do them* (Deuteronomy 5:1); לְהוֹשִׁיעֵנִי *to save me* (Isaiah 38:20).

The infinitive construct with ב and כ frequently yield a meaning tantamount to a temporal clause; e.g. וּבְבֹא מֹשֶׁה לִפְנֵי יהוה *and in the entering of Moses before Yahveh*, that is, *and when Moses entered before Yahveh* (Exodus 34:34); וַיְהִי בִּהְיוֹתָם בַּשָּׂדֶה *and it happened in their being in the field*, that is, *and while they were in the field* (Genesis 4:8); וַיְהִי בְּהַכְרִית אִיזֶבֶל אֵת נְבִיאֵי יהוה *and it happened in the cutting off of Jezebel the prophets of Yahveh*, that is, *and it happend while/when Jezebel was cutting off the prophets of Yahveh* (1 Kings 18:4). In like manner see also: וַיְהִי כִרְאוֹת אַחְאָב אֶת-אֵלִיָּהוּ *and when Ahab saw Elijah* (1 Kings 18:17); וַיְהִי כַּעֲבֹר הַצָּהֳרַיִם *and when noon had passed* (1 Kings 18:29); cf. also 1 Kings 19:13.

(b) *The Infinitive Absolute.* The infinitive absolute, like the infinitive construct, is a verbal noun, and so may be the subject of a nominal sentence, as in אָכֹל בָּשָׂר וְשָׁתוֹת יָיִן *eating meat and drinking wine* (Isaiah 22:13), or it may be the object of a sentence, as in לִמְדוּ הֵיטֵב *learn doing good* (Isaiah 1:17). It may also have an adverbial function; e.g. רִדְפוּ מַהֵר *pursue quickly (literally, pursue being quick)* (Joshua 2:5). Some infinitive absolutes of this nature, including מַהֵר, have become actual adverbs; so הַרְבֵּה, the hip'îl infinitive absolute of רבה, frequently appears with the meaning *greatly, exceedingly*, and so also *overly, too much*, as in יֵהוּא יַעַבְדֶנּוּ הַרְבֵּה *Jehu will serve him greatly* (2 Kings 10:18); אַל-תְּהִי צַדִּיק הַרְבֵּה *do not be righteous too much* (Ecclesiastes 7:16); and often with מְאֹד *very*, as in שְׂכָרְךָ הַרְבֵּה מְאֹד *your reward [shall be] exceedingly great* (Genesis 15:1).

The verbal character of the infinitive absolute may be seen when it appears to be a substitute for the ordinary verb, especially as an imperative; e.g. זָכוֹר אֶת-יוֹם הַשַּׁבָּת *remember[ing] the day of the Sabbath* (Exodus 20:8); אָכוֹל וְשָׁתוֹ כִּי מָחָר נָמוּת *eat[ing] and drink[ing], for tomorrow we die* (Isaiah 22:13).

Note that in all cases the infinitive absolute, unlike the infinitive construct, is *indeclinable* and can take no preformatives or afformatives. It stands uninflected, and simply expresses the basic idea of the verb root.

This suggests the most frequent use of the infinitive absolute, namely, to strengthen the force of the main verb of a sentence. When it is used *before the main verb*, it emphasizes the certainty and intensity of the verbal idea; e.g. the frequent phrase מוֹת תָּמוּת *dying you shall die*, that is, *you shall surely die*; see also קַנֹּא קִנֵּאתִי לַיהוה *being zealous I have been zealous for Yahveh*, that is, *I have been very zealous for Yahveh* (1 Kings 19:10, 14); אִם-שָׁמוֹעַ תִּשְׁמְעוּ בְּקֹלִי *if hearing you hear my voice*, that is, *if you truly/diligently hear my voice* (Exodus 19:5). When the infinitive absolute appears *after the main verb*, it emphasizes the continuance of the verbal idea; e.g. שִׁמְעוּ שָׁמוֹעַ וְאַל-תָּבִינוּ *hear hearing and do not understand*, that is, *go on hearing and do not understand* (Isaiah 6:9).

## 33 THE PARTICIPLE

See also *An Introduction*, §§ 36-37; Gesenius-Kautzsch, § 116; Davidson, §§97-100; and Williams, §§213-222.

Participles, like the infinitives, share the characteristics of both noun and verb. In form they are nominal, and so like nouns and adjectives are inflected, have gender, number and state, and may take the definite article, prepositions and pronominal suffixes. In meaning they are of verbal character, expressing continuing or imminent action, and may take direct and indirect objects.

(a) As a noun by itself, the participle expresses agency; it is basically impersonal, like a verb without an expressed subject, and may be translated simply as *one doing such and such*; e.g. יָרֵא *one fearing*, אוֹהֵב *one loving*, עֹשֶׂה *one making*; הַנִּמְלָט *the one escaping* (1 Kings 19:17).

Very often the participle takes on what is for English the meaning and usage of an ordinary noun; so יָרֵא is *a fearer*, אוֹהֵב *a lover, friend*, and עֹשֶׂה *a maker*. The common pair, אוֹיֵב ‖ קָם *enemy* ‖ *foe*, are actually participles: *one showing enmity* ‖ *one rising up*; cf. also the word frequently used with them, שֹׂנֵא *one hating*. Note also מוֹשִׁיעַ *one saving*, that is, *a savior*, and שׁוֹפֵט *one ruling*, that is, *a ruler*, a word often used in parallel with מֶלֶךְ *king*.

As a noun, the participle is often found in a construct relation; e.g. יֹדְעֵי טוֹב וָרָע *knowers of good and evil* (Genesis 3:5); מַגִּיעֵי בַיִת בְּבַיִת *joiners of house to house* (Isaiah 5:8);

יָדַעְתִּי כִּי-יְרֵא אֱלֹהִים אַתָּה *I know that you [are] a fearer of God* (Genesis 22:12), but cf. also וְלֹא יָרֵא אֱלֹהִים *and [you are] not fearing God* (Deuteronomy 25:18).

The participle as a *nomen agentis* is often most easily translated into English by a relative clause; e.g. הַנִּמְלָט *the escaping one, or the one who escapes* 1 Kings 19:17); וַאֲבָרְכָה מְבָרְכֶיךָ *and I will bless ones blessing you, or I will bless those who bless you* (Genesis 12:3). This is especially the case when the participle is in apposition; e.g. וְשָׁכַחְתָּ אֶת-יהוה אֱלֹהֶיךָ הַמּוֹצִיאֲךָ מֵאֶרֶץ מִצְרַיִם *and you forget Yahveh your God, the one bringing you out [who brought you out] from the land of Egypt* (Deuteronomy 8:14); see the continuation of participles in verse 15 and 16.

When used in apposition or as an adjective, the participle must agree in gender and number with its antecedent; e.g. יהוה צְבָאוֹת הַשֹּׁכֵן בְּהַר צִיּוֹן *Yahveh of Hosts, the one dwelling on Mt. Zion* (Isaiah 8:18); אִשָּׁה אַלְמָנָה מְקֹשֶׁשֶׁת עֵצִים *a widow woman gathering sticks* (1 Kings 17:10); אֵשׁ אֹכֵלָה *a devouring fire* (Deuteronomy 4:24).

(b) Verbally, the participle expresses continuing action, usually in the present (either actually or in the speaker's mind); e.g. כִּי-אַתָּה נֹתֵן אֶת-עַבְדְּךָ *that you are giving your servant* (1 Kings 18:9); רַבִּים אֹמְרִים *many are saying* (Psalm 3:3); אָנֹכִי מְלַמֵּד אֶתְכֶם *I am teaching you* Deuteronomy 4:1), but see Deuteronomy 4:12 where the participle is used in the context of past narrative: וַיְדַבֵּר יהוה אֲלֵיכֶם מִתּוֹךְ הָאֵשׁ קוֹל דְּבָרִים אַתֶּם שֹׁמְרִים *and Yahveh spoke to you from the midst of the fire; the sound of words you were hearing .....* Sometimes the verb היה is used to give emphasis to continuing action, especially in past narrative; e.g. וְעֹבַדְיָהוּ הָיָה יָרֵא אֶת-יהוה מְאֹד *and Obadiah was one fearing Yahveh greatly* (1 Kings 18:3); וּמֹשֶׁה הָיָה רֹעֶה אֶת-צֹאן יִתְרוֹ *and Moses was shepherding the flock of*

*Jethro* (Exodus 3:1). Often the participle carries with it a sense of imminence, that something is about to happen; e.g. כִּי לְיָמִים עוֹד שִׁבְעָה אָנֹכִי מַמְטִיר עַל-הָאָרֶץ *for yet seven days I am bringing rain on the earth*, that is, *in seven days I am about to bring rain on the earth* (Genesis 7:4). The sense of imminence is especially apparent when the clause is introduced by הִנֵּה *behold*; e.g. הִנֵּה יהוה עֹבֵר *behold, Yahveh is about to pass by* (1 Kings 19:11); הִנֵּה הָעַלְמָה הָרָה וְיֹלֶדֶת בֵּן *behold, the young woman is pregnant and about to bear a son* (Isaiah 7:14).

Since the participle, unlike the finite verb, does not contain a subject, the subject of the action must be separately expressed, and the participle must agree with it in gender and number; e.g. וְהָעֹרְבִים מְבִיאִים לוֹ *and the ravens were bringing to him* (1 Kings 17:6); וְעַבְדְּךָ יָרֵא אֶת-יהוה מִנְּעֻרָי *and your servant is fearing Yahveh from his syouth* (1 Kings 18:12); מַלְאֲכֵי אֱלֹהִים עֹלִים וְיֹרְדִים *and the angels of God ascending and descending* (Genesis 28:12). With no expressed subject with the participle a form of the third person is adopted; see above.

The subject for the action of a participle may be introduced by הִנֵּה with a pronominal suffix; e.g. וְהִנְנִי מְקֹשֶׁשֶׁת שְׁנַיִם עֵצִים *and behold I am gathering two sticks* (1 Kings 17:12). יֵשׁ *there is* and אַיִן *there is not* when used with pronominal suffixes may also express the subject of a participle; e.g. אִם-יֶשְׁךָ מוֹשִׁיעַ בְּיָדִי אֶת-יִשְׂרָאֵל *if you are delivering Israel by my hand* (Judges 6:36); אֵינֶנִּי נֹתֵן לָכֶם תֶּבֶן *I am not giving you straw* (Exodus 5:10).

Because participles are nouns, אַיִן, rather than לֹא, is used for the negative; e.g. וְאֵין-קוֹל וְאֵין עֹנֶה וְאֵין קָשֶׁב *and there was no sound, and there was no one answering, and there was no one paying attention* (1 Kings 18:29); אֵינֶנִּי שֹׁמֵעַ *I am not listening* (Isaiah 1:15).

## 34 THE SENTENCE IN GENERAL

In the following sections it is often difficult to make specific references works, because of differences in approach and so in organization and terminology. The treatment of the sentence as a whole comprises Chapter II of Gesenius-Kautzsch, "Part Three: Syntax," §§ 146-167. Very similar in treatment is Davidson, "Syntax of the Sentence," §§ 102-203. Reflecting the same tradition, but with some fresh insights, is Williams, "V. Syntax of Clauses," §§ 483-598. All reflect the traditional categories and terms of classical grammar. In the following reference is made to specific sections only where the subject matter clearly coincides.

A sentence is made up of a subject and predicate. There are two kinds of sentences: nominal and verbal. The *nominal sentence* has as its subject and predicate nominal forms (nouns, pronouns, adjectives, participles, numerals, adverbs and prepositional phrases). The *verbal sentence* has a nominal form as subject and a finite verb as the predicate; in the case of verbs, of course, the subject is included in the verbal form. Thus a single word, אָכַל *he ate*, or שָׁתָה *he drank*, is a verbal sentence. Usually, however, there are other words and phrases associated with the action of the verb, e.g. specified subjects, direct and indirect objects, prepositional phrases, adverbs, and so on.

The normal order of words in a sentence is subject--predicate, but this may be varied in many ways, depending upon emphasis and style. In the matter of word order, it should be remembered, of course, that in verbal sentences the subject is already part of the verb form itself. When the subject is further defined by a noun or proper name, it may stand before the verb, although more often it follows the verb as an extension of the subject already expressed in the verb.. This tendency to place the verb form first is only strengthened by the all-pervasive device of vāv consecutive, which requires this order. Because of this, it has been common to say (not very accurately since the subject is clearly defined in the verb form) that the normal order of words in a sentence is verb (predicate)--subject. In view of the actual variety within the biblical texts, however, it is better to say that the order of words in a sentence, nominal or verbal, is determined by what the author is doing, whether writing simple narrative, employing the tropes of poetry and elevated prose, making emphases, contrasts, or whatever. In matters like this one must learn to read a text and respond to it on its own terms.

## 35 THE NOMINAL SENTENCE

See also *An Introduction*, § 22; Gesenius-Kautzsch, § 141; Davidson, §§ 103-104; and Williams, §§ 483-493.

(a) As defined above in § 34, a nominal sentence has as its subject and predicate nominal forms: nouns, pronouns, adjectives, numerals, participles and infinitives, adverbs and prepositional phrases. The usual order is subject--predicate, although often this is reversed. Note the following examples: בָּנִים אַתֶּם לַיהוה אֱלֹהֵיכֶם *children [are] you to Yahveh your God* (Deuteronomy 14:1); יָדַעְתִּי כִּי אִישׁ אֱלֹהִים אָתָּה וּדְבַר-יהוה בְּפִיךָ אֱמֶת *I know that a man of God [are] you and the word of Yahveh [is] in your mouth truly* (1 Kings 17:24); עֹשֵׂה צְדָקוֹת יהוה *a doer of saving acts [lit. righteousnesses] [is] Yahveh* (Psalm 103:6); רַחוּם וְחַנּוּן יהוה *merciful and gracious [is] Yahveh* (Psalm 103:8); כִּי לְעוֹלָם חַסְדּוֹ *yea, forever [is] his steadfast love* (Psalm 136:1); וְאַנְשֵׁי סְדֹם רָעִים וְחַטָּאִים לַיהוה מְאֹד *and the men of Sodom [were] wicked and great sinners against Yahveh* (Genesis 13:13); note the emphasis suggested in יִוָּדַע כִּי-אַתָּה אֱלֹהִים בְּיִשְׂרָאֵל וַאֲנִי עַבְדְּךָ *let it be known that you [are] God in Israel and I [am] your servant* (1 Kings 18:24).

The predicate adjective, which frequently precedes the subject, must agree with the subject in gender and number, but does not have the definite article, even when the subject is definite; e.g. טוֹב הַדָּבָר *good [is] the matter* (1 Kings 18:24); see also above: Psalm 103:8 and Genesis 13:13. That the predicate adjective has no article, and that the common order is adjective--subject, helps to distinguish subject and predicate, especially when the subject has no article. Otherwise, as usual, the context is determinative.

(b) Since there is no copula in Hebrew, the subject and predicate of nominal sentences are simply juxtaposed. Sometimes, however, the third person pronoun (in the appropriate number and gender) is added, usually after the predicate, and has a kind of copulative significance; e.g. כִּי הַמִּשְׁפָּט לֵאלֹהִים הוּא *(lit.) for the judgment to God it*, that is, *for the judgment [is] God's* (Deuteronomy 1:17); or again, זֹה מַתַּת אֱלֹהִים הִיא *this the gift of God it*, that is, *this [is ]the gift of God* (Ecclesiastes 5:18). Occasionally, usually for emphasis, the pronoun is placed between the subject and predicate; e.g. יהוה הוּא הָאֱלֹהִים *Yahveh, he [is] the God* (1 Kings 18:39).

(c) In no case in a nominal sentence is there any indication of time or tense; this is determined only by our understanding of the context. See, for example, Amos 7:14: לֹא-נָבִיא אָנֹכִי וְלֹא בֶן-נָבִיא אָנֹכִי. Whether this is translated, *not a prophet [was] I, and not a son of a prophet [was] I*, or, *not a prophet [am] I, and not a son of a prophet [am] I,* depends on the overall interpretation of the passage and its issues. Even the kind of copula that one should supply is not always clear; is עָלַי קִלְלָתְךָ of Genesis 27:13 to be translated, *upon me [is] your curse*, or, *upon me [be] your curse*? Cf. also Exodus 12:2: הַחֹדֶשׁ הַזֶּה לָכֶם רֹאשׁ חֳדָשִׁים *this month [is / shall be] to you the first of months.* It should also be noted, that very occasionally היה *to become, to exist, to happen* is used as a virtual copula, perhaps to make the tense more definite or continuous, as, for example, Genesis 1:2: וְהָאָרֶץ הָיְתָה תֹהוּ וָבֹהוּ *and the earth was being formlessness and emptiness.*

(d) יֵשׁ is a noun expressing *existence* without, however, indicating tense; so, *there is*, or *there was*. Similarly, אַיִן / אֵין expresses *non-existence*: *there is not*, *there was not*. Cf. אִם-יֵשׁ-גּוֹי וּמַמְלָכָה *if there is a nation and a kingdom* (1 Kings 18:10);

וְאֵין קוֹל *and there was no sound* (1 Kings 18:26). There is a tendency to use both יֵשׁ and אֵין with the sense of a copula; e.g. אִם־יֶשְׁנוֹ בָאָרֶץ *if he is in the land* (1 Samuel 23:23); אֵינֶנִּי בְּקִרְבְּכֶם *I am not in your midst* (Deuteronomy 1:42).. They are especially used with participles and often have a pronominal suffix to introduce the subject of the participle; e.g. לָדַעַת הֲיִשְׁכֶם אֹהֲבִים אֶת־יהוה אֱלֹהֵיכֶם *to know whether you are loving Yahveh your God* (Deuteronomy 13:4). See above, § 33 (b).

## 36 THE VERBAL SENTENCE

See also Gesenius-Kautzsch, §§ 142-146; Davidson, §§ 105-116; and Williams, *passim.*

The verbal sentence has a nominal form as subject (frequently indicated only by the personal afformatives and preformatives of the verb itself, or as in the case of imperatives simply implied) and a finite verb as the predicate.

(a) When the subject is separately expressed (further defining the personal subject already expressed in the verb form), there is usually agreement in gender and number between it and the predicate (verb), although, as Davidson observes (§ 112), "There is less precision in the matter of agreement than there is in classical or other languages. . . . . There is a great tendency to construe according to the sense rather than strict grammatical law." So it is not surprizing that a collective noun, such as עַם *people*, may take either a singular or plural verb; cf. וַיָּבֹאוּ כָל־עַם הָאָרֶץ *and all the people of the land came* (2 Kings 11:18) and וַיִּשְׂמַח כָּל־עַם־הָאָרֶץ *and all the people of the land rejoiced* (2 Kings 11:20); וַיַּרְא כָּל־הָעָם וַיִּפְּלוּ עַל־פְּנֵיהֶם *and all the people saw (sg.) and they fell (pl.) on their faces* (1 Kings 18:39).

Similarly, a noun that is plural in form but singular in meaning, such as אֱלֹהִים, a plural of majesty, usually takes a singular verb form, e.g. וַיֹּאמֶר אֱלֹהִים *and God said* (Genesis

1:3), but see כַּאֲשֶׁר הִתְעוּ אֹתִי אֱלֹהִים מִבֵּית אָבִי *when God made me wander from the house of my father* (Genesis 20:13). Nouns in the dual usually take a plural form of the verb; e.g. וַיֵּלְכוּ שְׁנֵיהֶם יַחְדָּו *and the two of them went together* (Genesis 22:6).

With compound subjects the verb is usually in the plural when the subject comes before the verb; e.g. וְאַבְשָׁלוֹם וְכָל-הָעָם אִישׁ יִשְׂרָאֵל בָּאוּ יְרוּשָׁלִָם *and Absalom and all the people, the men of Israel, came to Jerusalem* (2 Samuel 16:15). When the verb form comes first, it may also be in the plural; e.g. וַיֵּצְאוּ מֹשֶׁה וְאֶלְעָזָר הַכֹּהֵן וְכָל-נְשִׂיאֵי הָעֵדָה *and went out Moses and Eleazar the priest and all the leaders of the congregation* (Numbers 31:13). More often, however, the verb form, when it precedes the compound subject, will agree in number and gender with the first element of the compound; e.g. וַיָּבֹא נֹחַ וּבָנָיו וְאִשְׁתּוֹ וּנְשֵׁי-בָנָיו אִתּוֹ *and entered Noah and his sons and his wife and the wives of his sons with him* (Genesis 7:7); וַתָּשַׁר דְּבוֹרָה וּבָרָק בֶּן-אֲבִינֹעַם *and sang Deborah and Barak the son of Abinoam* (Judges 5:1); וַיִּשְׁמְעוּ אֶחָיו וְכָל-בֵּית אָבִיו *and heard his brothers and all the house of his father* (1 Samuel 22:1); וַיִּתְחַבֵּא הָאָדָם וְאִשְׁתּוֹ *and hid himself (sg.) the man and his wife* (Genesis 3:8). Succeeding verbs that refer to the compound subject are, of course, in the plural; cf. וַתַּעַן רָחֵל וְלֵאָה וַתֹּאמַרְנָה לוֹ *and answered (sg.) Rachel and Leah, and they said (pl.) to him* (Genesis 31:14).

(b) Indefinite constructions are made in a variety of ways. Most common is the use of the third person masculine singular form of the verb, e.g. the ubiquitous וַיְהִי *and it happened.*; וָשָׁב וְרָפָא לוֹ *and he (= the people) turn and one heals him* (Isaiah 6:10); perhaps also אֶת-הַפָּר אֲשֶׁר-נָתַן לָהֶם *the bull that one had given them* (1 Kings 18:26; cf. 18:23). Less frequently the third feminine singular is used, e.g. לֹא-תַמְטִיר עָלֶיהָ *it [she] does not rain on it* (Amos 4:7). The third masculine plural is also used for the indefinite they; e.g. מִן-הַבְּאֵר הַהִוא יַשְׁקוּ הָעֲדָרִים *from that well they water the flocks* (Genesis 29:2); וְיִתְּנוּ-לָנוּ שְׁנַיִם פָּרִים *and let them give us two bulls* (1 Kings 18:23); הֲיִפְּלוּ

וְלֹא יָקוּמוּ *will they fall and will they not rise?* (Jeremiah 8:4), followed immediately by a similar proverbial statement, but in the third masculine singular. Plural participles can also express the indefinite; e.g. וְאֶת-כָּל-נָשֶׁיךָ וְאֶת-בָּנֶיךָ מוֹצִאִים אֶל-הַכַּשְׂדִּים *and all your wives and children they bring out to the Chaldeans* (Jeremiah 38:23); cf. Genesis 39:22). The use of the second person is very rare, but see עַד בֹּאֲכָה יִזְרְעֶאלָה *until your entering Jezreel* (1 Kings 18:46).

(c) Elements which complete the thought of the verbal sentence usually follow the verb, so that a typical order of words would be: verb with its subject--object--prepositional phrase--adverb. Of couse, as observed above in § 34, the actual order of any sentence is determined by the writer's style and emphases.

**37 THE NEGATIVE SENTENCE**

See also Gesenius-Kautzsch, § 152; Davidson, §§ 127-128; and Williams, §§ 395-428.

(a) The usual negative particle is לֹא . Used in both objective statements and formal commands, it usually appears before the verb; e.g. לֹא-הָיָה גֶשֶׁם בָּאָרֶץ *there was not rain in the land* (1 Kings 17:7); לֹא תִּגְנֹב *you shall not steal* (Exodus 20:15). Upon occasion לֹא is used with a noun; e.g. הוּא-חֹשֶׁךְ וְלֹא אוֹר *it [is] darkness and not light* (Amos 5:18); הֵם קִנְאוּנִי בְלֹא-אֵל *they made me jealous with a "not-God"* (Deuteronomy 32:21).

אַל is used primarily with the jussive. Standing before the verb, it is the way of expressing a negative command; e.g. אַל-תִּירָאִי *do not be afraid* (1 Kings 17:13); אִישׁ אַל יִמָּלֵט מֵהֶם *let not a one escape of them* (1 Kings 18:40).

(b) The particle אַיִן (usually in the form אֵין ) has the meaning of *not-being*, and so means *there is/was not*. It is used primarily with nominal sentences and participles; e.g. וְאֵין קוֹל

וְאֵין עֹנֶה *and there was no sound, and there was no one answering* (1 Kings 18:26). It frequently occurs with a pronominal suffix, especially with participles; e.g. וְאֵינֶנּוּ *and he was not* (Genesis 5:24); אֵינֶנִּי נֹתֵן לָכֶם תֶּבֶן *I am not giving you straw* (Exodus 5:10).

(c) Other negatives introducing negative clauses are: פֶּן *that not, lest*; אֶפֶס *nothing, save for*; טֶרֶם (usually with the preposition בְּ ): *not yet, before*; בַּל , poetic for לֹא ; בְּלִי *without* and בִּלְתִּי *without* (and לְבִלְתִּי ) *not, so that not.*

(d) It should be noted that two negatives together do not make a positive, but simply emphasize the negative force of the sentence; e.g. הֲמִבְּלִי אֵין-אֱלֹהִים בְּיִשְׂרָאֵל *(lit.) is it without [there being] no God in Israel, that is, Is there no God in Israel?* (2 Kings 1:3); cf. Exodus 14:11; 2 Kings 1:6, 16; and Zechariah 2:2.

## 38 THE INTERROGATIVE SENTENCE

See also Gesenius-Kautzsch, § 150; Davidson, §§ 121-126; and Williams §§541-545.

(a) Questions are frequently asked without the use of an interrogative particle, merely by the tone of voice. In a written text, however, where this cannot be heard and there are no marks of punctuation, the context must determine whether it is a question or not. The interrogative is clear in 1 Samuel 22:7: שָׁאוּל יִמְלֹךְ עָלֵינוּ *Will Saul rule over us?* It is not so clear in a passage such as Exodus 33:14: פָּנַי יֵלֵכוּ וַהֲנִחֹתִי לָךְ *my face (= I) shall go and I shall give you rest.* Some commentators feel that God is asking, *Shall I myself go and give you rest?* to which Moses replies in a quite natural and typical fashion (verse 15), *If your face (pl.) (= you) are not going, do not bring us up from here!* Cf. also Genesis 27:24; 2 Samuel 18:29; and Jonah 4:11.

(b) Most often, however, the simple question is introduced by the interrogative particle הֲ, attached dirctly to the first word; e.g. הֲשֹׁמֵר אָחִי אָנֹכִי *Am I my brother's keeper?* (Genesis 4:9); הֲלֹא כָל-הָאָרֶץ לְפָנֶיךָ *Is not all the land before you?* (Genesis 13:9); הֲלֹא הֻגַּד לַאדֹנִי *Was it not told to my lord?* (1 Kings 18:13).

(c) In a succession of questions the first is introduced by הֲ and the second by אִם or וְאִם; e.g. הֶהָיְתָה זֹאת בִּימֵיכֶם וְאִם בִּימֵי אֲבוֹתֵיכֶם *Has this happened in your days, and in the days of your fathers?* (Joel 1:2); הַאֱנוֹשׁ מֵאֱלוֹהַּ יִצְדָּק אִם מֵעֹשֵׂהוּ יִטְהַר-גָּבֶר *Will a mortal before God be righteous, before his maker will a man be pure?* (Job 4:17). As a means of continuing the question, אִם is often translated as or; for example הֲלָנוּ אַתָּה אִם-לְצָרֵינוּ *For us [are] you, or for our foes?* (Joshua 5:13).

(d) Indirect questions may be introduced either by the prefixed הֲ or אִם; e.g. לִרְאוֹת הֲקַלּוּ הַמַּיִם *to see whether the waters had abated* (Genesis 8:8); דִּרְשׁוּ בְּבַעַל זְבוּב אֱלֹהֵי עֶקְרוֹן אִם-אֶחְיֶה *inquire of Ba'al Zebub, God of Ekron, whether I shall live* (2 Kings 1:2).

(e) Interrogative clauses may also be introduced by the interrogative pronouns, מִי *who* and מָה *what, how*; e.g. מִי עָשָׂה זֹאת *Who did this?* (Judges 15:6); מֶה חָטָאתִי *What have I sinned?* (1 Kings 18:9); מַה-לְּךָ פֹה *What are you doing here (lit., what to you here?)* (1 Kings 19:9). A variety of other interrogative particles, often in combinations with prepositions, are also used to introduce questions; e.g. לָמָּה *why (lit. for what)*; אֵי , אַיֵּה , אֵיפֹה *where*; אֵיכָה / אֵיךְ *how*; בַּמָּה *by what*; כַּמָּה *how much*; מָתַי *when*; cf. עַד-מָתַי אַתֶּם פֹּסְחִים *how long (lit. to when) will you be limping* (1 Kings 18:21).

Sometimes the demonstrative pronouns, זֶה *this* and הוּא *that*, and also the enclitic אֵפוֹא *then*, are used with the interrogative, perhaps for rhythm or emphasis; e.g. מִי זֶה מַחְשִׁיךְ

עֵצָה *Who [is] this darkening counsel?* (Job 38:2); מִי-הוּא יַרְשִׁיעֵנִי *Who [is] that [who] will put me in the wrong?* (Isaiah 50:9); מִי-אֵפוֹא הוּא הַצָּד-צַיִד *Who then [is] he hunting game?* (Genesis 27:33). Cf. הַאַתָּה זֶה *(lit.) [Are] you this?*, that is, *Is this you?* (1 Kings 18:17).

## 39 DESIDERATIVE SENTENCES

See also Gesenius-Kautzsch, § 151; Davidson, §§ 133-135; and Williams, §§ 546-551 and *passim.*

(a) A wish may be expressed by the simple imperfect and its related forms, the jussive (often identical with the imperfect) and the cohortative; e.g. תֵּרָאֶה הַיַּבָּשָׁה *let appear dry land* (Genesis 1:9); יְהִי אוֹר *let there be light* (Genesis 1:3); אֶעְבְּרָה *let me / may I pass through* (Deuteronomy 2:27). The imperative may also express a desire or request, as שִׁפְטוּ-נָא בֵּינִי וּבֵין כַּרְמִי *judge between me and my vineyard* (Isaiah 5:3). A simple noun clause without a verb may also express a wish; e.g. אָרוּר אַתָּה *cursed [be] you!* (Genesis 3:14); עַל-עַמְּךָ בִרְכָתֶךָ *on your people [be] your blessing!* (Psalm 3:9).

(b) The interrogative מִי who, especially in the phrase מִי יִתֵּן *who will give* (which has the force of *O that* or *O had*) introduces a wish or desire, often impossible to fulfill; e.g. מִי-יִתֵּן מוּתִי אֲנִי תַחְתֶּיךָ *O that I had died (lit. who gives my dying) I instead of you* (2 Samuel 19:1). Cf. also 2 Samuel 23:15; Psalm 4:7; Job 6:8.

(c) The particles לוּ *O that, if only* and less frequently אִם *if only* also introduce a wish; e.g. לוּ-מַתְנוּ בְּאֶרֶץ מִצְרַיִם *O that we had died in the land of Egypt* (Numbers 14:2); לוּ יִשְׁמָעֵאל יִחְיֶה *O that Ishmael might live* (Genesis 17:18); אִם תִּקְטֹל רָשָׁע *if only you would slay the wicked* (Psalm 139:19).

## 40 COMPOUND SENTENCES

Much has been written about the kinds of clauses in biblical Hebrew, and how they are related, and what kinds of verb forms go where, and which follow. The discussions are very detailed and impressive; see, for example, §§ 140-167 on "Sentences" in *Gesenius' Hebrew Grammar* (revised by Kautzsch and Cowley in 1910), which still remains the standard reference grammar, and so has greatly influenced most presentations of biblical Hebrew. Unfortunately, however, its approach to the question of grammar and syntax, like most of the others, has been based primarily on the structure and categories of Greek and Latin and modern, especially western languages. The problem is that these categories do not really fit classical Hebrew, as the many variations and exceptions cited even in Gesenius clearly indicate. Instead of trying to understand Hebrew on its own terms, the tendency has been to put it into a *Philistine bed*, and make it conform to our classical and western languages and patterns of expression.

In doing this we miss much of the excitement and dynamic character of biblical expression. Hebrew, for example, is not a subordinating language like English and Latin, characterized by relative and dependent clauses and a regular sequence of tenses. Hebrew is primarily a coordinating language, as the use of vāv clearly shows. A וְ does not introduce a dependent clause, nor strictly speaking does the relative particle, אֲשֶׁר. Both וְ and אֲשֶׁר simply set together a series of realities, without, however, making explicit their precise relation to one another. It is left for the interpreter to decide, and the options are not always clear.

Indeed, as Joshua Blau wrote in his article on biblical Hebrew in the *Encyclopaedia Judaica*, XVI, 1983, "it is in the domain of clause formation that Hebrew has best preserved the ancient Semitic character. In contradisctinction to Arabic, it has not relinquished free sentence structure in favor of systematization." Blau goes on to say that "the boundary lines between main and subordinate clauses are blurred," and notes especially the use of vāv. "Moreover," he points out, "the number of subordinate conjunctions is relatively small."

In this connection the simple connective וְ *and* has been something of a martyr. It has been said to mean many things: *but, although, while, so then, or, in particular*, and so on. Accordingly, וְ has been given many special titles, such as *wāw adversitum, wāw concomitantiae, wāw explicativum, wāw adaequationis, wāw apodosis.* This variety of meanings and descriptions, of course, derives from the fact that ו is frequently used to introduce clauses that the interpreter understands as being adversative, circumstantial, subordinate, causal, comparative, final or consecutive. Doing this, however--assigning to ו a whole library of meanings--is to miss the point and character of Hebrew expression. That clauses joined by ו in a compound sentence may be given an adversative or concessive meaning in our interpretation does not change the fact that such a meaning is not explicit, and that ו is still a ו, the simple connective, and not כִּי אִם *but*, or אַף כִּי *although*, or *in order that*. A ו is a ו is a ו! How we set this ו into good English depends not upon a variety of meanings for ו, but upon our insight and understanding of the text. Cf. also § 31 (b) on vāv consecutive.

Despite these demurs with regard to the traditonal approach to the syntax of compound sentences in Hebrew, one must still consider relative and dependent clauses which are introduced by particles and subordinating conjunctions.

## 41 THE RELATIVE CLAUSE AND אֲשֶׁר

See also An Introduction, § 39; Gesenius-Kautzsch, § 138; Davidson, §§ 142-144; and Williams, §§ 462-469.

(a) The coordinate nature of Hebrew expression is clearly seen in the use of אֲשֶׁר, which is not strictly a relative pronoun in our English sense, but rather, as Williams describes it, merely "a particle of relationship" (*Hebrew Syntax*, § 462). אֲשֶׁר is a word which simply indicates that what has gone before is somehow related to that which follows, the precise nature of the relationship to be determined by the context. Sometimes this is quite straight-forward, as in וְנִסְתַּרְתָּ בְּנַחַל כְּרִית אֲשֶׁר עַל-פְּנֵי הַיַּרְדֵּן *and he hid by the Wady Kerit̲ that [was] to the face [NRSV: east] of the Jordan* (1 Kings 17:3); or as in כִּדְבַר יהוה אֲשֶׁר דִּבֶּר בְּיַד אֵלִיָּהוּ *according to the word of Yahveh that he spoke by the hand of Elijah* (1 Kings 17:16).

More often, however, the relationship is more complex; e.g. וַיַּעֲלֵהוּ אֶל-הָעֲלִיָּה אֲשֶׁר הוּא יֹשֵׁב שָׁם (1 Kings 17:19), where two quite independent clauses are joined by אֲשֶׁר: (1) *he brought him up to the upper chamber* and (2) *he was dwelling there.* אֲשֶׁר indicates a relationship between the two clauses, which we may translate into English as, *He brought him up to the upper chamber, where he was dwelling.* Still more complex is Genesis 45:4, where *NRSV* translates, *I am your brother, Joseph, whom you sold into Egypt*, but where the Hebrew text actually has two independent clauses joined by אֲשֶׁר: (1) אֲנִי יוֹסֵף אֲחִיכֶם *I am Joseph, your brother* and (2) מְכַרְתֶּם אֹתִי מִצְרָיְמָה *you sold me into Egypt*. Or again, Isaiah 7:16: תֵּעָזֵב הָאֲדָמָה אֲשֶׁר אַתָּה קָץ מִפְּנֵי שְׁנֵי מְלָכֶיהָ *the land will be forsaken before whose two kings you are in dread.*

When אֲשֶׁר is used, the interpreter should assume that a relationship is actually intended, and this should be clear in the translation, as complicated as this may sometimes be. In 2 Samuel 7:14, for example, the use of אֲשֶׁר significantly defines the understanding of the Davidic king as the son of God; to ignore it and make two independent clauses, as most modern translations do, may not drastically change the overall meaning, but does miss the intentional relationship between sonship and divine discipline. אֲנִי אֶהְיֶה-לּוֹ לְאָב וְהוּא יִהְיֶה-לִּי לְבֵן אֲשֶׁר בְּהַעֲוֹתוֹ וְהֹכַחְתִּיו בְּשֵׁבֶט אֲנָשִׁים וּבְנִגְעֵי אָדָם *I, I shall be to him as a father, and he, he shall be to me as a son whom when he commits iniquity I shall punish with the rod of men and the blows of the sons of man.* Cf. *NRSV: I will be a father to him, and he shall be a son to me. When he commits iniquity, I will punish him with a rod such as mortals use, with blows inflicted by human beings.* The translation misses the subtle contrast in relationship as well as the nuances related to sonship.

(b) אֲשֶׁר is sometimes omitted where one would expect it, especially in poetry and elevated prose; e.g. אֱלֹהִים לֹא יְדָעוּם *(lit.) gods they did not know them,* that is, *gods [that] they did not know* (Deuteronomy 32:17); וּבְיָדוֹ רִצְפָּה בְּמֶלְקַחַיִם לָקַח מֵעַל הַמִּזְבֵּחַ *and in his hand a coal [that] with tongs he took from the altar* (Isaiah 6:4); גּוֹי לֹא-תֵדַע לְשֹׁנוֹ *(lit.) a nation you do not know its tongue*, that is, *a nation [whose] tongue you do not know* (Jeremiah 5:15).

(c) What has been said concerning אֲשֶׁר applies also to the indeclinable relative pronoun זוּ as well as to the demonstrative זֶה in its rare use as a relative. Cf. יהוה זוּ חָטָאנוּ לוֹ *Yahveh against whom we have sinned* (Isaiah 42:24); הַר-צִיּוֹן זֶה שָׁכַנְתָּ בּוֹ *Mount Zion where you dwell* (Psalm 74:2).

## 42 DEPENDENT CLAUSES INTRODUCED BY PARTICLES AND CONJUNCTIONS

See also Gesenius-Kautzsch, §§153-165 *passim*; Davidson, §§ 129-155 *passim*; and Williams, §§ 429-461, 511-517, 533-535.

Although relatively few in number, a variety of conjunctions and articles are used to introduce dependent clauses. One of the most common and broadly used is כִּי *for, because, that (introducing both direct and indirect statemenmts), when*; e.g. כִּי לֹא-הָיָה גֶשֶׁם בָּאָרֶץ *because there was no rain in the land* (1 Kings 17:7); יָדַעְתִּי כִּי אִישׁ אֱלֹהִים אָתָּה *I know that you [are] a man of God* (1 Kings 17:24). כִּי also appears in a number of combinations, as for example, כִּי אִם, a strong adversative, *but, but rather*; e.g. לֹא עָכַרְתִּי אֶת-יִשְׂרָאֵל כִּי אִם-אַתָּה וּבֵית אָבִיךָ *I have not troubled Israel, but you and the house of your father* (1

Kings 18:18). Or again, עַד כִּי *until*, as in עַד כִּי-יָבֹא שִׁילֹה [ק״ שִׁילוֹ] *until Shiloh comes* (Genesis 49:10); cf. also אֶפֶס כִּי *except*. See below for the use of כִּי in legal formulations.

It should be noted that כִּי has also an asseverative use, expressing certainty, and that in this function, although it stands at the beginning of a clause, it does not in itself introduce a dependent clause; e.g. כִּי-לֶאֱוִיל יַהֲרָג-כָּעַשׂ *surely, for the fool vexation slays* (Job 5:2); אִם לֹא תַאֲמִינוּ כִּי לֹא תֵאָמֵנוּ *if you do not affirm, surely you will not be confirmed* (Isaiah 7:9); cf. also 1 Kings 18:27: קִרְאוּ בְקוֹל-גָּדוֹל כִּי-אֱלֹהִים הוּא *Cry in a loud voice! surely he is God!*

Among other conjunctions, besides those used in conditional and purpose clauses (see below), there are יַעַן *on account of, because*; פֶּן *lest*; and several expressing time, such as כַּאֲשֶׁר *when*; בְּטֶרֶם *before*; מֵאָז *since*, and the like. For the most part the meaning of all these is clear from a straight-forward reading of the text. Note, however, the patterns for sentences expressing conditions and purpose, which follow.

(a) *Conditional Sentences*. A conditional sentence has two main parts: the condition or supposition [*protasis*] and the result or consequence [*apodosis*]. The condition or supposition [the protasis] is introduced mostly by אִם if, כִּי *if, when*, לוּ and הֵן *if*. The result of the condition [the apodosis] may take a variety of verbal forms: perfect or imperfect, jussive, cohortative, imperative, or vāv consecutive; it is only seldom introduced by a particle, such as הִנֵּה *behold* or אָז *then*. Note the following examples: אִם-יְחַיֻּנוּ נִחְיֶה *if they keep us alive, we shall live* (2 Kings 7:4); אִם-יהוה הָאֱלֹהִים לְכוּ אַחֲרָיו *if Yahveh is the God, go after him* (1 Kings 18:21); אִם-תֵּלְכִי עִמִּי וְהָלָכְתִּי *if you go with me, I shall go* (Judges 4:8); וְאִם לֹא תַעֲשׂוּן כֵּן הִנֵּה חֲטָאתֶם *and if you do not do so, behold you have sinned* (Numbers 32:23). Of course, the order may also be reversed, e.g. לֹא אַשְׁחִית אִם-אֶמְצָא שָׁם אַרְבָּעִים וַחֲמִשָּׁה *I will not destroy, if I find there forty-five* (Genesis 18:28).

Two formulaic constructions related to the conditional sentence remain to be noted: the formulas for casuistic law and for oath-making.

(i) The formula for *casuistic law* with its several conditions is well-illustrated by Exodus 21:18-19, where כִּי introduces a series of general circumstances and אִם a series of modifying conditions. Note also that the apodosis is introduced by a vāv consecutive and continued by a relative clause introduced by רַק *only, except*.

וְכִי-יְרִיבֻן אֲנָשִׁים
וְהִכָּה-אִישׁ אֶת-רֵעֵהוּ בְּאֶבֶן אוֹ בְאֶגְרֹף
וְלֹא יָמוּת
וְנָפַל לְמִשְׁכָּב
אִם-יָקוּם
וְהִתְהַלֵּךְ בַּחוּץ עַל-מִשְׁעַנְתּוֹ
וְנִקָּה הַמַּכֶּה
רַק שִׁבְתּוֹ יִתֵּן
וְרַפֹּא יְרַפֵּא

When two men fight,
and one hits the other with a stone or fist,
and he does not die,
and he falls into bed [i.e., is laid up!]
if he gets up
and walks in the open with a staff,
the one hitting is cleared,
except he must pay his time of recovery
and see that he is fully recovered.

(ii) Upon first reading, the *oath formula* seems somewhat confusing. This is because the formula in its full form does not anywhere appear. It can, however, be reconstructed. To swear that something will not at all happen, the full formula is: *As Yahveh lives, thus may God do to me and thus may he add, if* [אִם, or sometimes

כִּי] *such and such happens!* It is a strong negative oath. Conversely, to swear that something will indeed happen, the full formula is: *As Yahveh lives, thus may God do to me and thus may he add, if not happens* [אִם לֹא] *such and such!*

So it is, that in the abbreviated manner in which oaths are made, אִם *introduces a negative oath*; e.g. חַי יהוה . . אִם-יִהְיֶה הַשָּׁנִים הָאֵלֶּה טַל וּמָטָר כִּי אִם-לְפִי דְבָרִי. *As Yahveh lives . . . if there is these years dew and rain except by my word*, which in view of the above formula means, *there shall not be dew and rain* (1 Kings 17:1). In a similar way אִם לֹא *introduces a positive oath*, as in David's promise to Amasa, כֹּה יַעֲשֶׂה-לִי אֱלֹהִים וְכֹה יוֹסִיף אִם-לֹא שַׂר-צָבָא תִּהְיֶה *Thus may God do to me and thus may he add, if you do not become commander of the host, meaning that he shall indeed be the commander* (2 Samuel 19:14).

(b) *Purpose Clauses.* Purpose may be implied by the simple juxtaposition of clauses, joined by vāv conjunctive or consecutive; e.g. קְחִי-נָא לִי מְעַט-מַיִם בַּכְּלִי וְאֶשְׁתֶּה *take for me a little water in a vessel and I shall drink*, or, as *NRSV* translates, *so that I may drink* (1 Kings 17:10). Purpose is explicitly expressed by the use of the infinitive construct (usually with ל ) and by the particles לְמַעַן and בַּעֲבוּר *in order that, for the sake of*; e.g. וַיְבַקְשׁוּ אֶת-נַפְשִׁי לְקַחְתָּהּ *and they seek my life to take it* (1 Kings 19:14); צִוִּיתִיךָ לְבִלְתִּי אֲכָל-מִמֶּנּוּ *I commanded you not to eat of it* (Genesis 3:11). For purpose introduced by the particles, note the following: כַּבֵּד אֶת-אָבִיךָ וְאֶת-אִמֶּךָ לְמַעַן יַאֲרִכוּן יָמֶיךָ *honor your father and your mother that your days may be long* (Exodus 20:12); הִנֵּה אָנֹכִי בָּא אֵלֶיךָ בְּעַב הֶעָנָן בַּעֲבוּר יִשְׁמַע הָעָם בְּדַבְּרִי עִמָּךְ *Behold, I am coming to you in the mass of cloud, in order that the people may hear my speaking with you* (Exodus 19:9).

---

# GLOSSARY

The glossary lists all words used in the Grammar except those in the fully-translated examples of textual problems in Chapter XV of the *Introduction.* The arrangement of the words follows the order of Brown, Driver, Briggs, *Hebrew and English Lexicon of the Old Testament.*

## א

אָב *n.m.* father; *pl.* אָבוֹת

אָבֵל-מְהוֹלָה *GN.* Abel-meholah

אֶבֶן *n.f.* stone

אָדָם *n.m.* humankind, man

אֲדָמָה *n.f.* land, ground, earth

אֱדוֹם *G.N.* Edom

אָדוֹן *n.m.* lord

אֲדֹנָי *n.m., pl. of majesty* Lord (= Yahveh)

אַדֶּרֶת *n.f.* cloak, mantle

אָהֵב *vb.* to love

אַהֲבָה *n.f.* love

אוּלַי *adv.* perhaps

[אור]

אוֹר *n.m. & f.* light; *pl.* אוֹרִים

מְאוּרָה *n.f.* hole, den (of a viper)

אָז *adv.* then, at that time

אֹזֶן *n.f.* ear

אֵזוֹר *n.m.* girdle, waistcloth

אָח *n.m.* brother

אַחְאָב *P.N.* Ahab

אֶחָד *adj. & numeral* one, each, a certain one

אַחֵר *adj.* other, another

אַחַר *adv.* after, behind

אַחֲרֵי *adv.* after, behind
אַחֲרוֹן *adj.* coming after, behind, last
אֲחֹרַנִּית *adv.* backwards
אֹיֵב / אוֹיֵב *pt. m.* enemy
אִיזֶבֶל *P.N.* Jezebel
אַיִן / אֵין *substantive, particle of negation* there is not, there are not
אִישׁ *n.m.* man, husband; *pl.* אֲנָשִׁים
אַךְ *adv.* surely, but
[אכל]
אָכַל *vb.* to eat, devour, destroy
אֲכִילָה *n.f.* food
מַאֲכֹלֶת *n.f.* fuel
אַל *adv. of negation* not
אֶל *prep.* to, unto
אֵלֶּה *demonstrative pron. m. and f. pl.* these
[אלה]
אֵל *n.m.* god
אֱלֹהִים *n.m. (usually taken as a plural of majesty)* god(s), God
אֵלִיָּהוּ *P.N.* Elijah
אֱלִישָׁע *P.N.* Elisha
אַלְמָנָה *n.f.* widow
אֶלֶף *n.m.* thousand
אֵם *n.f.* mother
אִם *conj.* if. אִם *is used to introduce a negative oath and* אִם לֹא *a postive oath; note also its use in continuing a question.*
[אמן]
אָמֵן *vb.* to be stable, firm; *hip̄'îl* to believe
אֱמוּנָה *n.f.* faithfulness, firmness, fidelity, faith
אֱמֶת *n.f.* truth, firmness, faithfulness
אָמַר *vb.* to say, command, order
אֲנַחְנוּ *pron. 1 c. pl.* we

אֲנִי *pron. 1 c. sg.* I

אָנֹכִי *pron. 1 c. sg.* I

[אנף]

אַף *n.m.* nose, anger

[אנשׁ]

אִשָּׁה *n.f.* woman, wife; *pl.* נָשִׁים; cf. אִישׁ

[אנת]

אַתְּ *pron. 2 f. sg.* you

אַתָּה *pron. 2 m. sg.* you

אַתֶּם *pron. 2 m. pl.* you

אַתֶּן *pron. 2 f. pl.* you

אָסַף *vb.* to gather

אָסַר *vb.* to tie, bind, gird, imprison

אַף *conj.* yea, indeed

אַף *See under* אנף

אַרְבַּע *See under* רבע

אַרְבָּעִים *See under* רבע

אַרְיֵה *n.m.* lion

אָרַךְ *vb.* to be long

אֲרָם *GN.* Aram

אֶרֶץ *n.f.* earth, land, country

אֵשׁ *n.f.* fire

אֶשְׁדָּת *n.f.; doubtful form, traditionally taken as a compound:* דָּת + אֵשׁ *with the meaning* fiery decree, fiery law

[אשׁר]

אַשְׁרֵי *pl. construct of* אֶשֶׁר *introducing a beatitude* happy, blessed

אֲשֵׁרָה *P.N. (and symbol of the goddess)* Asherah; pole, sacred tree

[אשׁר]

אֲשֶׁר *particle of relation* that

כַּאֲשֶׁר *conj.* when, just as

-אֶת / אֵת *nota accusativa, the particle placed before a definite direct object*

אֵת *prep.* with, at the side of

אַתְּ *See under* אנת

אַתָּה *See under* אנת

אַתֶּם *See under* אנת

אַתֶּן *See under* אנת

## ב

בְּ *inseparable prep.* in, by, with, at, against, from

בְּאֵר-שֶׁבַע *G.N.* Beer-sheba

[בדד]

בַּד *n.m.* separation; *with* ל alone, by itself

בְּהֵמָה *n.f.* animal, cattle, beast

בּוֹא *vb.* to come, enter; *qal perf.* בָּא

בָּחַר *vb.* to choose, elect; *the object is often introduced by* ב

בָּחִיר *n.m.* elect, chosen one

בָּטַח *vb.* to trust

בִּין *vb.* to understand, discern

בִּינָה *n.f.* understanding, discernment

בֵּין *prep.* between, among

בַּיִת *n.m.* house; *pl.* בָּתִּים

[בלה]

בִּלְתִּי *subst. used as particle of negation;* לְבִלְתִּי so as not

בָּלַס *vb.* to gather, tend figs

בֵּן *n.m.* son, child; *pl.* בָּנִים

בָּנָה *vb.* to build

בָּעַל *vb.* to marry, rule over

בַּעַל *n.m and P.N.* lord, owner, husband, master; Ba‘al

בַּעֲלָה *n.f.* mistress, wife

בָּקָר *n.m.* ox, cattle

בֹּקֶר *n.m.* morning

בִּקֵּשׁ *vb.* to seek

בַּר *See under* ברר

בָּרָא *vb.* to create, make

[ברה]

בְּרִית *n.f.* covenant

בָּרַךְ *vb.* to kneel, bend the knee; *intensive* בֵּרֵךְ to bless

בֶּרֶךְ *n.f.* knee

בְּרָכָה *n.f.* blessing

[ברר]

בַּר *adj.* pure, clean

בְּרִית *See under* ברה

בָּשָׂר *n.m.* flesh

בָּשַׁל *vb.* to boil

## ג

[גבר]

גִּבּוֹר *adj.* strong, mighty; *as a noun* warrior, hero

גְּבוּרָה *n.f.* strength, might

גְּוִיָּה *n.f.* body, corpse

גָּדַד *vb.* to cut

גְּדִי *n.m.* kid

גָּדַל *vb.* to be great, grow up

גָּדוֹל *adj.* great

גָּהַר *vb.* to bend, crouch

גּוֹי *nm.* nation, people

גּוּר *vb.* to sojourn, dwell; *qal perf.* גָּר

גֶּזַע *n.m.* stock, stem

גִּיל *vb.* to rejoice, be glad

גִּילָה *n.f.* rejoicing, joy, gladness

גָּלָה *vb.* to reveal, uncover

גָּלַל *vb.* to roll

גִּלְעָד *G.N.* Gilead

גַּם *adv.* also, moreover, even, yea

גָּמַל *vb.* to deal fully with, recompence, deal out; wean

גֶּפֶן *n.f.* vine

גֶּשֶׁם *n.m.* rain

## ד

דֹּב / דּוֹב *n.m.* bear
[דבר 1]
דָּבַר *vb.* to speak; *usually in the intensive* דִּבֵּר
דָּבָר *n.m.* word, thing, event
דַּבֶּרֶת *n.f.* word
[דבר 2]
מִדְבָּר *n.m.* wilderness
דּוֹב *See* דֹּב
דּוֹד *n.m.* uncle, beloved
דָּוִד *P.N.* David
דּוּמָה *n.f.* silence
דּוּמָה *G.N.* Dumah (Edom)
דִּין *vb.* to judge; *qal perf.* דָּן
דַּל *adj.* poor, low, weak
דָּם *n.m.* blood
דְּמָמָה *n.f.* silence
דַּמֶּשֶׂק *G.N.* Damascus
דֵּעָה *See under* ידע
דַּעַת *See under* ידע
דַּק *adj.* crushed, pulverized
דֶּרֶךְ *n.m. & f.* way, road
דָּת *n.f.* decree, law

## ה

-הֲ *interrogative particle*
הָדָה *vb.* to stretch out (the hand)
הֲדֹם *n.m.* stool, footstool
הָדָר *n.m.* splendor, majesty, honor
[הוא]
הוּא *pron. 3 m.s.* he, that
הִיא *pron. 3 f.s.* she, that

[הוה]

יְהוָה *P.N.* Yahveh

יָהּ *P.N.* Yah

יֵהוּא *P.N.* Jehu

הָיָה *vb.* to become, happen

הֵיכָל *n.m.* palace, temple

הָלַךְ *vb.* to go, walk

הָלַל *vb.* be boastful; *intensive* הִלֵּל to praise

הֵם / הֵמָּה *pron. 3 m.pl.* they, those

הָמוֹן *n.m.* sound, noise, crowd, abundance

הֵנָּה *pron. 3 f.pl.* they, those

הִנֵּה *demonstrative particle* behold, lo

הָרַג *v.b.* to slay, kill

הָרָה *vb.* to conceive, be pregnant

הָרַס *vb.* to throw down, break down, destroy

[הרר]

הַר *n.m.* mountain, hill, hill-country

הָתַל *vb.* to deceive, mock

## ו

וְ *conj.* and

## ז

זְאֵב *n.m.* wolf

[זבח]

זָבַח *vb.* to slaughter, sacrifice

זֶבַח *n.m.* sacrifice

מִזְבֵּחַ *n.m.* altar; *pl.* מִזְבְּחוֹת

זֶה *demonstrative pron. m.* this

זָהָב *n.m.* gold

זָכַר *vb.* to remember

[זמר]

מִזְמוֹר *n.m.* musical piece, melody, song, psalm

זָקֵן *vb.* to be old

זָקֵן *adj.* old; *as a noun* an elder

[זרח]

זָרַח *vb.* to rise (as the sun), come forth

מִזְרָח *n.m.* place of sunrise, east

זֶרַע *n.m.* seed

יִזְרְעֶאל *G.N.* Jezreel

## ח

חָבָא *vb.* to withdraw, hide

חָבַב *vb.* to love, cleave to

חֲבַקּוּק *P.N.* Habakkuk

חָבֵר *n.m.* companion, associate

חַג *n.m.* festival

חָדָשׁ *adj.* new

חָוָה *vb. appearing only in šîn tāv stem (causative reflexive)* הִשְׁתַּחֲוָה to prostrate oneself, fall down, worship

[חול 2]

חַיִל *n.m.* strength, wealth, army

[חיק / חוק]

חֵק / חֵיק *n.m.* bosom

חוּר *See under* חרר

חֲזָאֵל *P.N.* Hazael

חָזָק *adj.* strong, mighty

חָטָא *vb.* to sin

חֵטְא *n.m.* sin

חַטָּאָה *n.f.* sin, sin-offering

חֹטֶר *n.m.* branch, rod, shoot

חָיָה *vb.* to live, be alive

חַי *adj.* alive, living

חַיָּה *n.f.* living thing, animal
חַיִּים *n.m. pl.* life
חַיִל *See under* חול
חָכָם *adj.* wise
חָכְמָה *n.f.* wisdom
חָלָה *vb.* to be sick, be ill
חֳלִי *n.m.* sickness, illness
חָלָץ *n.f., only in dual* loins
חָלַק *vb.* to divide, share
חָמֵשׁ *n., numeral* five
חֲמִשִּׁים *n., numeral* fifty
חֶסֶד *n.m.* steadfast love, covenant loyalty, mercy, kindness
חָסִיד *adj.* faithful, pious, godly
חָסֵר *vb.* to lack, need
חָצִיר *n.m.* grass, herbage

[2 חרב]

חֹרֵב / חוֹרֵב *G.N.* Horeb

[3 חרב]

חֶרֶב *n.f.* sword
חָרַד *vb.* to tremble, be afraid

[3 חרר]

חוֹר / חֹר *n.m.* hole, den, hiding place
חָרַשׁ *vb.* to cut in, engrave, plow
חֹשֶׁךְ *n.m.* darkness
חָתַת *vb.* to be dismayed, shattered

## ט

טוֹב *adj.* pleasant, pleasing, good
טוֹב *n.m.* a good thing, benefit, welfare
טוֹבָה *n.f.* good, good things, benefit, welfare
טַל *n.m.* dew
טֶרֶף *n.m.* prey

## י

[יבל]
תֵּבֵל *n.f.* world
יָבֵשׁ *vb.* to be dry, be withered
יָד *n.f. & m.* hand, power
[ידע]
יָדַע *vb.* to know
דֵּעָה *n.f.* knowledge
דַּעַת *n.f.* knowledge
יָהּ *See under* הוה
יֵהוּא *See under* הוה
יְהוּדָה *G.N.* Judah
יְהוָה *See under* הוה
יוֹם *n.m.* day; *pl.* יָמִים
יִזְרְעֶאל *See under* זרע
יָחַד *vb.* to be united
יַחַד *n.m.* unitedness, together
יָכַח *vb. in causative* הוֹכִיחַ to decide, prove, reprove
יָלַד *vb.* to give birth to, bear
יֶלֶד *n.m.* child, boy, youth
יָם *n.m.* sea, ocean; *pl.* יַמִּים
יָמִין *n.f.* right hand, hand, south
יָנַק *vb.* to suck; *causative* הֵינִיק to give suck
יָסַד *vb.* to establish, found
יָסַף *vb.* to add, increase
יָעַד *vb.* to appoint; *reflexive* נוֹעַד to arrange, make an appointment
[יעץ]
יָעַץ *vb.* to advise, counsel
עֵצָה *n.f.* advice, counsel
יַעֲקֹב *See under* עקב
יַעַר *n.m.* forest, wood(s)
יָפַע *vb. only in hip̄'îl* הוֹפִיעַ to shine forth

יָצָא *vb.* to go forth, go out; *causative* הוֹצִיא to bring out
יִצְחָק *See under* צחק
יָצַק *vb.* to pour
יָקַץ *vb.* to awake
[יקשׁ]
מוֹקֵשׁ *n.m.* bait, lure
יָרֵא *vb.* to fear, be in awe, tremble
יִרְאָה *n.f.* fear, awe, dread
יָרַד *vb.* to go down, descend, flow
יַרְדֵּן / הַיַּרְדֵּן *G.N.* the Jordan
[ירה]
תּוֹרָה *n.f.* instruction, revelation, law
יְרוּשָׁלַםִ *G.N.* Jerusalem
יִרְמְיָהוּ *See under* 2 רמה
[ירשׁ]
מוֹרָשָׁה *n.f.* possession
יִשְׂרָאֵל *See under* שׂרא / שׂרה
יֵשׁ *substantive, particle of existence* there is, there are
[ישׁב]
יָשַׁב *vb.* to sit, dwell, be enthroned
תּוֹשָׁב / תֹּשָׁב *n.m.* dweller, inhabitant, sojourner
יָשֵׁן *vb.* to sleep, be asleep
[ישׁע]
יָשַׁע *vb.* to be wide, spacious; *causative* הוֹשִׁיעַ to save, deliver
יְשַׁעְיָהוּ *P.N.* Isaiah
יְשׁוּעָה *n.f.* salvation
[ישׁר]
יָשָׁר *adj.* upright
מִישׁוֹר *n.m.* uprightness
יְשֻׁרוּן *P.N., a poetic name for Israel* upright one
יָתַר *vb.* to remain over

## כ

כְּ *inseparable prep.* like, according to, as
כַּאֲשֶׁר *See under* אשר
[כבב]
כּוֹכָב *n.m.* star
כָּבֵד *vb.* to be heavy
כָּבוֹד *n.m.* glory
כֶּבֶשׂ *n.m.* lamb
כַּד *n..f.* jar
כֹּה *demonstrative adv.* thus, so
כֹּהֵן *n.m.* priest
כֹּחַ / כּוֹחַ *See under* כחח
כֹּל / כּוֹל *See under* כלל
כּוּל *vb.* to contain; *in pilpēl* כִּלְכֵּל to sustain, nourish
כּוּן *vb.* to be firm; *in causative* הֵכִין to establish
[כחח]
כֹּחַ / כּוֹחַ *n.m.* strength, power
כִּי *conj.* that, for, when, yea; *with* אִם *a strong adversative* כִּי אִם but rather; *in oath formulas* if, surely not
כֶּלֶב *n.m.* dog
כָּלָה *vb.* to be complete, spent, come to an end
כְּלִי *n.m.* article, utensil, vessel, tool
[כלל]
כֹּל / כּוֹל *n.m.* whole, all, every
כָּנָף *n.f.* wing, extremity
כִּסֵּא *n.m.* seat, throne
כָּסָה *vb.* to cover, hide, conceal
כֶּסֶף *n.m.* silver, money
[כפף]
כַּף *n.f.* hand, palm
[כפר 3]
כְּפִיר *n.m.* lion

כְּרִית *See under* כרת

כַּרְמֶל / הַכַּרְמֶל *G.N.* the Carmel

כָּרַע *vb.* to bow down, bend

[כרת]

כָּרַת *vb.* to cut; *cf. the idiom* כָּרַת בְּרִית to make a covenant

כְּרִית *G.N.* Cherith

כָּתַב *vb.* to write

## ל

לְ *inseparable prep.* to, for

לֹא *adv.* not, no

[לאך]

מַלְאָךְ *n.m.* messenger, angel

לֵב *n.m. & f* heart, mind, will; *pl.* לִבּוֹת

לֵבָב *n.m.* heart, mind, will

לְבַד *See under* בדד

לוּט *vb.* to wrap closely, enwrap, envelop

לוּן / לִין *vb.* to lodge, to pass the night

לָחַךְ *vb.* to lick

[1 לחם]

לָחַם *vb. in the reflexive* to fight, do battle

מִלְחָמָה *n.f.* battle, war

[2 לחם]

לֶחֶם *n.m.* food, bread

לַיִל / לַיְלָה *n.m.* night; *pl.* לֵילוֹת

לָכַד *vb.* to take, capture

לָמַד *vb.* to learn; *intensive* לִמֵּד to teach

לָמָּה *See under* מָה

לִפְנֵי *See under* פנה

## מ

מְאֹד *n.m. & adv.* muchness, abundance, exceedingly, very
מֵאָה *n.f. numeral* hundred
מְאוּמָה *indefinite pron.* anything
מְאוּרָה *See under* אור
מִדְבָּר *See under* 2 דבר
מָדַד *vb.* to measure
מָה *pron. interrogative & indefinite* what, how; *with prep.* לָמָּה for what? why?
מוֹקֵשׁ *See under* יקשׁ
מוּת *vb.* to die; *intensive and causative* הֵמִית to kill
מָוֶת *n.m.* death; *construct* מוֹת
מִזְבֵּחַ *See under* זבח
מִזְמֹר *See under* זמר
מִזְרָח *See under* זרח
מָחַץ *vb.* to smite
מַטֶּה *See under* נטה
מִטָּה *See under* נטה
מָטָר *n.m.* rain
מַיִם *n.m. only in dual* water, waters, sea, deep, drink
מִישׁוֹר *See under* ישׁר
מָלֵא *vb.* to be full, to fill
מְלֹא *n.m.* fulness, that which fills (= entire contents)
מַלְאָךְ *See under* לאך
מֶלַח *n.m.* salt
מִלְחָמָה *See under* 1 לחם
מָלַט *vb.* to escape; *intensive* to deliver, rescue
[מלך]
מֶלֶךְ *n.m.* king
מָלַךְ *vb. denominative* to be king, reign
מַמְלָכָה *n.f.* kingdom, reign
מִן *prep.* from, out of, at
מִנְחָה *n.f.* offering, gift, tribute

מִסְפֵּד *See under* ספד
מָגוֹג *See under* עוג
מְעוֹנָה *See under* עון
מְעַט *n.m.* a little, fewness, a few
מַעְיָן *See under* עין
מְעָרָה *See under* ערר
מַעֲשֶׂה *See under* עשׂה
מָצָא *vb.* to come upon, reach to, find
מִצְוָה *See under* צוה
מָקוֹם *See under* קום
מִצְרַיִם *G.N.* Egypt
[מרא]
מְרִיא *n.m.* fatling
מְרַאֲשׁוֹת *See under* ראשׁ
מַרְאֶה *See under* ראה
מִרְמָה *See under* 1 רמה
מָשַׁח *vb.* to smear, anoint
מָשִׁיחַ *n.m.* anointed one, messiah
מָשַׁל *vb.* to ruler (over); *often with* ב
מִשְׁמָע *See under* שׁמע
מִשְׁפָּט *See under* שׁפט
מִשְׁתֶּה *See under* שׁתה
מָתַי *interrogative adv.* when?
מֹתֶן *n.m. only in dual* loins

## נ

נָא *enclitic, not usually to be translated*
נְאֻם *n.m.* oracle, utterance, saying
[נבא]
נָבִיא *n.m.* prophet
נָבָא *vb. denominative* to be a prophet, prophesy
נָבַט *vb.* to look
נָגַד *vb. only in causative* הִגִּיד to tell, declare, narrate

נָגַהּ *vb.* to shine
נָגַע *vb.* to touch, strike
נָגַשׂ *vb.* to oppress, be a taskmaster
נָגַשׁ *vb.* to draw near, approach
נְדָבָה *n.f.* free-will offering
נָהַג *vb.* to lead, drive
נָהָר *n.m.* stream, flood, river; *pl* נְהָרִים / נְהָרוֹת
נוּחַ *vb.* to rest, settle down, be quiet; *qal perf.* נָח
נוּס *vb.* to flee, escape; *qal perf.* נָס
נוּעַ *vb.* to tremble, totter
נַחַל *n.m.* wadi, torrent, stream
נָחַם *vb.* to be sorry, relent; *intensive* נִחֵם to comfort, encourage

[נטה]

נָטָה *vb.* to stretch out, bend, incline
מַטֶּה *n.m.* staff, rod
מִטָּה *n.f.* bed
נָכָה *vb.* *mostly causative* הִכָּה / יַכֶּה to smite
נָכַר *vb.* to regard, recognize
נָמֵר *n.m.* leopard
נִמְשִׁי *P.N.* Nimshi
נָסַע *vb.* to journey, set out, travel
נַעַר *n.m.* boy, youth, lad, retainer
נְעֻרִים *n.f. pl.* youth (time of), early life
נָפַל *vb.* to fall
נֶפֶשׁ *n.f.* self, (living) being, life
נֵצֶר *n.m.* shoot, sprout
נָקִי *adj.* clean, free from, innocent
נָשָׂא *vb.* to lift up, raise, carry, take away, exalt
נְשָׁמָה *n.f.* breath
נָשַׁק *vb.* to kiss
נָתַח *vb.* to cut up, cut in pieces, divide
נָתַן *vb.* to give, set, appoint

## ס

סְאָה *n.f.* a measure of flour or grain, c. 10 quarts

[סאן]

סְאוֹן *n.m.* sandal, boot

[סבב]

סָבַב *vb.* to turn about, go around, surround

סָבִיב *adv. & prep.* round about, around

סֹבֶל *n.m.* burden

[סוג / שׂוג]

סִיג / שִׂיג *n.m.* a withdrawing. a moving away *(?)*

סוֹד *n.m.* council, counsel

סוּס *n.m.* horse

סוּסָה *n.f.* mare

סִינַי *G.N.* Sinai

סָלַח *vb.* to forgive, pardon; *the obect is introduced by* לְ

סֶלַע *n.m.* crag, cliff

סָעַד *vb.* to support, uphold

סָעִיף *n.m.* cleft, branch; *pl.* סְעִפִּים

[ספד]

סָפַד *vb.* to wail, lament

מִסְפֵּד *n.m.* wailing, lamentation, lament

[ספר]

סָפַר *vb.* to count; *intensive* סִפֵּר to recount, relate, tell

סֵפֶר *n.m.* book

מִסְפָּר *n.m.* number

סָתַר *vb.* to hide, conceal

## ע

עָב *See under* עוב

[עבד]

עָבַד *vb.* to work, serve

עֶבֶד *n.m.* slave, servant devotee.

עֹבַדְיָה *P.N.* Obadiah
עָבַר *vb.* to pass through, pass over, pass through
עֻגָה *See under* עוג
עֵגֶל *n.m.* calf
עַד *prep.* to, until, unto
[עוב]
עָב *n.m.* cloud
[עוג]
עֻגָה *n.f.* disc or cake of bread
מָעוֹג *n.m.* cake
עוֹד *adv.* still, yet, again
[עוה]
עָוֹן *n.m.* guilt, iniquity, punishment
עוֹלָם *See under* [2 עלם]
[עון]
מְעֹנָה *n.f.* dwelling place, habitation, den, lair
עוֹף *vb.* to fly; *qal perf.* עָף
עָזַב *vb.* to forsake, leave
[עזז]
עֹז *n.m.* strength, might
[1 עזר]
עָזַר *vb.* to help
[2 עזר]
עָזַר *vb.* to be strong, take hold
עַיִן *n.f.* eye
[2 עין]
מַעְיָן *n.m.* spring
עִיר *n.f.* city, town; *pl.* עָרִים
עָכַר *vb.* to stir up, disturb, trouble
עַל *See under* עלה
עֹל *See under* עלל
[עלה]
עָלָה *vb.* to go up, ascend
עֹלָה *n.f.* burnt offering, whole burnt offering

עֲלִיָּה *n.f.* upper chamber, roof chamber
תְּעָלָה *n.f.* water course, trench
עַל *prep.* upon, over, on behalf of, concerning, to, against
[עלל]
עֹל *n.m.* yoke
[עלם 1]
עַלְמָה *n.f.* young woman
[עלם 2]
עוֹלָם *n.m.* long duration, age, perpetuity, everlasting, world
עַם *See under* עמם
עִם *See under* עמם
עָמַד *vb.* to stand
[עמם]
עַם *n.m.* people; *pl.* עַמִּים
עִם *prep.* with
עִמָּנוּ-אֵל *P.N.* Immanuel
[ענה 1]
עָנָה *vb.* to speak, answer, respond
עֵת *n.f.* time; *pl.* עִתִּים / עִתּוֹת
עַתָּה *adv.* now
[ענה 3]
עָנָה *vb.* to be bowed down, afflicted, poor
עָנָו *n.m.* poor, afflicted, humble
עָנִי *adj.* poor, afflicted, humble
עָפָר *n.m.* dust, earth
עֵץ *n.m.* tree, wood
עֵצָה *See under* יעץ
עָצַר *vb.* to restrain, retain
[עקב]
יַעֲקֹב *P.N.* Jacob
[ערב 5]
עֶרֶב *n.m.* evening

[ערב 6]

עֹרֵב *n.m.* raven

עָרַךְ *vb.* to arrange, set in order

[ערר]

מְעָרָה *n.f.* cave

[עשׂה]

עָשָׂה *vb.* to do, make, work, create

מַעֲשֶׂה *n.m.* work, deed

עֶשֶׂר / עֲשָׂרָה *n. m. & f., numeral* ten

עֵת *See under* 1 ענה

עַתָּה *See under* 1 ענה

## פ

פָּארָן *G.N.* Paran

פֶּה *n.m.* mouth; *construct* פִּי

פֹּה *adv.* here

פּוּץ *vb.* to be dispersed, scattered

פַּח *n.m.* trap (for birds)

פִּי *See under* פֶּה

פֶּלֶא *n.m.* wonder

[פנה]

פָּנָה *vb.* to turn

פָּנֶה / פָּנִים *n.m. only in pl.* face

לִפְנֵי *prep.* before, in front of

פָּסַח *vb.* to limp

פַּעַם *n.f.* foot, anvil, occurrence, blow (*cf. French pas*)

פַּר *See under* 2 פרר

פֶּרֶד *n.m.* mule

[פרה]

פָּרָה *vb.* to bear fruit, be fruitful

פְּרִי *n.m.* fruit

פָּרַח *vb.* to sprout, bud

פָּרַק *vb.* to tear apart, tear away

[פרר 1]

פָּרַר *vb. in causative* הֵפֵר to frustrate, break

[פרר 2]

פַּר *n.m.* bull, steer

פָּרָה *n.f.* cow, heifer

פָּשַׁע *vb.* to sin, rebell, transgress

פֶּשַׁע *n.m.* sin, transgression

פַּת *See under* פתת

פֶּתַח *n.m.* opening, doorway, entrance

פֶּתֶן *n.m.* serpent, venomous snake

[פתת]

פַּת *n.f.* fragment, bit, morsel (of bread)

## צ

צָבָא *n.m.* host, army, time of service; *pl.* צְבָאוֹת

[צדק]

צֶדֶק *n.m.* righteousness, saving activity

צְדָקָה *n.f.* righteousness, righteous act, saving act

צָדֵק *vb.* denominative to be righteous, just

צַדִּיק *adj.* righteous, just; *as a noun* a righteous person

צֹהַר / צָהֳרַיִם *n.m.* noon, midday

[צוה]

צָוָה *vb. only in intensive* צִוָּה to command

מִצְוָה *n.f.* commandment

[צחק]

יִצְחָק *P.N.* Isaac

צִיּוֹן *G.N.* Zion

צֵל *n.m.* shadow

צַלְמָוֶת *n.f.* darkness

צָמֵא *vb.* to be thirsty

צָמָא *n.m.* thirst

צֶמֶד *n.m.* couple, pair, yoke

צָפוֹן *See under* צפן
צִפּוֹר *See under* צפר
צַפַּחַת *n.f.* jar, jug
[צפן]
צָפוֹן *n.f.* north
צִפְעוֹנִי *n.m.* poisonous serpent
[צפר]
צִפֹּר / צִפּוֹר *n.f.* bird
צָרְפַת *G.N.* Zarephath

## ק

קָבַץ *vb.* to gather, collect
קֶדֶם *n.m.* front, east, aforetime
קָדַר *vb.* to be dark
[קדשׁ]
קֹדֶשׁ *n.m.* holiness, separateness
קָדוֹשׁ *adj.* holy; *as a noun* a holy one = a god, (the) Holy One = God
קָדַשׁ *vb. denominative* to be holy, set apart, consecrated
מִקְדָּשׁ *n.m.* sanctuary
קָהָל *n.m.* assembly, congregation
קְהִלָּה *n.f.* assembly, congregation
[קוה]
תִּקְוָה *n.f.* hope
קוֹל *n.m.* thunder, noise, roar, voice; *pl.* קֹלוֹת
[קום]
קוּם *vb.* to stand, arise, establish; *qal perf.* קָם
מָקוֹם *n.m.* place
קָטַל *vb.* to kill
[קטן]
קָטֹן *vb.* to be small
קָטֹן *adj.* small

קֵיץ *See under* קצץ
קִישׁוֹן *G.N.* Kishon
קֶמַח *n.m.* flour, meal
קָנָא *vb.* to be zealous, jealous
קִנְאָה *n.f.* zeal, jealousy
קָסַם *vb.* to divine, soothsay
קָצִיר *See under* קצר
[קצץ]
קֵיץ *n.m.* end
[קצר]
קָצִיר *n.m.* harvest
1 קָרָא *vb.* to call, proclaim, read
2 קָרָא *vb.* to meet, encounter, befall
קָרַב *vb.* to draw near, approach
קֶרֶב *n.m.* inward part, midst
קָשַׁב *vb.* to give attention, be attentive
קֶשֶׁב *n.m.* attentiveness
קָשַׁשׁ *vb. denominative* to gather stubble

## ר

[ראה]
רָאָה *vb.* to see
מַרְאֶה *n.m.* sight, appearance
[ראשׁ]
רֹאשׁ *n.m.* head, top, summit
רִאשׁוֹן *adj.* first, former, chief
מְרַאֲשׁוֹת *n.f. pl.* a place at the head, head-place
[רבב]
רַב *adj.* many, much, great
רְבָבָה *n.f.* multitude, myriad, ten thousand
[רבה]
רָבָה *vb.* to be much, many, great
מַרְבֶּה *n.m.* abundance, increase

[רבע]
אַרְבָּעָה / אַרְבַּע *n. m. & f., numeral* four
אַרְבָּעִים *n. numeral* forty
רָבַץ *vb.* to stretch out, crouch
רֶגֶל *n.f.* foot
רָדָה *vb.* to subdue, rule, have dominion over
[רוח]
רוּחַ *n.f.* wind, breath, spirit
רִיחַ *vb.* denominative to take delight in
רוּם *vb.* to be high, exalted, raised up; *qal perf.* רָם
רוּץ *vb.* to run
רֶחֶם *n.m.* womb
רִיחַ *See under* רוח
רָכַב *vb.* to ride
רֶכֶב *n.m.* chariot, chariotry
[רמה 1]
מִרְמָה *n.f.* deceit, treachery
[רמה 2]
יִרְמְיָהוּ *P.N.* Jeremiah
רֹמַח *n.m.* spear, lance
רַע *See under* רעע
רֵעַ *See under* רעה 2
רָעֵב *vb.* to be hungry
רָעָב *n.m.* famine, hunger
[רעה 1]
רָעָה *vb.* to shepherd, pasture, tend
[רעה 2]
רֵעַ *n.m.* friend
[רעע]
רַע *adj. & n. m.* unpleasant, evil, harmful, calamity, misery, harm
רָעַע *vb. denominative* to be unpleasant, harmful, evil
רָעָה *n.f.* evil, calamity, misery, harm

רָעַשׁ *vb.* to shake, quake
רַעַשׁ *n.m.* quaking, shaking, earthquake
רָפָא *vb.* to make whole, heal
רִצְפָּה / רֶצֶף *n.f.* glowing stone, burning coal; *pl.* רְצָפוֹת
רָקִיעַ *n.m.* beaten-out expanse (of metal), firmament, vault of heaven
רָשָׁע *adj.* wicked
רֹתֶם *n.m.* broom plant, tree

## שׂ

שָׂבַע *vb.* to be sated, satisfied
שָׂדֶה *n.m.* open field, country, land; *pl.* שָׂדוֹת
שִׂיג *See under* סוג
שִׂיחַ *n.m.* musing, complaint
שׂוּם/ שִׂים *vb.* to put, place, set; *qal perf.* שָׂם
שָׂמַח *vb.* to rejoice, be glad, be joyful
שִׂמְחָה *n.f.* joy, gladness
שִׂמְלָה *n.f.* cloak, mantle
שָׂנֵא *vb.* to hate, be an enemy
שֵׂעִיר *G.N.* Seir
שָׂפָה *n.f.* lip, edge
[שׂרא / שׂרה]
יִשְׂרָאֵל *G.N. & P.N.* Israel
מִשְׂרָה *n.f.* rule, dominion
שַׂר *See under* שׂרר
שָׂרַף *vb.* to burn
שָׂרָף *n.m.* serpent, seraph
[שׂרר]
שַׂר *n.m.* prince

## שׁ

שָׁאַג *vb.* to roar
שָׁאַל *vb.* to ask, inquire
שָׁאַר *vb.* to remain, be left over
שְׁאֵרִית *n.f.* remnant, rest, that left over
[שׁבה]
תִּשְׁבִּי *G.N.* Tishbite
שֵׁבֶט *n.m.* rod, staff, scepter, tribe
[שׁבע]
שֶׁבַע / שִׁבְעָה *n. m. & f., numeral* seven
שְׁבִיעִית / שְׁבִיעִי *adj. m & f.* seventh
שָׁבַע *vb.* to swear
שָׁבַר *vb.* to break, shatter
[שׁדשׁ]
שֵׁשׁ / שִׁשָּׁה *n. m. & f., numeral* six
שָׁוְא *n.m.* emptiness, vanity
שׁוּב *vb.* to turn, return, repent; *qal perf.* שָׁב
שׁוּט *vb.* to go, rove about; *qal perf.* שָׁט
שׁוּל *n.m.* skirt of a robe, train
שָׁחַט *vb.* to slaughter
שַׁחַר *n.m.* dawn
שָׁחַת *vb.* to go to ruin; *mostly intensive and causative*
הִשְׁחִית / שִׁחֵת to destroy, ruin
שִׁיר *vb.* to sing; *qal perf.* שָׁר
שִׁירָה / שִׁיר *n.m. & f.* song
שִׁית *vb.* to place, set; *qal perf.* שָׁת
שָׁכַב *vb.* to lie down
שְׁכֶם *n.m.* shoulder
שָׁלוֹם *See under* שׁלם
שָׁלַח *vb.* to send, extend
שֻׁלְחָן *n.m.* table
שָׁלַךְ *vb.* to throw, cast away
שָׁלָל *n.m.* spoil, plunder, prey

[שׁלם]

שָׁלוֹם *n.m.* wholeness, well-being, prosperity, peace

[שׁלשׁ]

שָׁלוֹשׁ / שְׁלֹשָׁה *n. m. &. f., numeral* three

שְׁלִישִׁית / שְׁלִישִׁי *adj. m. & f.* third

שָׁלַשׁ *vb. denominative* to do a third time

שָׁם *adv.* there

שֵׁם *n.m.* name, reputation, fame; *pl.* שֵׁמוֹת

שָׁמַיִם *n.m. only in dual* heaven(s), sky

שָׁמֵן *vb.* to be fat, grow fat

שֶׁמֶן *n.m.* fatness, oil

[שׁמע]

שָׁמַע *vb.* to hear, obey

מִשְׁמָע *n.m.* that which is heard

שָׁמַר *vb.* to keep, watch over, guard

שֹׁמְרוֹן *G.N.* Samaria

[שׁנה 1]

שָׁנָה *vb.* to change

שָׁנָה *n.f.* year; *pl.* שָׁנִים / שָׁנוֹת

[שׁנה 2]

שָׁנָה *vb.* to repeat, do again

שְׁתַּיִם / שְׁנַיִם *n. m. & f., numeral, dual* two

שָׁנַס *vb.* to gird up

שָׁעַע *vb.* to sport, take delight in

[שׁפט]

שָׁפַט *vb.* to rule, judge

מִשְׁפָּט *n.m.* judgment, justice

שָׁפָט *P.N.* Shaphat

שָׁפַךְ *vb.* to pour out, shed

[שׁפר]

שֹׁפָר / שׁוֹפָר *n.m.* horn, ram's horn, trumpet

שִׁקְמָה *n.f.* sycamore tree

שֹׁרֶשׁ *n.m.* root, stump, stock

שֵׁשׁ *See under* שׁדשׁ

שָׁרַת *vb.* to serve, minister

[שׁתה]

שָׁתָה *vb.* to drink

מִשְׁתֶּה *n.m.* feast, banquet

שְׁתַּיִם *See under* 2 שׁנה

# ת

תֵּבֵל *See under* יבל

תֶּבֶן *n.m.* straw

תּוֹרָה *See under* ירה

תּוֹשָׁב *See under* ישׁב

תַּחַת *prep.* under, below, beneath

תָּכָה *vb., wholly doubtful root; traditional translations* to lead, assemble

תְּעָלָה *See under* עלה

תָּפַשׂ *vb.* to lay hold of, wield, handle, use skillfully

תִּקְוָה *See under* קוה

תָּקַע *vb.* to blow (a horn), give a blast

תֹּשָׁב *See under* ישׁב

תִּשְׁבִּי *See under* שׁבה

---

# INDEX OF SUBJECTS

I = Part One: An Introduction to Biblical Hebrew
II = Part Two: Continuing Biblical Hebrew

Matres lectionis, I 7, II 3a
*Plēnē* writing, I 8
Values (kinds) of vowels, I 6, II 3
Writing vowel points with consonants, I 9

Weak consonants, I 5, II 2e
Wish, expression of, II 39
By interrogative מִי, II 39b
By particles לוּ or אִם, II 39c

## INDEX OF HEBREW WORDS

------------------------------

# A GRAMMAR OF BIBLICAL HEBREW

## APPENDIX

### PARADIGM OF THE STRONG VERB

### VERBS WITH WEAK LETTERS AND GUTTURALS IN OUTLINE

Verbs with Pē Nûn [פ״ן]
Verbs with Lāmeḏ Hê [ל״ה]
Verbs with Pē Yôḏ and Pē Ālep̱ [פ״י and פ״ו]
Verbs with ‘Ayin Vāv and ‘Ayin Yôḏ [ע״ו and ע״י]
Verbs with ‘Ayin ‘Ayin [ע״ע]

Verbs with Pē Guttural
Verbs with Pē ’Ālep̱ [פ״א]
Verbs with ‘Ayin Guttural
Verbs with Lāmeḏ Guttural
Verbs with Lāmeḏ ’Ālep̱ [ל״א]

## PARADIGM OF THE STRONG VERB

| | | QAL | NIP̱‘AL |
|---|---|---|---|
| Perfect | 3 m.s. | קָטַל | נִקְטַל |
| | 3 f.s. | קָטְלָה | נִקְטְלָה |
| | 2 m.s. | קָטַלְתָּ | נִקְטַלְתָּ |
| | 2 f.s. | קָטַלְתְּ | נִקְטַלְתְּ |
| | 1 c.s. | קָטַלְתִּי | נִקְטַלְתִּי |
| | 3 c.p. | קָטְלוּ | נִקְטְלוּ |
| | 2 m.p. | קְטַלְתֶּם | נִקְטַלְתֶּם |
| | 2 f.p. | קְטַלְתֶּן | נִקְטַלְתֶּן |
| | 1 c.p. | קָטַלְנוּ | נִקְטַלְנוּ |
| Imperfect | 3 m.s. | יִקְטֹל | יִקָּטֵל |
| | 3 f.s. | תִּקְטֹל | תִּקָּטֵל |
| | 2 m.s. | תִּקְטֹל | תִּקָּטֵל |
| | 2 f.s. | תִּקְטְלִי | תִּקָּטְלִי |
| | 1 c.s. | אֶקְטֹל | אֶקָּטֵל |
| | 3 m.p. | יִקְטְלוּ | יִקָּטְלוּ |
| | 3 f.p. | תִּקְטֹלְנָה | תִּקָּטַלְנָה |
| | 2 m.p | תִּקְטְלוּ | תִּקָּטְלוּ |
| | 2 f.p. | תִּקְטֹלְנָה | תִּקָּטַלְנָה |
| | 1 c.p | נִקְטֹל | נִקָּטֵל |
| Imperative | m.s. | קְטֹל | הִקָּטֵל |
| | f.s. | קִטְלִי | הִקָּטְלִי |
| | m.p. | קִטְלוּ | הִקָּטְלוּ |
| | f.p. | קְטֹלְנָה | הִקָּטַלְנָה |
| Infinitive const. | | קְטֹל | הִקָּטֵל |
| Infinitive absol. | | קָטֹל | הִקָּטֹל |
| Participle | | קֹטֵל | נִקְטָל |
| (passive) | | קָטוּל | |

| PIʿEL | PUʿAL | HITPAʿEL | HIP̱ʿĪL | HOP̱ʿAL |
|---|---|---|---|---|
| קִטֵּל | קֻטַּל | הִתְקַטֵּל | הִקְטִיל | הָקְטַל |
| קִטְּלָה | קֻטְּלָה | הִתְקַטְּלָה | הִקְטִילָה | הָקְטְלָה |
| קִטַּלְתָּ | קֻטַּלְתָּ | הִתְקַטַּלְתָּ | הִקְטַלְתָּ | הָקְטַלְתָּ |
| קִטַּלְתְּ | קֻטַּלְתְּ | הִתְקַטַּלְתְּ | הִקְטַלְתְּ | הָקְטַלְתְּ |
| קִטַּלְתִּי | קֻטַּלְתִּי | הִתְקַטַּלְתִּי | הִקְטַלְתִּי | הָקְטַלְתִּי |
| | | | | |
| קִטְּלוּ | קֻטְּלוּ | הִתְקַטְּלוּ | הִקְטִילוּ | הָטְלוּ |
| קִטַּלְתֶּם | קֻטַּלְתֶּם | הִתְקַטַּלְתֶּם | הִקְטַתֶּם | הָקְטַלְתֶּם |
| קִטַּלְתֶּן | קֻטַּלְתֶּן | הִתְקַטַּלְתֶּן | הִקְטַלְתֶּן | הָקְטַלְתֶּן |
| קִטַּלְנוּ | קֻטַּלְנוּ | ה1תְקאטַּלְנוּ | הִקְטַלְנוּ | הָקְטַלְנוּ |
| | | | | |
| יְקַטֵּל | יְקֻטַּל | יִתְקַטֵּל | יַקְטִיל | יָקְטַל |
| תְּקַטֵּל | תְּקֻטַּל | תִּתְקַטֵּל | תַּקְטִיל | תָּקְטַל |
| תְּקַטֵּל | תְּקֻטַּל | תִּתְקַטֵּל | תַּקְטִיל | תָּקְטַל |
| תְּקַטְּלִי | תְּקֻטְּלִי | תִּתְקַטְּלִי | תַּקְטִילִי | תָּקְטְלִי |
| אֲקַטֵּל | אֲקֻטֵּל | אֶתְקַטֵּל | אַקְטִיל | אָקְטַל |
| | | | | |
| יְקַטְּלוּ | יְקֻטְּלוּ | יִתְקַטְּלוּ | יַקְטִילוּ | יָקְטְלוּ |
| תְּקַטֵּלְנָה | תְּקֻטַּלְנָה | תִּתְקַטַּלְנַה | תַּקְטֵלְנָה | תֻּקְטַלְנָה |
| תְּקַטְּלוּ | תְּקֻטְּלוּ | תִּתְקַטְּלוּ | תַּקְטִילוּ | תָּקְטְלוּ |
| תְּקַטֵּלְנָה | תְּקֻטַּלְנָה | תִּתְקַטַּלְנָה | תַּקְטֵלְנָה | תָּקְטַלְנָה |
| נְקַטֵּל | נְקֻטַּל | נִתְקַטֵּל | נַקְטִיל | נָקְטַל |
| | | | | |
| קַטֵּל | | הִתְקַטֵּל | הַקְטֵל | |
| קַטְּלִי | | הִתְקַטְּלִי | הַקְטִילִי | |
| קַטְּלוּ | | הִתְקַטְּלוּ | הַקְטִילוּ | |
| קַטַּלְנָה | | הִתְקַטַּלְנָה | הָטֵלְנָה | |
| | | | | |
| קַטֵּל | קֻטַּל | הִתְקַטֵּל | הַקְטִיל | הָקְטַל |
| קַטֹּל/קַטֵּל | קֻטֹּל | הִתְקַטֵּל | הַקְטֵל | הָקְטֵל |
| | | | | |
| מְקַטֵּל | מְקֻטָּל | מִתְקַטֵּל | מַקְטִיל | מָקְטָל |

# VERBS WITH WEAK LETTERS AND GUTTURALS IN OUTLINE

Only the most salient characteristics of verbs with weak letters and gutturals are presented in the following outlines, brief reminders of how these verbs modify the basic pattern of the strong verb. For details see the full discussion in *A Summary of Hebrew Grammar*. For paradigms of these and many other verbs see Abraham S. Halkin, *201 Hebrew Verbs Fully Conjugated in All the Forms*, Woodbury, N.Y.: Barron's Educational Series, Inc., 1970.

## VERBS WITH PĒ NÛN [פ״ן] (See II § 16)

When נ has no vowel of its own, it is assimilated into the following radical.

(1) Qal imperfect: יִגַּשׁ < יִנְגַּשׁ [נגשׁ] (cf. יִקְטֹל)

(2) Qal imperative:

(a) Verbs with _ in the imperfect drop the נ:

גַּשׁ < תִּגַּשׁ [נגשׁ]

(b) Verbs with ˙ in the imperfect usually keep the :;

נְפֹל < פֹּל < תִּפֹּל [נפל]

(3) Qal infinitive construct: Verbs dropping נ in the imperative do so here, adding ת to the remaining radicals and pointing as a second declension noun: גֶּשֶׁת < ת + גשׁ < גַּשׁ [נגשׁ]. Cf. Pē Vāv verbs.

Note also: נתן and לקח.

## VERBS WITH LĀMED HÊ [ל״ה] (See II § 17)

These verbs are originally ל״י (or, ל״ו), and the original י often reappears in composition.

(1) When ה is final the preceding vowel varies as follows:

(a) הָ with all perfects

(b) הֶ with all imperfects and participles absolute

(c) הֵ with all imperatives and participles construct

(2) When ה (properly י) is not final:

(a) with vocalic afformatives (except 3 f. s.) the ה drops; e.g.

עָשׂוּ < עָשְׂהוּ [עשׂה];

since the 3 f.s. afformative is הָ, the ה of the root becomes ת:

עָשְׂתָה < עָשְׂהָה [עשׂה]

(b) with consonantal afformatives:

(i) ֵי < ה with perfect passives

(ii) ִי < ה with perfect actives and hiṯpa‘ēl

(iii) ֶי < ה before -נָה of imperfects and imperatives

(c) The infinitive construct, instead of the final ה has וֹת; e.g. from עשׂה: עֲשׂוֹת (cf. קְטוֹל). The infinitive absolute follows the usual pattern.

## VERBS WITH PĒ YÔḎ AND PĒ VĀV [פ״י and פ״ו] (See II § 18)

I. PĒ YÔḎ.

(1) Qal imperfect: י quiesces with no change in vowel the thematic vowel is ַ

(2) Hip‘îl perfect: י quiesces and modifies the vowel: e.g. הֵינִיק < הִיְנִיק (cf. הִקְטִיל)

(3) Hip‘îl imperfect: י quiesces and modifies the vowel; e.g. יֵינִיק < יַיְנִיק (cf. יַקְטִיל)

II. PĒ VĀV

(1) The original ו reappears in the prefixing stems:

| | |
|---|---|
| Nip̄ʻal perfect | נוֹשַׁב [ישב] (cf. נִקְטַל) |
| Nip̄ʻal imperfect | יִוָּלֵד [ילד] (cf. יִקָּטֵל) |
| Hit̲paʻēl (sometimes) | הִתְוַדַּע [ידע] (cf. הִתְקַטֵּל) |
| Hip̄ʻîl perfect | הוֹשִׁיב [ישב] (cf. הִקְטִיל) |
| Hip̄ʻîl imperfect | יוֹשִׁיב [ישב] (cf. יַקְטִיל) |
| Hop̄ʻal | הוּשַׁב [ישב] (cf. הָקְטַל) |

(2) Qal imperfect has two forms:

(a) may be the same as פ״י: יִירָא [ירא]

(b) more often, however, the thematic vowel is ֵ,
the י is dropped and the preformative pointed
with ֵ,

יִישַׁב < יֵשֵׁב [ישב]

(3) Qal imperative is based on the imperfect, dropping the prefix; e.g. תֵּשֵׁב < שֵׁב

(4) Qal infinitive construct drops the י and adds ת to the second and third radicals, pointing as a second declension noun (cf. פ״ן verbs); e.g.

[ידע] דע + ת > דַּעַת    [ישב] שב + ת > שֶׁבֶת

Cf. also הלך which belongs to this class of verbs.

**VERBS WITH ʻAYIN VĀV AND ʻAYIN YÔD̲ [ע״ו and ע״י]**
**(MIDDLE HOLLOW VERBS) (See II § 19)**

The basic form for these verbs is the infinitive construct:
קוּם, שִׁיר, בּוֹא.

(1) Qal perfect is with ָ : בָּא שָׁר קָם

(2) Qal participle is based on this form:
בָּא בָּאִים (m.) and בָּאָה בָּאוֹת (f.)

(3) Qal imperfect is formed by using the basic form (= the infinitive construct) with the preformatives pointed with tone long ָ ; e.g. יָבוֹא יָשִׁיר יָקוּם

(4) Nip'al perfect has the thematic vowel וֹ with the preformative נָ : נָקוֹם
Nip'al imperfect has the thematic vowel וֹ with the regular preformative ִ and dāgēš fortē in the first radical: יִקּוֹם.

(5) Hip'îl has the usual ִי with preformatives pointed with tone long vowels:
   (a) Hip'îl perfect: הֵקִים < הִקִים (cf. הִקְטִיל)
   (b) Hip'îl imperfect: יָקִים < יַקִים (cf. יַקְטִיל)

(6) The intensive-repetitive stems are usually formed by doubling the last radical, or by doubling both the first and last radicals; e.g.
Pô'ēl: קוֹמֵם [קוּם] Pilpēl: כִּלְכֵּל [כּוּל] (cf. קִטֵּל)

**VERBS WITH 'AYIN 'AYIN [ע״ע] (DOUBLE 'AYIN VERBS) (See II § 20)**

The second and third radicals of these verbs are identical, and are frequently written as one letter, using dāgēš fortē where possible; e.g. קַל, קַלּוּ [קלל].

(1) The longer form (with both repeated radicals) is used:
   (a) when three radicals are required: סֹבֵב, סֹבֵּב
   (b) usually with the third person: סָבְבָה, סָבְבוּ

(2) Thematic vowels and preformatives for Qal imperfect:
  (a) active verbs have ֹ with ָ : יָסֹב (cf. יִקְטֹל)
  (b) stative verbs have ַ with ֵ : יֵרַךְ (cf. יִכְבַּד)

(3) Connecting vowels before consonantal afformatives:
  (a) perfect forms, ֹ / וֹ : סַב, סַבָּה, סַבּוֹתָ / סַבֹּתָ
  (b) imperfect form, ֶי : תְּסַבֶּינָה (cf. Nip'al תִּקָּטַלְנָה)

**VERBS WITH PĒ GUTTURAL (See II § 21)**

Note the following characteristics of the gutturals (see *A Summary of Hebrew Grammar*, § 2d for full details):

Gutturals and ר cannot take dāgēš fortē.
Gutturals require a composite ševâ.
Gutturals often prefer a vocal ševâ to a silent one.
Gutturals prefer *a* vowels, especially before them.
Ḥireq before a guttural becomes ֶ .

(1) Qal imperfect:
  (a) verbs with ֹ point the preformative with ַ except before א; e.g.
  יַעֲמֹד (cf. יִקְטֹל), but יֶאֱסֹף
  (b) verbs with ַ point the preformative with ֶ; e.g.
  יֶחֱזַק (cf. יִכְבַּד)

(2) Gutturals at the end of a syllable (where a silent ševâ would normally appear) usually take a composite ševâ.

(3) With vocalic endings the composite ševâ under a guttural necessarily changes to the corresponding short vowel; e.g.
  יַעַמְדוּ < יַעֲמְדוּ < וּ + יַעֲמֹד < יִעְמֹד [עמד]

(4) With Nip'al imperfect, imperative and infinitive, since gutterals and ר cannot be doubled, the preceding short vowel becomes tone long; e.g.

יֵעָמֵד < יִעָּמֵד (cf. יִקָּטֵל)

## VERBS WITH PĒ 'ĀLEP̱ [פ״א] (See II § 22)

A sub-class of Pē Guttural verbs, there are only five verbs: אבד *to perish*, אבה *to be willing*, אכל *to eat*, אמר *to say*, and אפה *to bake*. They are identical to the Pe Gutturals except in the Qal imperfect.

(1) The thematic vowel is _ , but in pause often .. .

(2) א quiesces with the preformative in the vowel ˙ ; e.g.

יֹאבַד יֹאבֶה יֹאכַל יֹאמַר יֹאפֶה

(3) In the first person only one א is written, e.g.

אֹמַר < אֹאמַר.

(4) The accent of אמר in vāv consecutive frequently retracts; e.g. וַיֹּאמַר, but frequently also וַיֹּאמֶר.

(5) The א of אמר quiesces with the ל of the infinitive construct; e.g. לֵאמֹר < לֶאֱמֹר < לְ + אֱמֹר

## VERBS WITH 'AYIN GUTTURAL (See II § 23)

(1) Gutturals prefer a vowels:

(a) Qal imperfect is usually formed with _ .

(b) Pi'ēl perfect frequently has _ for .. : e.g.

נִחַם < נִחֵם (cf. קִטֵּל)

(2) Gutturals require composite for simple vocal Ševâ; e.g. שָׁחֲטָה.

(3) With two vocal Šᵉvâs the first becomes the short vowel of the composite; e.g. in making an imperative:

שַׁחֲטוּ < שְׁחֲטוּ < תִּשְׁחֲטוּ .

(4) Gutturals and ר cannot be doubled. In intensive-repetitive stems compensation is not usually made for ה, ח, ע , but often for , and always for ר ;

בֵּרֵךְ < בִּרֵךְ    מֵאֵן < מִאֵן    נִחַם (cf. )

## VERBS WITH LĀMEḎ GUTTURAL (See II § 24)

Final gutterals must have an *a* sound before them.

(1) Qal imperfect is formed with _ ; e.g. יִשְׁמַע .

(2) A final guttural preceded by a long second or third class vowel requires a furtive pataḥ; e.g. שָׁמֹעַ < שָׁמֹע and הִשְׁלִיחַ < הִשְׁלִיח .

(3) A .. followed by furtive pataḥ contracts to _ , except (a) with infinitives and participles in the absolute and (b) with pausal forms.

(4) In the 2 f.s. perfect a helping vowel ( _ ) is placed before the afformative without, however, changing the original pointing of the ת ; e.g. שָׁלַחַתְּ < שָׁלַחְתְּ .

## VERBS WITH LĀMEḎ ʻĀLEP̱ [ל״א] (See II § 25)

א at the beginning of a syllable, is a full consonant.
א at the end of a syllable is quiescent.

*Appendix*

(1) א at the end of a syllable quiesces, and the preceding vowel is raised to its tone long; e.g.

מָצָא < מָצַא (cf. קָחַל ).

(2) Qal perfect active and qal imperfect active and stative have ◌ָ throughout: מָצָא, מָצְאָה, מָצָאתָ, מָצָאת, מָצָאתִי and so on; יִמְצָא, תִּמְצָא, תִּמְצָא, תִּמְצָא and so on.

(3) Qal perfect stative and all perfect stems other than qal active have ◌ֵ ; e.g. מָלֵא, מָלֵאתָ (cf. כָּבֵד ); נִמְלֵאתָ (cf. נִקְטַלְתָּ ); מִלֵּאתָ (cf. קִטַּלְתָּ ).

(4) All imperfects and imperatives have ◌ֶ before -נָה ; e.g. תִּמְצֶאנָה .

(5) Quiescent א is sometimes not written.

------------------------------